THE VERY SALT OF LIFE

WELSH WOMEN'S POLITICAL WRITINGS FROM CHARTISM TO SUFFRAGE

THE VERY SALT OF LIFE

WELSH WOMEN'S POLITICAL WRITINGS FROM CHARTISM TO SUFFRAGE

Edited by
JANE AARON and URSULA MASSON

HONNO CLASSICS

Published by Honno
'Ailsa Craig', Heol y Cawl, Dinas Powys
South Glamorgan, Wales CF6 4AH

First Impression 2007

The Very Salt of Life

© Foreword and introductions, Jane Aaron and Ursula Masson

British Library Cataloguing in Publication Data
A catalogue record for this book is available from
the British Library

ISBN 978 1870206 907

Published with the financial support of the Welsh Books Council

Cover image: Evan Walters; detail from poster for the 1926 National
Eisteddfod, reproduced with permission of the Estate of Evan Walters.
Printed in Wales by Gomer

DEDICATION

To Deirdre Beddoe
in grateful appreciation of her contribution to
Welsh women's studies

ACKNOWLEDGEMENTS

We owe a debt of thanks to a number of friends and colleagues who have drawn our attention to sources used here, and sometimes provided transcripts. In particular, we would like to thank Neil Evans, for the letter from the Chartist women of Blackwood, and the reports of the north Wales suffragists from the 1913 Suffrage Pilgrimage; Bill Jones, for the articles by Margaret E. Roberts from *Y Drych*; and Ryland Wallace, for material by Helena Jones and discussions about Alice Abadam and Rachel Barrett.

Thanks are also due to the staff of the archives of the Museum of London for permission to reprint the writings of Alice Abadam and Rachel Barratt and for providing copies of the work; and to the staff of the Local Studies Collections of Cardiff Central Library, the Swansea Central Reference Library and the National Library of Wales for help in locating some of the other texts reproduced in this volume.

We are also grateful to the following for permission to reproduce illustrative materials: to Elisabeth Bennett and the staff of the Archives, University of Wales, Swansea, for the photograph of south Wales suffragists in the 1913 Suffrage Pilgrimage; to the Women's Library for the cartoon of Lloyd George and 'Miss Wales'; to the National Library of Wales for Hugh Hughes' cartoon of Jane Williams and the photograph of Cranogwen; and to Llandovery College for the image of Augusta Hall.

Contents

Foreword by Jane Aaron and Ursula Masson i

Part I. Chartism, Nationalism and Language Politics
Introduction by Jane Aaron...3

1. Members of the Blackwood Female Patriotic
Association 15
*Address of the Female Patriots of Blackwood to Messrs
H. Vincent, Townsend, Edwards & Dickenson (1839)....................15*

2. Jane Williams, Ysgafell 18
***Artegall** or Remarks on the Reports of the Commissioners
of Inquiry into the State of Education in Wales (1848) 18*

3. Augusta Hall, Lady Llanover 51
*Anerchiad i Gymraësau Cymru (An address to the Welsh
women of Wales, 1850)..51*
An Address to the Welsh Women of Wales 57

**Part II. Feminist Dissent in the Pulpit, in Education and
in the Temperance Movement**
Introduction by Jane Aaron..67

4. Margaret Evans Roberts 77
Diystyru y Merched (Ignoring the Women, 1878) 77
Ignoring the Women...79
Merched yn y Pwlpud (Women in the Pulpit, 1894) 82
Women in the Pulpit...86

5. Cranogwen (Sarah Jane Rees) 91
Esther Judith (Cymraeg, 1880-1) 91
Esther Judith...100

6. Elizabeth Phillips Hughes... 109
The Higher Education of Girls in Wales (1884)...........................109

7. Dilys Glynne Jones.. 123
*The Duty of Welsh Women in Relation to the Welsh
Intermediate Education Act (1894) 123*

8. Buddug (Catherine Jane Pritchard) 136
*Paham yn arbenig y dylai merched bleidio dirwest (Why
women in particular should plead temperance, 1880)................136*
Why women in particular should plead temperance 137

Na Chaffed Hudoles Fyw (Let not an enchantress live, 1900)....140
Let not an enchantress live 141

9. Ellen Hughes 142
Merch – ei Hawliau a'i Hiawnderau (Woman – Her Claims
and Her Rights, 1892) 142
Woman – Her Claims and Her Rights 146
Angylion yr Aelwyd (Angels in the House, 1899)........................150
Angels in the House...152

Part III. Gender, Class and Party: Liberal and Labour Movement Writings

Introduction by Ursula Masson...................................... 159

10. Nora Philipps... 172
An Appeal to Welsh Women (1893)...172

11. Women's Liberal Associations............................... 177
Rules and Objects of Welsh Women's Liberal Associations
(1891, 1893) 177

12. Mrs D. M. Richards.. 180
The Duty of Women and Wives to try for places on the Parish
Councils, &c. (1894) 180

13. Nora Philipps... 184
Notes on the work of Welsh Liberal Women (1895)....................184

14. Nora Philipps and Miss Elsbeth Philipps 198
Progress of Women in Wales (1896)..198

15. Anna Jones... 206
Women and Religious Freedom (1895) 206

16. Gwyneth Vaughan.. 210
Women and their Questions (1897) 210

17. 'Un o'r ddau Wynne' (Alis Mallt Williams).......... 213
Patriotism and the Women of Cymru (1898) 213

18. 'Matron'... 215
i. On Women's Work in the Family, Poverty and Housing...........215
Out-Heroding Herod: The Infantile Mortality of the
Rhondda..215
An Eight Hour Day for Women..220
The Housing Question and the Lessening of Women's
Hours of Work..222
'Household Gods'..223

ii. On Women's Equality and the Political Parties *224*
Woman Suffrage: The Socialist Position and the
Promised Reform Bill *224*
Untitled *225*
Women and the Liberal Party *227*
Women in the Labour Movement *230*

19. 'R.C.' 235
The Women's Labour League *235*
Women and the Labour Movement *237*
The Women's Labour League *239*

20. Mrs Scholefield.. 243
Annual Report of Cardiff Women's Labour League (1913)..........*243*

Part IV. The Cause: Writings from the Women's Suffrage Movement

Introduction by Ursula Masson......................................249

21. Cardiff Suffragists ditch the Liberal Party: letters. 260
Dr Erie Evans (1909) *260*
Olive Stephenson-Howell (1910)..................................*262*
Cardiff Women's Liberal Association (1911).................*264*

22. North Wales Suffragists on Pilgrimage 265
Newspaper Reports (1913)...*265*

23. Who's Who (1913) 282
KEATING HILL, MRS. MARY..*282*
MANSELL-MOULLIN, MRS. EDITH RUTH *282*

24. Dr Helena Jones... 284
Women's Votes in Wartime (1916).................................*284*
Women as Citizens (1916) *286*

25. Alice Abadam 288
The Feminist Vote: Enfranchised or Emancipated? (1918/19)...*288*

26. Gwladys Perrie Williams.. 295
Woman's Opportunity (1919)...*295*

27. Rachel Barrett.. 298
Autobiography (c. 1924)...*298*

28. Margaret, Lady Rhondda....................................... 303
This was My World (1933)...*303*

Foreword
BY JANE AARON AND URSULA MASSON

Today, in the early summer of 2007, the appointment of an equal number of male and female ministers to a new Welsh National Assembly Cabinet has caused no surprise: it is what contemporary Wales expects. Many aspects of the new Cabinet – its size, its distribution of responsibilities, the geographical location of its members – have provoked controversy, but its gender balance is taken for granted. Since the first National Assembly election of 1999, when 26 out of the 60 new Assembly members were women, Welsh people have become used to seeing political power fairly distributed between the sexes. And yet this is very much a new development for Wales: in 1996, just before the referendum which ushered in devolution, only one of the country's 38 Westminster MPs was a woman (Ann Clwyd), and throughout the twentieth century few Welsh women, with the notable exception of Megan Lloyd George (MP from 1921-51 and from 1957-66) and Eirene White (MP from 1950-1970), can be said to have made their mark in constitutional politics. The abruptness of this shift from gross under-representation to equality, at least at the Assembly level, could be seen as indicative of a fragility in the new order; what came about so suddenly might be interpreted as the consequence of ideological movements not indigenous to Welsh life, which have temporarily displaced a more rooted patriarchy. But to think in such terms is to ignore the long history of Welsh women's struggle, in constitutional and grass-roots politics and in many different spheres of life, for a greater voice in Welsh affairs.

The aim of this anthology, the first of its kind, is to bring that history vividly to life through the participants' own strongly-felt words, and to explode the notion that Welsh women of previous generations did not struggle for gender equality in the homes, schools, chapels, workplaces and voting-booths of Wales. Defining the 'political' in a broad sense, to encompass women's engagement with all aspects of the public life of the nation, as well as their goal of emancipation, it includes a diverse range of texts, in both Welsh and English, with the Welsh-language pieces translated here by Jane Aaron. For some of our contributors, the issue which incited them to take up their pens was not gender inequality; many of them were more likely to protest against perceived injustices in the social class system, or against cultural imperialism. But in speaking out at all as women they were inevitably participating in the struggle against the subordination and silencing of the 'second sex'.

Culled from a wide range of sources, including political party archives and periodical literature, and incorporating contributions by Welsh women to American as well as British periodicals, most of this book's contents have not been previously reprinted. Initially it had been our intention to produce one anthology, covering the whole of the nineteenth and twentieth centuries, but so swamped were we by the sheer mass of potential contributions, that it became necessary to limit this first volume to one century of Welsh women's political writings, from the 1830s to the 1930s. We have divided the material into four thematically-organised parts which span the century chronologically, and have introduced each section separately, thus enabling a full appreciation of the historical and political context of the pieces, even by readers new to Welsh studies, women's studies, or both.

The first section, which covers the 1830s and 40s, focuses on two key events of those decades, the growth of the Chartist movement in Wales culminating in the 1839 Newport Rising, and the impact of the 1847 Report on the State of Education in Wales, which caused national consternation, not least because of its defamation of Welsh women as sexually wanton. The second part includes the testimonies of women protesting against their subordinated position within the Nonconformist chapels of Wales, and those leading the struggle to achieve a better education for Welsh women. Also represented in this section is the voice of the Welsh women's temperance movement, which did much to empower its participants and bring them out of their homes to organise and protest. Part III provides representative examples from the writings of those women who by the final decades of the nineteenth century were participating in influential numbers in the party political organisations of their period, including Liberal women in the period of the Cymru Fydd, or Young Wales, movement, and women working for socialism and the Labour movement during its early years in Welsh political life. Finally, the last section is devoted to the writings of the Welsh suffragists, militant and constitutional, working within the Votes for Women campaigns of the first decades of the twentieth century.

A volume like this one could not, of course, have been produced without the contribution of pioneering earlier works by Welsh feminist historians and cultural critics, and, as the references in the following introductory sections indicate, we are heavily indebted to them. Angela John's edited essay collection *Our Mothers' Land: Chapters in Welsh Women's History 1830-1939* (1991), was largely instrumental in opening up the field with its many seminal chapters, such as Ceridwen Lloyd-Morgan's study of the Welsh women's temperance movements, Siân Rhiannon Williams' account of the nineteenth-century Welsh-language women's periodicals, and Kay Cook's and Neil Evans's work on the suffrage movement. W. Gareth Evans's *Education and Female Emancipation: The Welsh Experience, 1847-1914* has proved indispensable to researchers of Welsh women's education since its first appearance in 1990; similarly Gwyneth Tyson Roberts' book on the 1847 Report, *The Language of the Blue Books: The Perfect Instrument of Empire* (1998) provided the first sustained exploration of women's responses to the Report. For the later period covered in this collection Deirdre Beddoe's *Out of the Shadows: A History of Women in Twentieth-Century Wales* proved an indispensable guide.

We could not hope to include in this one volume all those political issues which emerged for women as 'the very salt of life', as Margaret Haig Thomas vividly described the militant suffrage movement. One cause to which many Welsh women throughout the twentieth century dedicated themselves was the peace movement: a future volume might begin again in the pre-First World War period with Welsh women's contributions to the anti-militarist and anti-imperialist debates. The question of women's relationship to nation and to language saw the emergence of new forms of activism, and new subjects for writing, in the development of Plaid Cymru in the 1920s and the Welsh Language Movement in the 1960s. Similarly, the equal rights agenda of suffragists and the focus of socialist women on the needs and welfare of working-class mothers, have a continuous history from the pre-1914 writings of 'Matron' reprinted here, through to the Women's Liberation Movement of the 1970s and 80s and beyond. Sexuality, the body, and personal relationships were newly politicised in the campaigns of the second wave of feminists, but the poverty of women, and their unequal position, though increasing presence, in the workforce remained contentious issues.

Once again, in a second volume, we expect to be spoilt for choice as to what to include, just as we have been in the compiling of this present collection. In today's changing world, when women's place in the political parties and in representative institutions has been reinvigorated in Wales by the move to devolution, it is all the more important to remember and to reclaim, as a significant part of our political inheritance, these previously forgotten voices of the past.

Part I

Chartism, Nationalism
and Language Politics

ARTEGALL, or THE WHIPPING.

1. 'Artegall, or, The Whipping', by Hugh Hughes, 1848. The cartoon shows Jane Williams chastising the three commissioners of the 1847 *Report on the State of Education in Wales* (reproduced by permission of the National Library of Wales).

2. Augusta Hall, Lady Llanover, by C. A. Mornewick, 1862 (reproduced by permission of the warden of Llandovery College).

INTRODUCTION
BY JANE AARON

The decades with which this anthology begins and closes, the 1830s and the 1930s, were both eras of marked political turbulence in Wales, which peaked in the 1830s with the Chartist rising at Newport in November 1839. During that decade Welsh women as well as men campaigned for the 'Six Points' of the Chartist movement, demanding reform of a corrupt electoral system in which only one male out of every seven could vote. The imprisonment of four Chartist leaders in Monmouth gaol in August 1839 aroused the industrial population of the south-east valleys, suffering acutely as they were from the brutalising work and living conditions of early industrialism. Henry Vincent, a young and particularly popular Chartist speaker, and William Edwards, a Newport baker, with William Townsend and John Dickensen, had been charged with attending illegal meetings, and gaoled in Monmouth. Many wrote in their defence to the radical newspapers of the day, and the journal *Western Vindicator* included in its pages the first entry of this collection, by the Members of the Blackwood Female Patriotic Association.

The Western Vindicator, published weekly, covering Chartist activity in south Wales and the west of England, was owned and produced by Henry Vincent.[1] His enthusiasm for women's involvement in political life was strongly felt: the first issue of the *Vindicator* carried on its front page an article by Vincent, headed 'What have Women to Do with Politics?', to which question he answered, 'All – everything!'. Using the familiar analogy between the family and the nation, and

---

[1] Owen R. Ashton, 'The *Western Vindicator* and the early Chartists', in Joan Allen and Owen R. Ashton, *Papers for the People: a Study of the Chartist Press,* (London, 2005).

emphasizing the 'separate spheres' notion of women's moral and educational influence in the family, he claimed that 'in the nation the feelings, habits, desires and patriotism of its people spring from the influence of the majority of the mothers of the people'.[2] In the radical discourses of the nineteenth century, potentially conservative views of women as essentially maternal and domestic could be used to argue for the necessity of their presence in the political public sphere. The *Vindicator* frequently included descriptions of the numerous and lively presence of women at meetings and demonstrations, and 'Female Patriots', as the Chartist associations called themselves, used its columns to send sisterly greetings and exhortations to each other – from Bristol and Bath to south Wales, for example, or, as here, to express solidarity with the political prisoners, and with the nationwide struggle. Vincent and others were in fact imprisoned more than once in the course of the year, before the November rising. Hardly had the Female Patriots of Newport written to congratulate him on his 'liberation from the gaol of our tyrants',[3] than the Female Patriots of Blackwood were penning their outrage at his re-incarceration.

Were the Chartist women feminists? The demand for universal suffrage in the Charter was for male suffrage, and it has been argued that Chartism, by its use of a conservative rhetoric of the family and gender difference, was essentially inimical to women's rights. In the 'Address of the Female Patriots' the stress is on the sympathetic sisterhood and solidarity of women with men rather than with one another as women. Nevertheless, in so far as demands for women's political rights were made in this decade, they came from men or women working within, or sympathetic towards, Chartism.

The identity of the 'Address's' author is unknown, but it

---

[2] *The Western Vindicator*, no. 1, February 23 1839.

[3] *Vindicator*, no. 23, July 23 1839.

is clear from the letter's command of English that its writer, or writers, were educated woman, probably of the same class as some of the ring-leaders of the ill-fated march: two of those who were eventually transported to Australia for their involvement in the uprising, John Frost and Zephaniah Williams, were born to middle-class prosperity. Zephaniah owned a house in Blackwood, and his son Llewellyn led the local youth branch of the movement; his wife Joan, the daughter of a wealthy Machen landowner, may well have been one of the letter-writers. Though Welsh was the language in which Zephaniah corresponded with her, during the long years of his Australian imprisonment before she joined him in Tasmania, the family Bible in which Joan inscribed (in English) her children's births and death was in English.[4] If not she herself, it must have been similarly positioned Blackwood women who wrote the 'Address'. But for all its high level of literacy, the 'Address' clearly identifies with the labouring population and its sufferings under a harsh capitalism; it expresses a determination to seek 'the undeniable birth right of the working classes', pressing 'our just claims' on the attention of the middle classes.[5] And it makes use of the characteristic discourse of Chartism to legitimate protest and physical force – the use of '*their right arms if need be*' – in terms of the ancient rights of the people, stolen from them by corruption and despotism.

If the 'Address' does not refer specifically to the political cause of women as women, it concerns itself even less with

---

[4] See John Humphries, *The Man from the Alamo: Why the Welsh Chartist Uprising of 1839 Ended in a Massacre* (St. Athan, 2004), for further information on Joan Williams and the 1839 Chartist uprising.

[5] There is a very large literature on Chartism. For more on Chartism in Wales, and on women Chartists, see David J.V. Jones, *The Last Rising: the Newport Insurrection of 1839 (Oxford, 1985)*; D.J.V. Jones, 'Women and Chartism', *History*, vol. 68, no. 222 (February, 1983); Dorothy Thompson, *The Chartists, Popular Politics in the Industrial Revolution* (London & New York, 1984).

the political cause of the Welsh people as Welsh, but the same
can by no means be said of the next two pieces included in
this anthology. Both were written in the immediate context of
an 1847 government report on the state of education in Wales,
which became known as the 'Treason of the Blue Books'. It
was the Chartist uprising of 1839 and the Rebecca Riots of the
early 1840s which in March 1846 incited the Welsh MP for
Coventry, William Williams, to request that 'an Inquiry…be
made into the state of Education in the Principality of Wales,
especially into the means afforded to the labouring classes
of acquiring a knowledge of the English language.' Three
monoglot English Commissioners (Messrs Lingen, Symons
and Johnson) were duly sent into Wales to inquire into the
levels of education attained by a population still in many
parts monoglot Welsh. Not surprisingly, their report, when
it appeared in December 1847, found that the standard of
education in Wales in general was deplorably low, particularly
with regard to the teaching of English.

The *Report* connected this lack of educational access to
English civilization with what it claimed to be the barbarity
and primitive backwardness of the population, and went way
beyond its brief in producing a document of unprecedented
official condemnation of Welsh morality. The Commissioner
Jelinger C. Symons gave it as his considered opinion that
though 'the Welsh are peculiarly exempt from the guilt of great
crimes', yet there are 'few countries where the standard of
minor morals is lower'.[6] 'Petty thefts, lying, cozening, every
species of chicanery, drunkenness (where the means exist),
and idleness' were characteristic failings of the Welsh, a race
incapable of greatness even in crime, except for one large-
scale vice: many of the witnesses to the *Report* informed its

---

[6] *Report of the Commission of Inquiry into the State of Education in Wales…In
Three Parts. Part I, Carmarthen, Glamorgan and Pembroke. Part II, Brecknock,
Cardigan, Radnor and Monmouth. Part III, North Wales* (London, 1847), ii, 56.

Commissioners that 'want of chastity is the giant sin of Wales.'[7] This laxity was said to be encouraged by the Nonconformist religious sects; according to the *Report*, Welsh women's sexual incontinence was 'much increased by night prayer-meetings, and the intercourse which ensues in returning home'. And it affected not just the lower classes in Wales, but the people as a whole: Welsh 'want of chastity,' reported the Commissioners, 'is not confined to the poor. In England, farmers' daughters are respectable; in Wales they are in the constant habit of being courted in bed.'[8] Courting in bed referred to the practice of acknowledged lovers getting to know one another better while lying, supposedly fully clothed, in the woman's bed. For lack of any other private space during the winter months, the practice had been common in other parts of rural Europe too before the mid-century,[9] but the Victorian morality of middle-class England, with its stress upon the sanctity of the marriage bed, was by now demanding a change in sexual mores.

No earlier report on Wales had preached on the ethical failings of the inhabitants so extensively, and none had previously focused on extramarital sexuality as a particularly Welsh weakness. The *Report* demonstrated a typically Victorian double standard in its attribution of blame for heterosexual misconduct to the female partner only, and in its assertion that her corruption struck at the moral root of her society generally: according to Symons, 'want of chastity in women…is sufficient to account for all other immoralities, for each generation will derive its moral tone in a great degree from the influences imparted by the mothers who reared them.'[10] Not only was the *Report* misogynistic, it was also

---

[7] Ibid., 60.

[8] Ibid., iii, 67-8.

[9] See Martine Segalen, *Love and Power in the Peasant Family*, trans. Sarah Matthews (Oxford, 1983), 20.

[10] *Report*, 1847, ii, 57.

racist in its claims that the flaws it condemned belonged to the Welsh *per se*, as an aspect of their ethnicity, rather than as attributes belonging to any one group or class within the nation. Such was the outrage it aroused in Wales that it succeeded in drawing together the various forces of public opinion in opposition to it, unintentionally encouraging an ultimately positive re-assessment of Welsh national identity.

The first lengthy critique of the *Report*, reprinted for the first time here in an abridged version, was published in 1848 by Jane Williams, Ysgafell (1806-1885). London-Welsh by birth and an Anglican, Williams was also deeply sympathetic to the Puritan and nonconformist tradition in Wales, which considered itself most particularly insulted by the *Report*. The bardic name she chose for herself signified her pride in her own republican ancestors: 'Ysgafell' was the name of the Montgomeryshire farmhouse in which her Roundhead forefather, Henry Williams, had campaigned with Vavasor Powell in 1654 against Cromwell's attempt to take power from the people during the Interregnum period. Her *Artegall; or Remarks on the Reports of the Commissioners of Inquiry into the State of Education in Wales*, is a sustained analysis of the way in which the *Report* attempts to justify an English governmental take-over of the educational system and curriculum in Wales. The title of the piece conveyed its fighting spirit from the outset: Artegall, the hero of Edmund Spenser's *The Faerie Queene* (1590-6), is portrayed in the fifth canto of the poem as a valiant fighter for Justice. In it, Williams exposes the Commissioners' technique of making much of all the negative evidence they had collected, and little of the more positive material. She rubbishes the arguments they put forward on the alleged lack of chastity of Welsh women, for example, by pointing firstly to the fact that 'Mr. Evan Jones, of Tredegar' – that is, the Nonconformist minister and author Ieuan Gwynedd – had published statistics showing that there was only 0.8 per cent difference between the numbers of illegitimate births in Wales and those in England,[11] and secondly, by showing that many of the witnesses to the Commissioners found much to praise in the women of Wales, but their testimony was given no prominent place in the Report.

What shocks her sense of justice most strongly is the Report's attempt to attribute the blame for all the alleged national faults it finds in the Welsh to the continuing existence of the Welsh language, and she closes her diatribe with an earnest plea to the people of England for help to withstand the likely intervention of their Government in Welsh freedom. '[T]he direct and unprecedented interference of the Executive Government, in the regular management and inspection of Schools' demands, she says, 'Preventive Opposition from the watchful Friends of BRITISH LIBERTY'.[12] This final appeal is arrived at unexpectedly through a comparison between the Welsh situation under English rule in the nineteenth century and the situation of the Saxons under Norman rule during the early medieval period. She is attempting to alert her English readers to the injustice of their Government through reminding them that Britishness supposedly glories in the idea that Britons 'never, never, never shall be slaves'. If that is their boast, then they should defend their British neighbours, the Welsh, from the imperial nineteenth-century 'Normans' who once again were threatening the freedom of Britons in the name of an oppressive civilisation.

Nor was she, of course, the only Welsh writer to be thus animated into political engagement by the 'Treason of the Blue Books'. Two of the most powerful but hitherto divided forces in mid-nineteenth century Wales were drawn closer together

---

[11] See Evan Jones [Ieuan Gwynedd], 'A Vindication of the Educational and Moral Condition of Wales...' (1848), in Brinley Rees (ed.), *Ieuan Gwynedd: Detholiad o'i Ryddiaith* (Caerdydd, 1957), 87-91.

[12] See below, p. 50.

in reaction against it: the world of the Welsh Nonconformists on the one hand, (previously not generally concerned with issues of national identity,) and that of the Anglican Welsh antiquarians and nation-builders on the other. During the late eighteenth and early nineteenth century, the Romantic movement in Wales had been characterized by increased scholarly interest in antiquarianism and nation-building, as well as a marked growth in the numbers of dissenters. Patriotic societies such as the Cymmrodorion, established in 1751 and the Gwyneddigion, established in 1770, commissioned and published for the new mass audiences of the printing presses Welsh grammars, dictionaries and histories, and edited bardic 'specimens' whose survival had hitherto depended on manuscript collectors.[13] As students of Welsh 'remains' they participated in what came to be known as the Celtic revival of the second half of the eighteenth century, instrumental in the construction of modern concepts of Scottish, Irish and Welsh nationhood. In 1818, as the hub of Welsh antiquarian activity moved from the London-Welsh taverns to the parlours of a group of Anglican clergy in Wales, the societies became more easily accessible to women, and the contribution of female members to the Cambrian Society's activities seems to have been particularly welcomed. During the first of the Eisteddfodau held under the Society's auspices, at Carmarthen in 1819, a woman was amongst the recipients of bardic orders, and in 1834, when the Eisteddfod was held at Cardiff, a woman won the prize-winning essay on the topic 'The advantages resulting from the preservation of the Welsh language and national costumes of Wales'. At the time and for decades to

[13] Prys Morgan, 'From a death to a view: the hunt for the Welsh past in the Romantic period', in Eric Hobsbawm and Terence Ranger (eds)*, The Invention of Tradition* (Cambridge, 1983), 43-100; Gwyn Alf Williams, 'Romanticism in Wales', in R. Porter and M. Teich (eds), *Romanticism in National Context* (Cambridge, 1988), 9-36.

come, few were more active and zealous in furthering the cause of the Welsh language than the writer of the essay, Augusta Waddington Hall, later Lady Llanover (1802-96), the probable author of the third piece included in this anthology.

Born in Llanofer, near Abergavenny, to English parents who had purchased the estate some ten years previously, and married in 1823 to Benjamin Hall, MP for Monmouthshire, Lady Llanover, or Gwenynen Gwent (the Bee of Gwent) to give her her bardic name, used her own and her husband's not inconsiderable wealth to enlarge Llanover House and establish it as a centre for the promotion and preservation of Welsh culture. In a border-country locality in which the Welsh language was otherwise rapidly losing ground during this period of intensive anglicization, she funded Welsh-language schools, made a spectacular success of a series of lavishly celebrated Eisteddfodau in Abergavenny, peopled her home and estates with Welsh-speaking servants and tenantry, established a harp factory to save the Welsh triple harp, did her utmost to support the flagging Welsh flannel industry, and welcomed to Llanover House a coterie of like-minded Welsh and Celtic aficionados, including a number of gifted women. Jane Williams, Ysgafell, was herself one of these; others who made significant contributions to the Welsh culture of their day were the antiquarian Angharad Llwyd; Maria Jane Williams, the collector of Welsh folk music; and Lady Charlotte Guest, the translator of the *Mabinogi*.

In 1850, when Ieuan Gwynedd, in the furtherance of his own continued attack upon the 1847 Report, published the first periodical for Welsh women, *Y Gymraes* (The Welshwoman, 1850-1), Lady Llanover became its chief patron. The journal's first number included an 'Address to the Welsh women of Wales' (*'Anerchiad i Gymraësau Cymru'*), by an author who signed herself 'Gwenllïan Gwent', which echoed many of the ideas expressed in Lady Llanover's prize-winning 1834 Eisteddfod essay. Accordingly, the general critical assumption has always

been that she was its author,[14] and it is included under her name
in this anthology, in the original Welsh and in translation. A
'wake-up' call to its readers, it attempts to persuade them to
adopt high moral standards, in tune with the explicit aims of
the new periodical which were to show that women brought
up in Welsh-language culture were more virtuous than their
sisters elsewhere, rather than less so. A Welsh woman worthy
of that title must defend the good name of her nation through
publicly exemplifying her purity and high-mindedness,
while at the same time emphasizing her Welshness through
speaking her national language and wearing Welsh national
costume. Lady Llanover is probably best remembered today
for her creation and very successful popularization of the so-
called 'traditional' Welsh costume for women: the high black
beaver hat, trademark of the Welsh tourist-trap shop, was, in
particular, her own invention.[15] Encased in Welsh flannel and
helmeted in her hard hat, the Welsh woman would be armed
against any aspiration to emulate the English leisured classes;
instead, she would persevere with the traditional role of her
mothers and grandmothers. It is once again the woman's
role as 'mother of the nation' which is primarily emphasized
here; Lady Llanover was a nation-builder *par exemplar*, but
no feminist. Nevertheless her 'Address' at least depicts its
idealized Welsh woman as very actively and self-consciously
the mainstay of her politicized and resistant society, bearing
upon her shoulders the chief responsibility for the future of
Wales as Welsh-speaking, self-respecting, and a nation in its
own right. As we shall see in the next part of this anthology,
for the generation of women who came of age after the trauma

---

[14] Siân Rhiannon Williams, 'The true "Cymraes": images of women in
women's nineteenth-century Welsh periodicals', in Angela V. John (ed.),
Our Mothers' Land: Chapters in Welsh Women's History 1830-1939 (Cardiff,
1991), 73.
[15] For further material on Augusta Hall's invention of the 'traditional' Welsh
costume, see Morgan, 'From a death to a view', 80-1.

of the 'Blue Books' the domestic sphere was increasingly being experienced as too narrow a field in which to limit the potential of the awakened Welsh woman.

1. Members of the Blackwood Female Patriotic Association

Address of the Female Patriots of Blackwood to Messrs H. Vincent, Townsend, Edwards & Dickenson

Western Vindicator 31 August 1839

RESPECTED PATRIOTIC BROTHERS, – We the Female Patriotic Association of Blackwood address you in the language and feelings of sisterly affection. As members of the same human family, we ought at all times to cultivate a friendly feeling towards each other, and do all we possibly can to alleviate the distress of our fellow creatures, and more especially to evince our sympathy for those persecuted patriots who, by their council and advice, are endeavouring to ameliorate the condition of the suffering millions of our unhappy country – who, for advocating truth and justice to all members of the community, have been selected by a tyrannical portion as objects for their *fiendish* persecution. We should consider ourselves unworthy of those humane principles you have justly taught from time to time, could we not sympathise with your *unmerited persecution*. Gracious heavens! What a system of *misrule* and tyranny! A man to be dragged from his home, shut up in a dungeon, deprived of the privilege of an interview with his best friends, and treated like a common felon, for holding forth the principles of truth and justice, and publicly exposing villainous and tyrannical oppression – for dragging the '*triple-headed monster*' from its hiding place, and exhibiting it in all its hideous gaze of the oppressed millions – for unfolding the prison doors of the accursed Bastille, and showing to the world the reward laid up in store for honest poverty – for holding forth to the public gaze the pale emaciated factory child, in short, for advocating the undeniable birth right of the working classes – for labouring and exerting yourselves to awaken the producing millions to a sense of their duty (a duty they owe to their country and their God) – the hideous monster of despotism and tyranny has stretched forth its homicidal talons, and thought proper to fix them upon you as fit objects for their hated persecution.

By glutting their vengeance upon some individuals, our rulers think to put a stop to our just cause; and proceed blindly on, without any consideration as to what the consequences will be. Let them have a care – *the more persecution, the more determination.* You by your energetic circuits, have implanted in our bosoms, and that of our brothers, principles which will never be eradicated, until we are laid in the silent tomb, free from all the cares and turmoils of this life.

RESPECTED BROTHERS, – We consider it is a duty incumbent upon us as a society, with the combined assistance of our sisters in England, Scotland and Wales, to ease the rugged path of persecution – by condolence to soothe the cares of our brothers in persecution – by our kindness, and by showing them that we are determined to render all the assistance in our power towards carrying the principles of the Charter into law, and by urging our just claims upon the middle classes of the community. We are determined to do all in our power towards supporting those that will support our cause; and to encourage our brethren by urging them on to a sense of duty they owe to those persecuted patriots who suffer in our just and righteous cause – to urge them on to render all the assistance possible with their money and with *their right arms if need be.*

RESPECTED BROTHERS, – The period is not far distant when justice shall sway its sceptre over our oppressed country

– when the patriotic sons and daughters of Britain shall be rewarded according to their respective merits. We hail the auspicious day when the sons and daughters of Britain shall assemble together, and with one accord make the valleys to ring

'BRITONS NEVER SHALL BE SLAVES!'

– when the tottering fabric of superstition and tyranny shall be hurled into oblivion – when the arm of despotism shall wither beneath the gigantic power of the people – when tyranny, with its baneful hand, shall be hurled from its tottering throne – when the whole fabric of corruption shall be rooted to its very foundation – when the banners of old England shall flutter in the breeze, and liberty resound from pole to pole – when the temple of tyranny shall shrink by the power of the people to its native nothingness, and a temple based upon its ruins, dedicated to the goddess of freedom. That the patriotic sons and daughters of Britain shall have the pleasure of witnessing and experiencing the blessings of freedom, is the prayer of your affectionate sisters, THE MEMBERS OF THE BLACKWOOD FEMALE PATRIOTIC ASSOCIATION.

2. Jane Williams, Ysgafell

Artegall or Remarks on the Reports of the Commissioners of Inquiry into the State of Education in Wales (1848)

'Now take the RIGHT likewise,' said Artegall,
'And counterpoise the same with *so much wrong*'.
(*Faery Queen*, Book V, Canto ii, Stanza xlvi)

I. Introduction

The Reports of the Commissioners of Inquiry into the State of Education in Wales, have done the people of that country a double wrong. They have traduced their national character, and in so doing, they have threatened an infringement upon their manifest social rights, their dearest existing interests, comprised in their ordinary modes of worship and instruction, their local customs, and their mother tongue.

The British public appear too generally to have received the Commissioners' personal Reports as a judicial summing up of the Evidence they have adduced. Those reports are, on the contrary, the partial inferences of advocates, the special pleadings of Counsel for the prosecution, in the case Shuttleworth *versus* Wales.[1]

The Commissioners were sent forth with instructions

---

[1] James Phillips Kay-Shuttleworth (1804-77) a civil servant and educationist, argued strongly in *The School in its Relation to the State, the Church and the Congregation* (1847) for central government involvement in education.

to make out a case, and they have diligently and faithfully laboured to accomplish it. But ere, on the strength of such allegations, the Principality is allowed to be made the subject and the victim of a new educational experiment, the attention of British Legislators is earnestly requested to an examination of the Evidence on which they rest.

The statements of the Commissioners are altogether absolute, and not, as they ought to be, balanced by comparison. The Commissioners evidently wanted that enlarged and comprehensive view of society, as it is in various counties, and as it has been in different ages, which could alone have prepared and enabled them to receive and to communicate correct pictures of the moral, physical, and educational condition of any several and separate nation. They wanted too a knowledge of the Welsh language, and of many other things.

The ideal of perfection may be rightly applied as an incentive to excellence, but it ought never to be used by the frail and the fallible for the condemnation of their brother sinners. They have brought an abstract principle, a transcendental notion of what education and condition ought to be, mercilessly and directly to bear upon the people of the Principality. They have condemned their customs, habits, and conduct by it, without the slightest reference to comparative merit as regards those of England and other countries. With cursory and superficial observers, first impressions too often become permanent and indelible. That very 'salient nature of the facts' spoken of by Commissioner Symons, should have warned him and his confederates of the truth, that defects naturally stand out upon the surface of society, while all that is good lies close within. They laid hold of those salient points, and refused to search deeper for the real state of things. They have precipitately generalized upon isolated instances. They have judged of a large and healthy family by its invalid members. They have mistaken particular cases for indicative and representative facts. They have given undue prominence to the evil: they have depreciated or suppressed the good; and this with the apparently charitable intention of having the evil remedied. They have garbled and perverted the evidence afforded by their own returns, whenever it tended to contradict their preconceived opinions. They procured a conflicting host of valuable, neutral, and worthless depositions, and often gave more credit to deponents whose ill will, inexperience, ignorance or prejudice rendered them incompetent, than to those of real weight and thorough knowledge. Their production gives the chaff without the wheat, the occasional sin without the predominating virtue, the single deviation apart from the prevalent tenor of Cambrian life. By a sort of Platonic process of world making, they fictitiously theorize a national character out of the refuse dregs that have filtered through from its higher and better state. Every beautiful picture that intrudes is unfavourably hung in the sub-gallery of an appendix; clouds, fogs, and storms envelop all their scenery. Nothing bad is omitted. The most trivial and offensive details are dwelt upon. The very countenance of a poor silent schoolboy is satirized as 'a look of entire vacancy'. They have used the very shreds of truth to plume the poisoned arrows of calumny.

The Government and the public were for a time misled by the delusive statements in the Report of 'The Children's Employment Commission.' Thorough examination and better testimony have since exposed those fallacies. Time, that great revealer of truth, will surely subject the Reports of the Education Commissioners to the same stern censors, and prove that they have borne unfaithful testimony to Wales.

2. Evidence

[…] 'I took written evidence,' says Commissioner Symons, 'from various persons in widely different classes in life, in whose knowledge, intelligence and integrity I had reasons to confide.'

Great importance is attached in this Report to the evidence of the Rev. R. H. Harrison of Builth, and it is quoted six or seven times to substantiate various charges made against the inhabitants of Builth, and of the Principality, and in support of the Commissioner's opinions. 'The State of this neighbour-hood, and perhaps of the Principality appears to be this,' says Mr Harrison, and then indulges in suppositions as to how things are, and how they came to be so. The closing sentence of his deposition is the following, 'The above remarks on the intemperance of the people, and the number of the injurious effects of the public houses apply to the Principality also.' Mr Harrison is an Englishman; he was presented to the Perpetual Curacy of Builth in September 1844, and consequently had resided there about two years at the period of his giving evidence. He had no previous acquaintance with Wales, and his subsequent experience has been closely limited to his own locality. His whole deposition therefore is impeachable on the grounds of his personal want of 'knowledge and intelligence,' and all consequences deduced from it by the Commissioner are nought. […]

It is probable that the 'intelligence' of the Reverend Mr Morgan, Rector of Machen, and Rural Dean, may be considered, by those who take the trouble of reading his depositions, as very questionable; and consequently, according to the Commissioner's own test, of little worth. Take the following specimens: 1. 'In my opinion a tram-road for the conveyance of coal from the hills to the sea-port, for exportation, tends to demoralize the district through which it passes to an inconceivable degree. The results are theft, drunkenness, and prostitution!' 2. 'From what I have seen within the last few days as regards the different works and collieries in my immediate neighbourhood, the sad, nay almost total ignorance on religious matters of children ripening into manhood, the total indifference of their masters, and I regret to add almost equally so of their parents, (beyond the obtaining the day's work on the part of the former, and the daily earnings on that of the latter) all convince me of the imperious necessity of even a compulsory system for the education of the working classes!'

It is much to be deplored that this gentleman's discoveries in his own 'immediate neighbourhood' being only a 'few days' old, he necessarily wanted time for attempting their compulsive remedy, and for the formation of those 'matured opinions' to which Commissioners of Inquiry justly attach such high importance.

Concerning a particular portion of the Evidence, Mr Symons states in a prefixed memorandum, 'The answers were numbered to correspond with the following questions, which were addressed only to such persons as were deemed likely to have a correct knowledge of the facts, and matured opinions on the general topics of the inquiry, and who, from their station or position were likely to know and represent the feelings as well as circumstances of different classes of the people.' The Rev. James Denning, Curate of St. Mary's Brecknock, is one of the standard bearers in this chosen band. As regards his 'matured opinions on the general topics of inquiry,' let it be remembered, that at the date of his deposition, Mr Denning had been less than two years a resident in the town of Brecknock, and to that place all his small knowledge and short experience of Wales was confined. The threefold Rev. J. Hughes, Rector of Llanhilleth via Newport, may afford him a wholesome lesson of reproof for his presumptuous assertions in the following words, addressed to Commissioner Symons; 'I have only lived 5 years in Monmouthshire, and I have carefully abstained from adverting to any points which I have not perfect knowledge of, lest I might possibly mislead you.' But no such conscientious scruples had Mr. Denning. Take a specimen of his 'correct knowledge of facts.' He represents Wales as 'sunk in comparative heathenism,' evidently labouring under the delusion that his parish in the town of Brecknock is Wales.

The Rev. Rees Price, Curate of St. John's in the same town says, 'If it be safe to judge of people's religious character by their regular attendance at places of worship, I think I may pronounce of a great portion of the people of this place that they are a religious people. It is pleasing to witness so many on the Lord's Day on their way to and from their several places of worship.'

Mr Denning in the same general manner says, 'The poor seem ignorant on most subjects except how to cheat and speak evil of each other.'

Mr Davies, Theological Professor of Brecknock College, a man who has 30 years experience as a Dissenting Minister in Wales, gives the following counter-testimony, 'On certain subjects there is much ignorance, such as history, &c., but on the subject of religion there is considerable information. They are generally ignorant of the English language, but it would be a sad mistake to judge of their knowledge by the ignorance of the English.' The Rev. W. L. Bevan, Vicar of Hay, deposes, 'I should not consider the poor as more ignorant than the generality of the poor in England.' He is competent to speak thus, being a Welshman educated in England.

Mr Denning asserts, 'The defect in morals which is most remarkable to a stranger is their double-dealing. No person here ever asks the sum he intends to take for an article. The seller vows and declares he will not dispose of an article for a less sum than he at first asks, but presently he lowers the price, if he sees you unwilling to buy – morals are very low indeed with regard to buying and selling. Truth is not regarded when money is concerned.' This passage is quoted as authentic evidence in proof of Brecknockshire morals, in the Commissioner's Report. Now the three parishes comprised in the county town contain a population of 5,746. Is it probable, is it even possible, that such an accusation can be true of *all* its tradesmen? Mr Davies states, 'I do not think their morals are generally defective – during my residence of 8 years in this neighbourhood I have never noticed anything particularly amiss or disorderly in the character of the inhabitants. The people appear to me to be generally quiet, and peaceable, and not meddling or given to change.'

Let us now consider Mr Denning as 'from station or position likely to know and represent the feelings as well as circumstances of different classes of the people'. In answer to question 8, 'Is the English language gaining ground, &c.,' Mr Davies replies, 'In the towns it may, though this may be doubtful, judging from the fact, that religious worship is generally conducted in all the Welsh towns in the Welsh language. In the country is it altogether Welsh, except on the borders. Twice as many use the Welsh language now as did 40 years ago. It would be a great benefit to have the English better taught, to introduce the Welsh to sources of general information.'

Concerning the 'violent suppression' of the vernacular tongue, Mr Griffith, President of the Independent College, Brecknock, says, quoting from the Llandovery Conference, 'That would be utterly impracticable even if desirable. The slightest hint of the kind would outrage our most cherished sympathies as a people.' The Rev. Rees Price of St. John's deposes that, 'The really Welsh portion of the people are very tenacious of their native language, and would regard with displeasure any means of doing away with it'. E. D. Thomas, Esq. of Wellfield, speaks of his fellow Cambrians as 'cherishing their well known national antipathy to strangers, and hostility to the settlement of English among them.' The sincerity and sympathy with which the feelings of the people are represented in the above depositions are unquestionable. In direct contradiction to them, Mr Denning exclaims, 'I cannot too strongly express my opinion about the necessity of getting rid of the Welsh language. Banish the Welsh language, and Englishmen will come and reside here, and thus a healthy tone will be given to society,' &c. Cambrian appreciation of such prophetic promises may be inferred from the previous paragraphs. Mr Denning is an Anglo-Irishman, and has fully manifested his perfect incapability of 'knowing and representing the feelings and circumstances of the people.' Yet this man's deposition is a high authority, a treasury of citation to Commissioner Symons!

In answer to question 3, 'Are their morals defective, and if so in what respects? State instances and facts which illustrate this.' L. V. Watkins, Esq. Lord Lieutenant of the county, residing in the parish of Battle, near Brecknock, says, 'I know of none.' To question 6, 'Would better education tend to improve the morals and conduct of the people?' he replies, 'I think them generally well-behaved.' Many of the deponents knowing nothing of any other country, county, or district than their own, naturally enough think its doings of all sorts unparalleled. Richard Williams, M. D. Aberystwyth, after maligning the morals of the poor, acknowledges, 'In justice I should say that many strangers have informed me, the lower classes of Wales are far superior to those of the same class in other parts of the kingdom.' He testifies that, 'The Welsh generally are sober and peaceable,' and that, 'Sunday is most religiously and devoutly observed by all classes.'

The majority of the witnesses had a direct personal interest in furthering the plan of the Commissioners. The landowners hoped to save their money, and the clergy and ministers their care and toil, by commending the schools to the proffered charge of the Executive Government, and therefore they endeavoured to give the worst possible account of the moral necessities of the people and to enforce the strength of their belief in the reformatory powers of secular education.

Prefixed to the Memorial of the Dissenters of Llanfair Caereinon, &c. is a very significant memorandum, made by Commissioner Johnson, implying that opinions of a certain tendency were both sought and sanctioned, and were acceptable in any casual varieties of form, ranking under the same species;

while against the intrusion of another this exculpatory protest was required, 'for the opinions as well as the statements which follow, the memorialists are alone responsible.' Among those reprobated opinions stands the following, delivered by Mr Robert Dafydd Thomas, 'The Dissenters of Wales are determined to make efforts to furnish the children of all classes and denominations with secular and liberal education, upon the plan and principles of the British and Foreign School Society, and that voluntarily. The only thing they wish is, that the government would not interfere any further with the education of the people, than by encouraging and assisting voluntary efforts of the people themselves, should they think it necessary, and that without any distinction.' […]

4. Character of the People I

Commissioner Johnson is content with accusing Wales of one vice: 'The besetting sin of North Wales – the peculiar vice of the Principality – incontinence.'[2] England, including Wales, is divided into 11 parts, for the purpose of the Registration Act. Mr Evan Jones, of Tredegar, gives a table of the percentage of illegitimacy in each of these divisions, and shows that out of the 11 divisions, five are in this respect more guilty than Wales; where prostitution and adultery are confessedly unknown.[3] Commissioner Lingen's accusation extends to four vices. 'A wide spread disregard of temperance, whenever there are means of excess, of chastity, of veracity, and of fair dealing.' In his parochial notes the character of 'sober' continually recurs. If it be lawful to entertain the supposition that the people are so merely from the absence of temptation, then may the indigent in all lands be accounted intemperate too. Of veracity and fair dealing, he appears, according to

---

[2] For 'incontinence' read 'sexual promiscuity'.

[3] See Evan Jones [Ieuan Gwynedd], 'A Vindication of the Educational and Moral Condition of Wales...' (1848), in Brinley Rees, ed., *Ieuan Gwynedd: Detholiad o'i Ryddiaith* (Caerdydd: Gwasg Prifysgol Cymru, 1957), 87-91.

his known notes, to have met with multitudinous cases, and brings no personal proof that he ever met with the contrary. Commissioner Symons not only prefers all the above charges, but terribly augments the list of offences, 'There are perhaps,' he remarks, 'few countries where the standard of minor morals is lower. Petty thefts, lying, cozening, every species of chicanery, drunkenness (where the means exist,) and idleness prevail to a great extent among the least educated part of the community, who scarcely regard them in the light of sins.' The attempt at fixing a foregone conclusion appears in the following passage, from the deposition of Cecil Parsons, Esq. of Presteigne, cited by Mr. Symons in his Report. 'It appears, from the Parliamentary Returns, that the proportion of illegitimate children in Radnorshire exceeds that of any other county.' Surely the Commissioner, if he required the aid of public documents, might have referenced to them himself, without blazoning the intervention of so weak a deputy in this second-hand mimicry of evidence. Again, Commissioner Symons says, 'In Radnorshire the morals of the people are of a very low standard.' Yet even Saxonized Radnorshire, the least moral county in Wales, may seem worthy perhaps, on the strength of the following evidence, to be compared with any county in England. R. Price, Esq. M.P. of Norton Court, says of his neighbours, 'I consider them as a sober and moral race of people.' F. Phillips, Esq. of Abbey Cwmhîr, says of the neglected people around him, 'They are, especially the women, civil and obliging in answering inquiries, showing the road, giving shelter or a cup of spring water; they knit stockings for their families.' […]

From the inevitable progress of good or evil habits in this probation world, the vices assigned to the Welsh by the Commissioners, must of necessity, if they really existed, have grown up into crimes, and earned the utmost penalties of the Law for a commensurate number of the depraved. The contrary however is proved by the following extract from Commissioner Symon's Report. 'Not-withstanding the lamentable state of morals the gaols are empty. The following comparison between the relative criminality of the three counties in my district, with that of the neighbouring agricultural county of Hereford, exhibits this moral anomaly in the Welsh character very forcibly.'

Counties of	Population in 1841	Committals for Trial at Assizes and Quarter Sessions for the 5 years ending with 1845	Centesimal proportion of offenders to Population.
Brecknock	55,603	261	0.46
Cardigan	68,766	135	0.19
Radnor	25,356	140	0.55
Hereford	113,878	1,198	1.05

'Crimes therefore are twice as numerous in Herefordshire as in Radnorshire, and five times more so than in Cardiganshire. I attribute this paucity of punishable offences in Wales, partly to the extreme shrewdness and caution of the people but much more to a natural benevolence and warmth of heart, which powerfully deters them from acts of malice and all deliberate injury of others; and I cannot but express my surprise, that a characteristic so highly to the credit of the Welsh people, and of which so many evidences presented themselves to the eye of a stranger should have been left chiefly to his own personal testimony.'

Here is reproof, the strongest, the keenest, the most contemptuous, which words can convey from the Commissioners, to the very hearts and consciences of their chosen auxiliaries, those traitors in the Welsh camp who have belied and betrayed their country. Here is an acknowledgement of the partial view given of Welsh character by the unqualified statements of evil in many of the depositions. As regards the 'mental condition of the children,' Commissioner Symons asserts, 'that it would be better ascertained by measuring results than by minute observation of the means used to produce them.' Yet here he virtually denies the effect of the same principle applied to men. This is at once illogical and unfair. The commissioners prefer, that the paucity of crime in Wales, should stand as a 'moral anomaly,' to the recognition of that powerfully exercised principle of conscience which really controls and regulates the ardent temperament of the people. Mr Symons says himself in another place, when hinting the likelihood of their becoming seditious, 'Their passions are easily excited, and their ignorance renders this excitability peculiarly hazardous.' What then becomes of their 'shrewdness, caution, and benevolence?' Prudential motives are indeed strong with most Welshmen, but moral motives are stronger, and religious ones strongest of all. Commissioner Johnson states, 'Whatever may be the defect of Society in North Wales, it is free in the five northern counties, from crimes of a heinous nature, and no signs of disaffection or sedition have appeared within the memory of man.' He adds in a note to the same sentence, 'The proportion of commitments for North Wales is 61.2 below the calculated average for all England and Wales, on the same amount of male population of the like ages.'

Lord John Russell, in his speech of July 16, 1846, in the

House of Commons, said, 'The amount of ignorance in this country [England], the want of education, the degree in which the gospel is entirely a sealed and unknown book is a lamentable fact.' The following evidence therefore cannot fail to be highly consolatory, so far as the Principality is concerned. The Rev. H. Griffiths, President of the Independent College at Brecknock, says, 'Taken as a whole, I believe the Welsh peasantry are decidedly superior to the English. Having spent 12 years as a Minister in England, and in daily communication with the poor, I may perhaps be allowed to speak with some confidence.' Again, he mentions the inhabitants of the 'purely Welsh towns,' as 'familiarized with truths which feed the heart, and which thereby quicken their minds and improve their manners. Hence in Wales, the education of the people is independent of, and therefore must not be measured by the extent of their school attainments.' He adds, 'In hundreds of our cottages at this day, you may find men of most elevated habits of thought and feeling, who never read a page in their lives but the Bible. The pulpit has been our national teacher, and nobly has it done its Work.' The Very Rev. the Dean of St. David's testifies that, 'The people derive a wonderful degree of biblical knowledge from their habit of questioning one another in the Sunday Schools.' The Rev. Edward Davies, of Brecknock College, a man much commended for his learning, piety, and zeal by Commissioner Symons, asserts, 'There are no people in the world so well provided with the means of religious instruction as the Welsh, as regards accommodation for religious worship, preaching, Sunday School instruction, and religious books.' And again, 'Very gross and mistaken statements have been made as regards education in Wales, parties not distinguishing, either from ignorance, or from some other cause, between secular education and that which is moral and religious. My position and standing as a Minister of the Gospel, and as a tutor of youth destined for the Welsh Ministry, enable me to say that the Principality will bear comparison with any country under the sun, in point of piety, good morals and religious information.' Commissioner Johnson felt, and acknowledges among the Welsh, 'The energetic working of a missionary spirit in Religion.' He says, 'The intelligence of the poorer classes in North Wales corresponds with the means afforded for education; far superior to the same class of Englishmen, in being able to read the Bible in their own language, supplied with a variety of religious and political literature, and skilled discussing with eloquence and subtlety abstruse points of polemic theology, they remain inferior in every branch of practical knowledge and skill. Their schools, literature and religious pursuits have cultivated talents for preaching and poetry, but for every other calling they are incapacitated.'

What secular information would do, is altogether an assumption on the part of the Commissioners and their allies; what religious education has done, and what it is doing, are obvious facts to every informed and intelligent observer. 'The Welsh,' declares J. Johnes, Esq. of Dolaucothi, 'are essentially a religious people, and desirous of knowledge.'

5. Character of the People II
'The Welsh,' announces Commissioner Symons, 'are peculiarly exempt from the guilt of great crimes. There are few districts in Europe where murders, burglaries, personal violence, rapes, forgeries, or any felonies on a large scale, are so rare.' Their generous and kindly, their social and brotherly feelings also, are proved even to him, by 'The ancient practice among neighbouring families of assisting the marriages of each other's children, by loans or gifts of money, at the 'biddings' or marriage meetings, to be repaid on a similar occasion in the family of the donor; as well as the attendance of friends at times of death, or adversity.'

They honour the Sabbath day. Commissioner Lingen says, 'When not in chapel the people are generally at their own homes, for they are not to be met any where on Sunday excepting on their way to and from the chapels.'

They are personally neat and clean. 'Sunday,' he says, 'is to him (the Welsh labourer) more than a day of bodily rest and devotion. It is his best chance all the week through, of showing himself in his own character. He marks his sense of it by a suit of clothes, regarded with a feeling hardly less Sabbatical than the day itself. I do not remember to have seen an adult in rags in a single Sunday School throughout the poorest district. They always seemed to me better dressed on Sundays than the same classes in England.' He attests that the children too are usually 'neat and well clad.' Their dissent is of the most tolerant and liberal character, and not only many members of the chapel congregations, but often the very ministers themselves attend the Welsh service at church. The peculiar affection of the people for the very name of the land of Canaan, as the native land of their Bible, and of their Redeemer, and the type of their Heavenly home, caused an informant of Mr Lingen's to say, that they were generally 'better versed in the geography of Palestine than of Wales.' […]

Mr Symons says, 'superstition prevails. Belief in charms, supernatural appearances, and even in witchcraft sturdily survives all the civilization, and light, which has long ago banished these remnants of the dark ages *elsewhere*.'

Does *elsewhere* mean England? Does it include London? Here is the counter testimony of a Public Reviewer. 'If there be any who think that astrology has subsided into a mere matter of harmless amusement, we tell them they are mistaken. Ask the second-hand booksellers if works on astrology and magic do not keep up their prices, and meet with a rapid sale; ask the auctioneer the same question. There are shops in London which deal in nothing but this pernicious diet.' The same Journal devotes successive articles to the exposure of the superstitious almanacs of Moore, Raphael, Merlinius Liberatus, Zadkiel, &c.

Mr Johnson distinctly states, that the morality of the people, 'is found to grow worse on approaching the English border.' The Rev. E. Davies, of Brecknock College, says, 'I believe the influence of bad example to be much more injurious to the morals of our poor than the want of education.' Yet Mr Lingen rejoices that, 'Rail-roads and the fuller development of the great mineral beds are on the eve of multiplying the points of contact.' […]

The Welsh small farmer lives harder than the English labourer, and the Welsh labourer harder still; and Commissioner Lingen found pretty and intelligent children 'quite hearty and happy' who did not remember when they had last tasted meat. […]

An instance of the way in which false deductions are drawn from facts occurs at page 56 of the Report of Commissioner Symons. He happened in the 'small town of Tregaron' to see a woman admit a sow into her cottage, and close the door, and hence he infers that, 'The pigs and poultry form a usual part of the family.' Once, and once only in the course of more than 20 years' experience of the 'Moral and Physical Condition of the People,' the writer witnessed a similar fact, two pigs were thus admitted to a neat kitchen, and on inquiring the cause of so strange a proceeding, was told by the tidy mistress of the cottage, that there was no back way to the premises, and therefore the pigs were obliged to be taken across the kitchen to their sty. Once, and once only, the writer found poultry a part of the indoor family. A solitary and very aged woman cherished a pet hen, which would sit on her knee or at her feet, and follow her about like a dog. When doors are open, and pigs and poultry are roaming about, they will often go prowling and prying into cottages, but their presence is never allowed or tolerated there. On several occasions the Commissioners betray their unacquaintance with the general habits of a rural population. One of them expresses surprise at not finding brick chimneys to cottages, in a region where brick is with difficulty procurable by the wealthy. Another, mentioning the women says, 'It would appear that household duties of a material nature, (whereof several are naturally picked up in the common routine of agricultural employment) were not altogether neglected.' Any Welsh matron would readily inform him, that practical skill in domestic occupations was never yet 'picked up' in the fields. Mr Symons, in trying to account for the fact, that the day schools in a rural district were attended more numerously by boys than girls, heightens his difficulty by the consideration that 'the labour of the boys becomes first available.' He knew such to be the case in the mining districts, and assumed it to be so everywhere, though any cottager could have told him that the girls' home services become first available, that they have not 'more leisure,' and cannot 'be better spared.'

These gentlemen cannot realize the necessities of rustic life, or they would not be so much surprised or offended at the interruption of a schoolboy's studies to go and look for the stray dog, or to drive a trespassing pig out his mother's garden, nor so very sadly annoyed by 'the whirring of a spinning wheel.' In his Report of the Mining Districts of Monmouthshire, Mr Symons says, 'In fact the parents who allow their children to remain in school a sufficient time to be well educated, must sacrifice from three shillings to ten shillings a week, besides the prospect of their remaining afterwards on their hands, owing to their incompetency to enter the business of which they had failed to pass through the noviciate.' If prolonged schooling has the effect of permanently disabling the children from earning their own living, it is very natural and proper that the prudent foresight of the parents should avert so dread an evil, however prosperous their own present circumstances may be. In the rural districts matters are very different. The same Commissioner states, 'The people in my district are almost universally poor. In some parts of it, wages are probably lower than in any part of Great Britain.' Children above 10 or 11 years of age, are therefore employed either in outdoor occupations which contribute more or less to their maintenance, or in taking care of infants, to enable the mother to pursue her labours. Mr Symons knows all this, and mentions 'The summer vacation, when every effort is directed to the accumulation of a small fund for the winter, and each child adds his quota to the labour which produces it.' He knows that the consequent irregularity of the children's attendance at day schools cannot be remedied, unless by a complete change in the circumstances of the people. Yet he can sneer at the poor mother, who boasted of sending her four children in quarterly turn to give equal advantages to each, and at the master who 'spoke of it as a very natural arrangement,' and terms it 'their driblet of schooling.' Commissioner Johnson, who appears to have understood rather better what to expect among the poor, also mentions 'the quarterage schools in Wales.' Neither of the Commissioners found it possible to ascertain precisely, the average duration of the children's attendance, but from their calculation, it would appear not to be lower than is usual 'elsewhere.' The Rev. R. Burgess, Secretary to the London Diocesan Society, says in his published Letter to Dr. Hook, 'I have taken some pains to ascertain one very important fact, as especially bearing upon religious instruction. I mean the average time for children remaining in our best schools, when we get them there; and I believe it will be found that the average does not extend in large towns and manufacturing districts to more than 15 months for boys, and something less for girls. In some of our seaports I find it extends to two years and a half, and occasionally 3 years, but I have little hesitation in affirming that throughout England, the average time passed by the children of our poor and industrious classes does not exceed two years, and if we confine ourselves to the populous places, 18 months will be an ample allowance under the most favourable circumstances.'

6. Day Schools
The three Commissioners agree in reporting the general

unfitness or incompleteness of the school buildings and furniture, apparatus, and all requisites, in the inefficiency of the master and mistresses, and the worthlessness of the Welsh Day Schools. It is some consolation to poor Cambria, under their sweeping censure of all her habits and institutions, painfully conscious as she is of the mote in her own bright eye, and anxious to remove it, compassionately to recognize that beam, which dazzles and overshadows her giant sister's vision. Read the following account of the Day Schools of England: one might suppose that the Commissioners had written it only of Wales. 'The Report of the Inspectors of Schools disclosed that a great number of instances even the primary arrangements for enclosing the school site, providing proper offices, completing the drainage and ventilation of the building, furnishing it with proper means of warmth in winter, and with desks and benches for the scholars, were either executed in meagre and insufficient manner, or were, in some cases, entirely neglected. […]'

Conscious of failure in the attempt to make out a case for Government interference on the ground of deficient quantity of educational means in Wales, the Commissioners endeavour to effect their object by depreciating and disparaging their quality. It appears from the following paragraph, that the intention of the Commissioners in questioning the children, was rather to convict of ignorance, than to fathom the depth of attainable knowledge. 'My examinations' says Mr Symons, 'have been essentially catechetical, and having in view the catholic nature of the inquiry, they were not confined to the limited scope of the subject taught in the schools visited, but were extended to most branches of ordinary information.' Proceeding on this principle, it is not surprising that he found cause for terming the poor children's answers to his questions 'grotesque guesses and wild efforts.'

It is not many years since the conviction that it is right to diffuse general information among the labouring classes has been acknowledged even in England. Old and honoured opinion long pronounced it needless and wrong. At length it was allowed that they might safely, and perhaps profitably, be taught to read their Bibles; and then the slow concession of writing and arithmetic doubtfully and reluctantly followed. At this stage in the educational progress of opinion, many of the patrons of the Welsh Day Schools are now quietly halting. Under these circumstances sufficient regard has not been shown by the Commissioners in the examination of particular schools, to what has been designed and attempted there. They have used an improper test, and elicited false results. Every thing is wrong in their eyes; even the Infant Schools are '*too exclusively infantile.*'

The wide and superficial culture, and the precocious fruits of the new system, are all to them. That system, however, has many faults, and is often brought to bear too strongly upon the feeble effort of incipient thought. It is a strain on childish reason more injurious in effect, than over-exertion is to the tender muscles of the frame. It is a process of stove-forcing supplied to a British forest tree, insuring precocious maturity, and enfeebling its object for ever. Many of its examinations are like tearing open a spring blossom to seek in it the undeveloped germen of autumn fruit.

'The organic and essential inefficiency of the Welsh Day Schools,' is dilated upon in the Commissioners' Reports, with an air of positive complacency. The masters are held up to ridicule, and the scholars to contempt. A special company of blunders is drawn out from their crowded depot in the Appendix, to parade on the conspicuous platform of each Report. No adequate allowance is made there for the throng of difficulties with which the children have at once to contend in such examinations. Among those difficulties must be reckoned an extemporaneous translation made from one language into another, which remarkably differs from it in construction and idiom. Many of the subjects too, required recollection and thought, while the children's self possession was disturbed, and their attention led astray by the presence and interference of strangers. They were also embarrassed by timidity, and by that greatest of all hinderances to successful exhibition, the wish to appear to peculiar advantage.

One of the Commissioners indeed seems to have taken an almost malicious pleasure in producing consternation in the master, and confusion in the scholars, not only by his '*exhaustive examinations*', but by taking an 'opportunity,' as he says 'of going suddenly into schools.' Perhaps a similar course of examination upon all the various types of instruction, carried on in the French language, might not have elicited more satisfactory or more grammatical replies from the pupils of most English boarding schools. Some of the questions proposed were certainly very puzzling. It is complained that, 'The children were very ignorant, and could not say what an angel is.' Who can? The wisest do but express the same idea by another term, using three words instead of one. Again, 'No one in the school could explain "mock," except that it was an unkind thing to do.' Might not the Commissioner have perceived, that a single truth, thus thoroughly understood by an independent act of mind, really gives it more invigorating exercise, than hours of the most ingenious cross-questioning upon words and second notions? Take the following list of answers as a proof of the perplexing order of the Commissioners' school questions: 'The coldest quarter is the east; the pupils were not agreed whether the East Indies are a hot or cold country. On my saying "right" to a girl who answered "hot," and then asking what was the climate of the West Indies, they all said "cold".' This proves at least that the poor catechumens trusted more to their misled reason, than to memory. They are accused of not knowing the use of prepositions and conjunctions; but they appear once at least to have taught the learned Commissioner himself the correct application of the adverb. Instead of 'What is gunpowder made of?' the Commissioner put the question, 'How is gunpowder made?' and was immediately answered 'By the invention of man,' on further explanation, the reply was given, 'Of Charcoal and Sulphur.' Here was a manifest distinction made between the means employed, and the materials used. [...]

Commissioner Symons remarks, 'I have asked the boys selected by the master as his grammarians, in several schools, which is the adjective in the sentence, 'I am going to beat the dog,' or the adverb in, 'I shall stir the fire,' and have rarely found them fail to guess half the words in the sentence, so thoroughly devoid of thought, or inculcation of principle is the whole system of teaching.' The Commissioner would have done more justice in giving them credit for the deference which could not believe he would suggest an error, and for the native courtesy, which even when it was discerned, restrained them from apparently contradicting him, by saying that neither adjective nor adverb was there. By way of extenuating his harshness, Commissioner Symons pleads to begin, 'The rigorous impartiality enjoined us by your Lordships.' Cato the Censor was not more rigorous! Cicero against Anthony showed not less impartiality! As to singing, he allows, 'The children have great capacity for it, and their voices are not devoid of melody.' While Commissioner Lingen was evidently, and often touched by the sweetly sung, 'Old fashioned carol tune, rude and simple, yet pleasing; and the singularly simple and plaintive hymn tune,' which he 'never heard before. It is owned, that these poor children say their lessons, 'Frequently and with wonderful accuracy and rapidity,' though, 'in a Welsh screech.' Take the same Commissioner's testimony to their remarkable powers of memory. 'The proficiency of the children in spelling is wonderful. I have found complete mastery over the puzzling question of the precedence of the *e* and *i* in receive, believe, perceive, mischief, grief &c. and plough, crow, cough, through, and though, have been correctly spelt, by certainly a majority of the Welsh children to whom I have put them in a great number of schools.' He also states, 'In arithmetic, the natural ability of the children is clearly displayed. I have witnessed more proficiency after a small amount of instruction, than I ever witnessed in any schools, either in England or on the Continent.'

The general ignorance of geography and grammar is very shocking to all the Commissioners. It is a somewhat awkward fact, that their own Assistants occasionally make an ungrammatical record of the grammatical errors they have detected, 'nor could neither – How much coals,' &c. The syntax of one of these critical Commissioners moreover is remarkable for almost transatlantic inelegance. It is allowed, that wherever languages and the sciences were properly taught, the children excelled in them; and that some of their drawings were admirable. Commissioner Lingen admits in the appendix, where all favourable admissions lie hid in safe obscurity, 'I rarely found that the children were so utterly ignorant and irrational as they appeared, at first, if one could stay long enough with them. – They are above their education, owing to their natural intelligence.' […]

9. Language

The words of Mr Williams's Motion of March 10, 1846, in the House of Commons, strike the key-note of all that follows, and 'the means afforded to the labouring classes of obtaining a knowledge of the English language,' are made the test of 'the State of Education in the Principality of Wales.' Commissioner Johnson says, 'The Sunday schools, as the main instrument of civilization in North Wales, have determined the character of the language, literature, and general intelligence of the inhabitants. The language cultivated in the Sunday Schools is Welsh, the subjects of instruction are exclusively religious; consequently the religious vocabulary of the Welsh language has been enlarged, strengthened, and rendered capable of expressing every shade of idea; and the great mass of the poorer classes have been trained from their childhood to its use.' Commissioner Symons testifies, 'The Celtic race therefore, who have learned English, are a mere fraction of the population, confined chiefly to the towns of Brecknock, Aberystwyth, Crickhowel, and Talgarth, and a small number of people in the town of Cardigan, whose Celtic origin is questionable.' Commissioner Lingen describes the part of his district where English is spoken, as 'Lying to the south of the London mail-road, i.e. the entire southern coast line, and the depth of a few miles behind it, from Cardiff to the coast of the Irish Sea, with the exception of the interval between Swansea and St. Clares, where the south-eastern corner of Caermarthenshire reaches down to the British channel. Throughout the rest of my district, especially in those quarters which are inland and rural – there is no general and popular acquaintance with it.'

'The Welshman,' he adds, 'possesses a mastery over his own language, far beyond that which the Englishman of the same degree possesses over his.' And again, 'Readiness and propriety of expression, to an extent more than merely colloquial, is certainly a feature in the intellectual character of the Welsh.' And yet, still further on, he deploringly explains, 'Language is not cultivated further than to be on a level with the use that is to be made of it.' At Llanelltyd, *a wise and excellent plan*, which Commissioner Johnson terms '*an experiment!*' has been tried by 'Sir Robert and Lady Williames Vaughan, who are anxious to bring up the children of their tenantry in the principles of the Established church, and believe that this can only be effected by *teaching them religion according to those principles in the Welsh language.* Hence the charity children in the schools at Llanelltyd and Llanfachreth are *required* to learn to read Welsh first, and when they can read Welsh with ease, are at liberty (if they stay long enough) to learn to read English.'

The first Report among the memorials from the Dissenters of Llanfair Caereinon, Castell Caereinon, and Manafon, in the county of Montgomery, states 'There are some people of the Welsh nation, that are in the habit of speaking English with their children from their infancy, and consequently there are many children of the Welsh people that cannot speak their mother tongue. We consider this a very bad practice, because those children can speak no language perfectly, and generally cannot enjoy the privileges of our Sunday Schools, because they are conducted in the Welsh language. Every child has a right to know the language of his parents. To deprive them of that is an insult to our nation, language, and country. We greatly abhor this practice, but it is the case generally on the borders of England; and this is one reason why Offa's Dyke is like Sodoma and Galilee of the Gentiles, in ungodliness and ignorance, &c.' This Report is authorized by eleven Dissenting Ministers and Teachers, and signed by a twelfth.

Commissioner Lingen admits that, 'There is no inconsiderable number of the clergy, both established and dissenting, who would have Welsh still popularly taught, and not simply employed in teaching.' He intimates that the native clergy, who speak Welsh, and have been wholly educated in Wales, are therefore a hindrance to their country's educational progress; and covertly hints that the poor provision which the Church offers to 'an educated man,' prevents it having the advantage of Englishmen's services. Not considering that the religious ministrations of foreigners are almost as offensive to the Cymry now, as they were in the days when usurping Gregory sent Augustine the charge, 'The Bishops of the British Churches I confide wholly to thee,' almost as irksome, as the spiritual pastors from Normandy, who forced themselves upon the native Welsh, to their 'intolerable annoyance.' The respect ever shown by Bishop Burgess to Welsh nationality, was honourable alike to himself and to the people. The discreet and wise regulations of the present Bishop of St. David's concerning the Ordination and Induction of the clergy of his diocese, and the fact that he has himself learned their language and preaches in it, sufficiently prove the high importance which is attached by the most competent judges to the use and cultivation of the vernacular tongue.

Throughout these Reports, multitudinous ill-effects are attributed to the Welsh language. It is accused of facilitating and encouraging perjury. Mr. Hall, of Newcastle Emlyn, says, 'The Welsh language is peculiarly evasive, which originates from its having been the language of slavery.' Commissioner Symons enunciates, 'The Welsh language is a vast drawback to Wales, and a manifold barrier to the moral progress and commercial prosperity of the people. It is not easy to overestimate its ill-effects. It is the language of the Cymry, and anterior to that of the Ancient Britons. It dissevers the people from intercourse which would greatly advance their civilization, and bars the access of improving knowledge to their minds. As a proof of this, there is no Welsh literature worthy of the name.' This is such manifest tirade as scarcely to deserve a comment. Is the language of the Ancient Britons the language of slavery? Tacitus characterizes that nation as a 'Warlike people, independent, fierce, and obstinate.' In that language, he, whom his enemies praise as 'that heroic chieftain,' Caractacus, incited his fellow-warriors to struggle unwearied through long and successive years, for an 'era of liberty.' In that language Boadicea spoke, when she asserted 'the cause of public liberty.' In that too, after retreating before the Saxons to the strongholds of Cambria, the Bards rejoiced that the Cymry could still preserve 'Their country, their language, and their God.' It is a nation proverbial through all ages for buoyancy and elasticity of spirit; for passing lively hope through all discouragements; for always arising from defeat with fresh alacrity; for having endured even conquest without subjugation.

Mr Symons's reference to the antiquity of that language

was at once misplaced and impolitic. Who can desire that a
language so venerable, so hallowed by associations, should
die? It is still the living utterance of all that is most tender,
most sacred, and most precious to the Cymry. Since the
days of the Apostles, they have worshipped in its words; for
centuries they have read their Bible in that language; of late
years it has been the medium of renewed religious diligence;
it is now the great and mighty agent which is working out their
temporal and eternal good.

Of its *secular* advantages or disadvantages, they may
surely be allowed to judge for themselves. Of its religious
worth, the proofs are undeniable. One result of England's
missionary experience in foreign lands is, the ascertained
principle that native missionaries in every country can alone
be depended on effectively to carry out the work of national
instruction. Nowhere is nationality more strongly felt, or
more fondly valued, than in Wales. Why then, lying close to
England's border, should she be denied a privilege, of which
the enjoyment is sanctioned in the remotest isles of Anglican
enterprise?

A passage has been already quoted, in which Commissioner
Symons asserts that 'There is no Welsh literature worthy of
the name.' Commissioner Johnson's Assistant, Mr James,
gives however a goodly catalogue of books, though limited
merely to those 'Of a character to be commonly read by the
people.' General ignorance cannot possibly exist where such
books are commonly read and understood. After severely
criticizing, in critic's sourest mood, the Welsh Periodicals,
Commissioner Symons adds, 'Nevertheless they have partially
lifted the people from that perfect ignorance and utter vacuity
of thought, which otherwise would possess at least two thirds
of them.'

It is this mode of condemning the people for what they
possibly might have been or done, under some non-existent
contingencies, which strikingly betrays, upon many occasions,

the want of candour, the pervading partiality and prejudice of their Reports. The people are considered to be temperate, merely from poverty; poor from idleness; submissive from want of rebel leaders; free from great crimes from aversion to punishment; and would doubtless have experienced 'vacuity of thought,' if their minds had not been stored with information.

The Hon. E. M. L. Mostyn, M.P., Lord Lieutenant of the county of Merioneth, mentioning the English language, says, 'The acquisition of which is necessary to prevent the demoralization consequent upon a state of ignorance.' The Commissioners seldom received any influential testimony so precisely to their purpose as this. The words of the Rev. William Evans, of Aberayron, convey the summary meaning of the Welsh deponents generally upon this subject. 'I think it beneficial for them to learn English, *but not forget their own language.*'

Look down the Commissioner's pages of cited passages, from competent authorities, on the subject, and they amount to no more. Mr Lingen believes it impossible to make the Welsh language the vehicle of necessary secular information. He cannot mean that such information is indissolubly amalgamated with the English Language, for all the European states are actively contributing their several quotas to the world's supply. The whole vocabulary of modern science has been added to the English dictionary since the days of Dr. Johnson; and its terms are principally derived from sources as familiarly known to the learned men of Wales as to those of England. It is very difficult to believe, that a language copious enough to afford a most energetic and noble vision of the Bible, can be found insufficient for any other human use.

After multiplying and magnifying the short comings and misdoings of the Welsh, the whole aggregate of imputed enormities is traced, according to Mr Williams's directing index, to one origin, their ignorance of the English language, in utter forgetfulness of that sad taint of hereditary sin which 'infects every person born into this world,' and alike the Saxon and the Celt. Gazing too intently upon their scarlet catalogues of Welsh iniquities, the Commissioners never fail to see, floating before their closed eyes, that verdant accidental colour, the English language.

Yet confessedly some obstacles occur in changing a nation's vernacular speech. 'In proportion,' bewails Commissioner Lingen, 'as the teacher adheres to English he does not get beyond the child's ears; in proportion as he employs Welsh, he appears to be superseding the most important part of the child's instruction.'

It is owned too that a certain schoolmaster complained, it took him a full month to make his boys remember the English names for numerals instead of the Welsh ones. Yet amid difficulties of this kind, which evidently bewilder his faculties, Commissioner Lingen is anxious to advise and to encourage the patronizing Committee of Council, in assaulting that 'wall of brass' – 'the popular language.' He says, 'Schools are not called upon to impart in a foreign, or engraft upon the ancient tongue a factitious education, conceived under another set of circumstances, (in either of which cases the task would be as hopeless as this end unprofitable,) but to convey in a language which is already in process of becoming the mother tongue of the country, such instruction as may put the people on a level with that position which is offered to them by the course of events. If such instruction contrast in any points with the tendency of old ideas, such contrast will have its reflex and justification in the visible change of surrounding circumstances.' It is to be hoped the Secretary has a key to this cipher; to the uninitiated it reads very much like *nonsense*. 'My district,' says Commissioner Lingen, 'exhibits the phenomenon of a peculiar language isolating the mass from the upper portion of society.' This phenomenon which strikes the commissioner so much is not without many parallels in history. One of them, familiarly known, may be appositely

mentioned here. Through many centuries Norman French
was the language of the English Court, and of the English
nobility and judicature, yet the depressed and despised
Saxon clung to his native literature, and worked quietly on,
speaking the foreign language just as much as business made
necessary, and no more time; enriching his mind meanwhile
with the information it conveyed, and enlarging his own
copious language with all its best words. That Saxon treasury
possessed already vast stores of verbal wealth from Celtic
and Latin sources, and at last it absorbed also the dialect of
its conquerors. They would *if they could* have forced their
language – barbarous dialect, and mere patois though it was,
upon conquered England. They tried various means to effect
it, *and they failed.*

Liberty is better appreciated, and far better understood in
our days. England expects a liberal government, free trade,
the freedom of the press, and universal religious toleration,
yet oh, most strange anomaly! should her rulers deny to their
Cambrian fellow-subjects mere freedom of speech, the use of
their ancient mother tongue! Can tyranny itself go farther,
unless it touch the unuttered and indignant thought? The
language of the Cymry, once spoken by Cassibelaunus, has
lived on under Roman and Norman domination. The wish to
destroy it is unworthy of the Englishman. The cleaving of the
Jews to Hebrew, which, through no longer a living tongue,
is still understood by almost every one of those wanderers
among the nations, speaking, as they do, all the various
languages of the earth, is not more tenacious than that of the
Cymry to their ancient mother tongue. They love it still, as
that enthusiastic Welshman of the twelfth century did, who
told King Henry, 'Thy power may weaken, and in part ruin
this nation, but to destroy its integrity of existence the wrath
of God is alone sufficient. In the day of Final Judgement, I
believe, that no other race, no other tongue, but that of the
Cymry, will give answer for this corner of the earth to the

Sovereign Judge.'[4]

10. Conclusion

This inquiry has avowedly been made, 'In order that her Majesty's Government and Parliament may be enabled, by having these facts before them, in connexion with the wants and circumstances of the population of the Principality, to consider what measures ought to be taken for the improvement of the existing means of education in Wales.' Mr. Symons declares, that himself and his colleagues were aware of their 'Entire powerlessness to effect the Inquiry by authority, the very semblance of which would be obnoxious to the Welsh people; and of the perfect facility with which they could render the investigation abortive, if indisposed to its execution.' 'I am enabled to state,' he adds, 'that throughout my district I have met with the utmost facility, and the most willing and valuable cooperation from all classes of the community. Facilities and hospitality have everywhere abounded.' The other commissioners make similar acknowledgements. With the guileless simplicity of those who have nothing to hide, the Welshmen threw open their schools and their homes to those gentlemen. With native courtesy they welcomed them as strangers, with inborn loyalty they respected and honoured them as government Commissioners.

But ere Mr Symons had completed his inquisitorial researches, he found that their purport had become thoroughly understood and was utterly abhorrent to the people. He says, 'The hostility evinced towards your Lordships' Minutes of Council of 1846 made known just previously to my arrival in Monmouthshire, in some measure, and in some cases, extended itself to my Inquiry, and impeded its execution.' The Commissioners would have found that hostility everywhere,

---

[4] The 'old man of Pencader' to Henry II, according to Giraldus Cambriensis, *Descriptia Kambria* (1163).

on making their tour over again. The Rev. Edward Davies, of Brecknock College, one of the most influential Dissenting ministers in Mr Symons's district says, 'A considerable change has come over the views of many dissenters since the appearance of the reports on Education in Wales. I have seen my country cruelly libelled, and needlessly caricatured, and all for a certain purpose, which he who runs may read.'

As regards the pecuniary means possessed by the Principality for educating its own poor, the Hon. Mr Mostyn, Lord Lieutenant of the county of Merioneth, states, 'I have no hesitation in saying, so far as North Wales is concerned (with the whole of which I am intimately acquainted) that no means whatever exist for providing a sound elementary education for the children of the labouring classes, except in a very few localities, and in those places the means are not sufficient and partially applied.' Mr Johnson on the contrary states, in his Report, concerning the permanent School Endowments of North Wales, 'The sum at present available for education from this source considerably exceed £4,000, exclusive of lost charities, and certain large endowments, which being under litigation have not been returned.' And again, 'The amount annually raised by charitable contributions of the rich is (in round numbers) £5,675, that raised by the poor £7,000,' and he further remarks thus upon this £7,000, 'an income which, when compared with that given by the rich for the support of schools, £5,675, disproves the universal complaint of the indifference of the poor towards education, and which, if combined with the latter and the endowments at present wasted, might support a system of education not wholly disproportionate to the wants of the inhabitants.' The School endowments in the six counties of South Wales amount to £2,388. 3s 5d., the annual contributions of the rich to £6,280. 1s 1d., and the pence of the poor to £12,239. 3s 9d. As regards the Mining Districts, commissioner Lingen says, 'Mr Price (of Neath Abbey) was one of the proprietors of Works who introduced the custom of weekly stoppages for the support of a school. Mr Price considered that the Masters in South Wales, had the power by these means to provide effectually for the education of the people without further assistance.'

It has been satisfactorily shown, from the Commissioners' own Tables, and from earlier official returns, that the proportion of Day Scholars to population, which was as one to twenty-six in the year 1830, had increased to one in nine, or nine and a half, in 1846-7; and that the Welsh Sunday Schools are attended by one in every three and a half of the whole working population, men, women and children.

Hence it is apparent, that the extraordinary talents and capacities of this ever intelligent people are now going through the most effectual of all mental and moral training, in that education which genius works out for itself.

And acquaintance with religious truth has widely excited among them that consciousness of responsibility, which, involving the principle of duty, insures at once the good conduct of the subject and the security of the state.

If Secular Education had been found abounding, and Religious Education more or less neglected, that circumstance might indeed have afforded grounds for urging increased diligence upon its proper superintendents and guardians, the clergy, and other Ministers of Religion. But even then, the direct and unprecedented interference of the Executive Government, in the regular management and inspection of Schools, would still have demanded, as it now imperatively does, Preventive Opposition, from the watchful Friends of BRITISH LIBERTY.

3. Augusta Hall, Lady Llanover

Anerchiad i Gymraësau Cymru (An address to the Welsh Women of Wales)

Y Gymraes, I, 8-11, 1850

Fy Nghydwladesau, – Er efallai y synnwch wrth weled testun yr ysgrif hon, ac y bernwch y buasai anerchiad i 'Ferched Cymru' gyfleu *ystyr* fy mwriad, eto credaf yr addefwch ar ôl darllen y llinellau hyn fod gwahaniaeth mawr rhwng y Gymraes o Gymru a'r ddynes sydd yn byw yng Nghymru, er y dichon eu bod wedi eu geni yno, a hyd y nod [sic] o rieni Cymreig; ond yr hon nis gall honni yr enw o Gymraes o Gymru, oblegid nad yw erioed wedi ymdrechu yn ei gwlad ei hun nac allan ohoni i gyflawni dyletswyddau y dosbarth anrhydeddus hwn. Oblegid *anrhydeddus* y rhaid eu bod pa un bynnag ai tlawd ai cyfoethog, mewn rhagoroldeb moesol, os gwir deilyngant eu galw yn 'Gymraësau o Gymru', ac i gael eu hystyried fel merched cywir y wlad sydd wedi ei breintio gan ragluniaeth mewn cynifer o ffyrdd nodedig.

Bwriadaf yn y lle cyntaf nodi allan y dylanwad a feddiennir gan ferched.

Yn ail y gwrthrychau y dylid [sic] gwir Gymraësau eu dwyn oddi amgylch.

Yn drydydd, y budd a ddeilliai oddi wrth lwyddiant yr ymdrechion a gymeradwyir gennyf, yng nghyd â'r drygau a ochelid.

Gallu merched yw *eu dylanwad*, ac y mae eu dylanwad

priodol yn annherfynol. Mae dynion yn ddibynnol arnynt am
holl gysuron eu bywyd. Hebddynt hwy ni chaent ymborth
parod i'w fwyta, na gwisgoedd addas i'w dodi am danynt. Ond
gall fy narllenasai ddywedyd fod gan lawer a ddarllenant y
llinellau hyn, wasanaethddynion i goginio a gwnïo iddynt. Ond
ail ddywedaf y rhaid i dadau, brodyr, gwŷr a phlant, ddibynnu
ar eu merched, eu chwiorydd, eu gwragedd, a'u mamau er
hynny. A pha fwyaf o gynhorthwy a dderbynnir oddi wrth
wasanaethddynion, a phersonau dibynnol arnynt, mwyaf oll yr
ymestyn eu dylanwad, cynydda fel ceinciau pren, heb leihau
yn y mesur lleiaf yn ymyl y gwraidd. Ar ôl rhagymadrodd
fel hyn, dichon y disgwylir fy mod yn myned i gynnig rhyw
ymdrech anghyffredin o eiddo y meddwl neu'r deall, yr hon
nas gall ond ychydig ferched gyrraedd, a'r hon nas gallai ond
llai fyth gael amser na hamdden i ymwneud â hi. Ond gall
pawb wneud fy nghyngor heb golli un awr, na gadael y cylch y
mae Duw wedi eu gosod ynddo. Mae fy nghyfarwyddiadau yn
gymwys i bawb o'r bwthyn i'r palas, a gallaf sicrhau iddynt os
dilynant hwy y byddent yn *ddedwyddach* o'r herwydd, heb sôn
am fwynhau yr ymwybodolrwydd o'u bod yn gwneud yr hyn
sydd iawn. Ond nid wyf yn myned i bregethu i chwi, – gadawaf
hynny i weinidogion eich gwahanol enwadau crefyddol. Bydd
iddynt hwythau nodi allan eich prif ddyletswyddau ar y ffordd
i'r nef. Eto, y mae dolennau yng nghadwyn ein dyletswyddau
ar y ddaear, y rhai a mynych dorrir neu esgeulusir, ond y rhai,
pe y gofelid am danynt a wnaent ein llwybr drwy y byd hwn
yn ddiogelach a hyfrytach, ac a esmwythaent yr anawsterau
i gyrraedd byd gwell. Yr wyf yn cyfeirio yn fwyaf neilltuol
at feithriniad ysbryd *cenedlgarol*, yr hwn sydd nid yn unig y
mwyaf diniwed, ond yn un o'r pethau mwyaf llesol y gellir
llanw meddwl dyn ag ef. Y mae *cenedlgarwch* wedi ei blannu
ynddom gan Ragluniaeth ddoeth a da, ac fel pob dawn arall os
esgeulusir ef, y mae *drwg yn sicr o ddilyn*. Er y mynych arferir
y gair *cenedlgarwch*, ychydig sylw a delir i'w bwysigrwydd,
ac ni ddeallir ei natur ond yn dra amherffaith. Os gofynnir,

pa beth yw *cenedlgarwch*? bydd llawer o'm darllenesau yn barod i ateb, mai 'cariad at ein gwlad ein hunain, a gofal neilltuol am ein cydwladwyr a'n cydwladesau'. Can [sic] belled ac y mae hyn yn myned, y mae o'r gorau, ond ni bydd y fath genedlgarwch â hwn byth yn rhinwedd gweithgar a ddylai dreiddio drwy ein holl feddyliau, teimladau a syniadau beunyddiol, ac arwain i ddaioni yn y cyfan. Y cenedlgarwch sydd *weithgar*, ac a brawf ei hun mewn *gweithredoedd* yn gystal â *geiriau*, ydyw yr hwn wyf yn cymeradwyo i'm cydwladesau, a'r hwn y bwriada yr ysgrif hon eu tueddu i'w arferid yn gystal â'i ganmol. Ni wada ein gelyn pennaf nad yw Cymru yn wlad deg a phrydferth. Nid ydyw cyfaddef y ffaith hon, gan hynny, yn arwydd o rinwedd na doethineb; ac nid hawdd i'r rhai a anwyd ac a fagwyd yn y wlad hon, beidio â theimlo yn falch pan fawrygir ei cheinion a'i chynhyrchion lluosog. Ond nid yw hyn ond cysgod o genedlgarwch, nid yw ond teimlad yr hwn nas gellir braidd ei ochelyd; ymdaena yn ddiymdrech dros y meddwl, a diflanna yn ddisylw, ac yn fynych ni ddychwel byth i'r galon seriedig ac oerllyd o'r hon yr ymadawodd.

Ni a drown yn awr at wir genedlgarwch, gan ddangos pa fodd y *dylai* ddylanwadu ar bob gwir Gymraes, pa un bynnag y byddo yn mwynhau y fraint o drigo yn ei gwlad enedigol neu ym mhell mewn bro estronol. Perthyn i'r genedl rai pethau neilltuol, ac y mae doethineb ein cyd[sic]-dadau wedi eu hystyried yn deilwng o barch a chyson dyfalbarhad. Yr wyf yn cyfeirio yn neilltuol at ein hiaith werthfawr. Rhodd Duw yw iaith. Nid oedd dyn yn alluog i'w ffurfio; y mae yn wyrth safadwy, ac yn brawf o allu y Creawdwr. Y mae rhai ieithoedd yn burach, ac yn fwy cynhwysfawr, a helaethach nac eraill. Mae yr iaith Gymraeg nid yn unig ym mysg yr henaf, ond yn un o'r rhai mwyaf aruchel, oherwydd ei gallu darluniadol, sydd wedi ei diogelu ar y ddaear. Y mae ei phrif elfennau yn anghyfnewidiol ers cyfnod mor henafol fel na all hanesyddion ddywedyd, gydag un radd o sicrwydd, pa bryd *nad oedd* ein cenedl yn siarad yr un iaith â ninnau, yn preswylio Ynys Brydain.   Yn yr iaith hon yr addolodd ein cyd[sic]-dadau y Duw yr ydym ninnau yn addoli.   Gwyddom fod Duw wedi defnyddio ein hiaith fel offeryn a'n cadw rhag llawer o drueni a ddygodd llygredigaeth ar y Saeson.   Mae y dyn neu'r ddynes sydd yn ymfodloni ar gyhoeddiad moesol o fath lyfrau Cymreig y dywysogaeth, yn sefyll gwell cyfle i arwain buchedd sobr, gyfiawn, a duwiol ymarweddiad, o gael ei barchu yn y byd hwn, ac o gyrraedd dedwyddwch yn y byd a ddaw, na'r rhai y gwenwynir eu meddyliau gan y wasg Seisonig.   Lledaenir y rhai hyn ym mysg bechgyn a genethod eu hysgolion, a gall y sawl â ddarlleno y papurau Seisonig o bryd i bryd, weled ynddynt ardystiadau gan rieni a noddwyr plant yn erbyn y llyfrau dychrynllyd hyn.   Eto y maent mor aml, fel y mae nifer luosog o bersonau yn ennill eu bywoliaeth wrth eu cyfansoddi, a chyhoeddi.   Diolch i Dduw, nid ydym ni yng Nghymru yn gwybod ond ychydig am bethau fel hyn, ond cofiwn os nad bydd i ni goleddu a meithrin ein hiaith ein hunain, yr hon sydd wedi ei chadw mor rhyfeddol i'r dibenion puraf, ac yn yr hon y mae yn barod fwy o lyfrau, nag y gall y doethaf eu myfyrio yn drwyadl mewn can' mlynedd, y bydd i ni golli amddiffynfa gref ein rhinwedd a'n dedwyddwch, ac y gosodir ein plant yn agored i'r holl ddrygau y cyfeiriasom atynt.   Famau Cymru! siaradwch Gymraeg wrth eich plant.   Eich esgeulustod beius chwi, a brad eich calon fydd yr achos, os na bydd i'ch hiliogaeth floesg swnio eu geiriau cyntaf yn yr iaith a roddodd Duw i'n henafiaid ym more y byd.   Oddi wrthych chwi (ac nid eu tadau) y dysgant garu Duw yn eu hiaith eu hunain.   Ar y llaw arall, os esgeuluswch chwi eich dyletswydd, drwyddoch chi y deuant yn epil gymysgryw, yr hon na arddelir gan neb, ond a ddiystyrir gan bawb, a wyddent fod iddynt unwaith genedl, ac iaith, ond i'w mamau 'werthu eu genedigaeth fraint am saig o gawl.'[1]

---

[1] Hebreaid, xii, 16.   Cyfeirir at stori Esau yn Genesis, xxv, 29-34.

Can [sic] belled ag y mae tynged eich meibion a'ch merched yn eich llaw chwi, Famau Cymru, na adewch iddynt ddysgu iaith *hawdd* yr estron, hyd nes y medront iaith *anhawdd* eu gwlad eu hunain; ac *yna*, os bydd amgylchiadau bydol yn gofyn y Saisonaeg, bydd ychydig o wythnosau yn ddigon i'w meistroli. Ond bydded iaith yr aelwyd, ac iaith crefydd, yr hon a osododd Duw yn rhan i'r Cymry, a chyhyd ag y cadwont hi, ni raid iddynt ofni na bydd iddynt darian ac astalch yn erbyn Satan a'i gynllwynion. Ffurfiwch yn meddwl eich plant, a chefnogwch yn eich gŵyr, benderfyniad i amddiffyn iaith Cymru. Nac arweinier chwi ar gyfeiliorn gan wag-falchder, ac na chymhellwch hwy i ddynwared eu bod yn Saeson. Gwerthfawrogwch eich cymdogion Seisonig am yr hyn sy dda ynddynt, a gochelwch y drwg. Ond cedwch eich hawl ddiymwad i fod yr hyn y gwnaeth eich Duw chi – i siarad yr iaith a ddysgwyd i chwi gan Dduw – ac uwchlaw y cyfan i'w addoli Ef yn eich iaith eich hunain; yr hon, yn nesaf at hynny, sydd i chwi ac i'ch plant yn rhagfur o gadernid yn erbyn ymosodiadau arferion drwg a llygredigaethau.

Heblaw hyn, arferwch eich GWLANENNI CENEDLAETHOL, y rhai sydd wedi bod er amser anghofiadwy yn wisgoedd ein cenedl. Diau fod yr arferiad o honynt wedi ei [sic] cadw am y meddant gynifer o ragoriaethau. Diogelant y corff rhag effeithiau niweidiol lleithder a glaw. A mwy na hynny y maent yn diogelu y rhai â'u gwisgant rhag tân. Ni chlywsom sôn erioed am faban mewn dillad gwlanen wedi llosgi i farwolaeth, ond pa gynifer o famau a adawsant i'w plant drengi, o herwydd eu balchder ffôl, yn eu dilladu mewn cotwm gwael – cotwm y gymalwst, fel y galwai yr hybarch Carnhuanawc ef,[2] a'r hwn nid yw'n addas ond i drigolion yr India – am y tybient fod hynny yn foeswych. Fel hyn y mae mamau wedi talu am eu ffoledd ar eu haelwydydd eu hunain â bywydau y mabanod diniwed â ymddiriedwyd i'w gofal.

---

[2] Thomas Price (Carnhuanawc, 1787-1848), un o'r 'hen bersoniaid llengar' a ddylanwadodd yn fawr ar Augusta Hall a'i chylch.

Cyn gadael y gwisgoedd, yr wyf am ddywedyd gair am HET Cymru wrth fy nghydwladesau. Yr wyf am eich cymell yn awr ac am byth i arfer (neu adferu) y gorchudd priodol hwn i'r pen, a'r hon sydd yn briodol gyda gŵn wlanen dda, ac nad ydyw yn gofyn am wellt nag ysnodenau. Bydded i'r Gymraes YMDDANGOS YR HYN YDYW, ymddangosed fel ei hunan, yn lle gwisgo *mwgwd*, a gall ymddibynu y bydd iddi deimlo ei fod yn llawer haws, yn gystal ag yn llawer mwy parchus, iddi ymddangos yn ei chymeriad ei hun, a bod yr hyn ydyw, na mabwysiadu gwisg Seisonig, a chymryd arni fod yr hyn nad yw, a'r hyn y dylai bob amser ddymuno bod, gan fod Duw wedi ei gwneud yn Gymraes. Yn hytrach nag ymwisgo mewn dillad anaddas i'r arferion bywiog a gweithgar a ddylent fod yn ymffrost pob un o ferched Cymru, dylid arfer gwisgoedd Cymreig, pe y costient fwy; ond nid felly y mae. Yn y dull hwn dygwch i fynnu eich meibion a'ch merched a thra byddo y meddwl yn ystwyth gwnewch argraff arno. Dysgwch hwy i brisio yr oll sydd yn dda yn eu gwlad eu hunain, a dysgwch hwy ym *mha le*, ym *mha fodd*, a *phaham*, y mae llawer o bethau yng Nghymru yn well nag mewn gwledydd eraill; a hefyd pa fodd a phaham y byddai pethau da mewn gwledydd eraill yn niweidiol yn y wlad hon. Dysgwch hwy i fyfyrio hanes hynafiaethol Cymru, ac i ddeall a gwerthfawrogi cynhyrchion eu gwlad. Byddent iddynt adnabod rhinweddau ei llysiau a'i blodau cynhenid, melusder [sic] neilltuol cig ei defaid, a chynhesrwydd ei gwlân. Dysger hwy i olrhain llwybrau ein hafonydd ac ansawdd ei ffynhonnau, amrywiaeth a defnydd ei meteloedd, yng nghyd â'r dull gorau i ddiwyllio eu tir eu hunain. Llanwer eu meddyliau â rhyfeddodau natur, a dysger hwy i ddyrchafu eu calonnau at Dduw natur. Addysger hwy yn holl gelfyddau bywyd, y rhai a berthynant yn neilltuol i'w gwlad ei hunain, ac sydd fwyaf angenrheidiol ynddi.

Y mae hyn oll o fewn eich cyrraedd chwi, Gymraësau, a phan lanwer eich meddyliau chwi a'ch plant â chariad at eich iaith a'ch gwlad eich hunain, y pryd hynny ac nid yn gynt y gallwch ystyried eich hunain yn *genedlgarol*, ac yna chwi â llawn ddeallwch fod cenedlgarwch yn amddiffyniad a bendith, yn felysydd llwyddiant, a chysur mewn adfyd. Bydd ei feithriniad yn wrthglawdd yn erbyn drwg, drwy lanw pob cilfach wag o'r meddwl, y rhai y cymerir meddiant prysur ohonynt gan nwydau, y rhai a wnaent eu perchennog yn druenus. GYMRAËSAU CYMRU! Bydded i chwi astudio a gwir ddeall cenedlgarwch; mawrhewch a meithriniwch ef ym mhob dull yn eich gallu drwy eich bywyd. Dyma yw awydd gwresog un sydd yn gwybod drwy brofiad ei fod yn dda mawr, ac nid yn sŵn gwag. Felly y didwyll ddymuna eich cyfeilles,

GWENLLÏAN GWENT

An Address to the Welsh Women of Wales

My Compatriots – Though you may be surprised to see the subject of this essay, and may judge that an address to 'the Women of Wales' would have conveyed the *meaning* of my intention, yet I think you will admit after reading these lines that there is a great difference between the Welsh Woman of Wales and the woman who lives in Wales, though she may have been born there and even to have Welsh parents, but who cannot claim the name of a Welsh Woman of Wales, because she has never exerted herself in her country or out of it to fulfil the duties of this honourable class. For *honourable* they must be, whether poor or wealthy, in moral excellence, if they truly deserve to be called 'Welsh Women of Wales', and to be considered true daughters of that country which has been blessed by providence in so many remarkable ways.

I intend in the first place to set out the influence which women have.

Secondly, the objects which true Welsh women should bear about with them.

Thirdly, the good which will result from succeeding with

the efforts I recommend, along with the evils which will be avoided.

The power of women is *their influence*, and their proper influence is endless. Men are dependent upon them for all comforts throughout their lives. Without them, they would have no food to eat or suitable clothing to wear. But my readers may object that many who read these lines have servants to cook and sew for them. But I repeat that, for all that, fathers, brothers, husbands and children depend on their daughters, sisters, wives and mothers. And the more help women receive from servants and dependents the more their influence extends, increasing like the branches of a tree, without decreasing in the least at its root. After such an introduction, no doubt it will be expected that I am going to suggest some extraordinary effort of the mind or the understanding, which only a few women will be able to achieve, and with which even fewer will have the time or leisure to concern themselves. But everybody can adopt my counsel without losing one hour, and without leaving the circle in which God has placed them. My advice is appropriate for everybody from the cottage to the palace, and I can assure them that if they follow it they will be *happier* as a result, quite apart from enjoying the consciousness of doing that which is right. But I am not going to preach to you, I leave that to the ministers of your various religious sects. Let them point out your chief responsibilities on the way to heaven. Yet there are links in the chain of our responsibilities on earth, which are often shattered or neglected, but which, if we take care of them, will make our path through this world safer and pleasanter, and which will smooth out the difficulties in reaching a better world. I refer most particularly to the adoption of a *patriotic* spirit, which is not only the most innocent, but one of the most beneficial things with which the human mind can be filled. *Patriotism* has been planted in us by a wise and good Providence, and like every other talent if it is neglected *evil is certain to follow*. Though the term *patriotism* is often used, little attention is paid to its importance, and its nature is but imperfectly understood. If asked, what is *patriotism*, many of my readers would be ready to reply that it is 'love for our country, and a particular care for our compatriots'. That is all very well, as far as it goes, but such a patriotism as that will never become an active virtue, capable of penetrating through all our thoughts, feelings and daily ideas, and leading to goodness in all of them. The patriotism which is *active*, and which proves itself in *actions* as well as *words*, is the one I am recommending to my female compatriots, and the one which this essay intends to persuade them to practice as well as praise. Our worst enemy would not deny that Wales is a fair and beautiful country. Confessing that fact, therefore, is not a sign of virtue or wisdom, and it would be difficult for anyone born in this country not to feel proud when its beauties and multiple productions are praised. But this is only the shadow of patriotism, only a feeling which can barely be avoided; it spreads thoughtlessly across the mind, and disappears without trace, often never returning to the cold and seared heart it has left.

We will now turn to true patriotism, and show in what way it *should* influence every true Welsh woman, whether she enjoys the privilege of living in her native country or afar in a strange land. Some special characteristics belong to the nation, and the wisdom of our forefathers has deemed them worthy of respect and persistent longevity. I refer in particular to our precious language. Language is a gift of God. Man was not capable of creating it; it is a standing miracle and proof of the power of the Creator. Some languages are purer, and more comprehensive and more extensive than others. The Welsh language is not only amongst the oldest, but, because of its descriptive capacities, it is one of the highest to have been safeguarded on earth. Its primary elements have remained unchanged since a period so ancient that historians cannot state with any certainty at what time a people talking the same language as we do *did not* inhabit the Isle of Britain. In this language our forefathers worshipped the God that we worship. We know that God has used our language as an instrument to protect us from the wretchedness that has brought corruption on the English. The man or woman who is satisfied with moral publications typical of the Welsh books of the principality stands a better chance of leading a sober, righteous life, piously conducted, likely to be respected in this life and to arrive at bliss in the world to come, than those whose minds are poisoned by the English press. These publications are distributed amongst the boys and girls of their schools, and he who reads the English papers from time to time can see in them attestations from parents and children's guardians protesting against these terrible books. Yet they are so frequent, that a numerous group of people earn their livelihood from writing and publishing them. Thanks be to God, we in Wales know but little of these things, but let us remember that if we do not cherish and nurture our language, which has been so strangely preserved for the purest ends, and in which there are already more books than the wisest could digest thoroughly in a hundred years, we will lose the strong defense of our virtue and contentment, and our children will be exposed to all the ills to which we referred. Mothers of Wales! speak Welsh to your children. Your blameworthy carelessness and your heart's betrayal will be to blame, if your lisping descendants do not sound their first words in the language which God gave our forefathers in the morning of the world. From you (and not from their fathers) they will learn to love God in their own language. On the other hand, if you neglect your duty, through you they will become a mongrel brood, unclaimed by anybody, but disregarded by all, who will know that they once had a nation and a language, but that their mothers 'for one morsel of meat sold their birthright'.[1]

In so far as the fate of your sons and daughters are in your

---

[1] Hebrews, xii, 16. The reference is to the story of Esau in Genesis, xxv, 29-34

hands, Mothers of Wales, do not let them learn the *easy* tongue of the stranger before they can speak the *difficult* tongue of their own country; and *then*, if worldly circumstances require English, a few weeks will suffice to master it. But let the language of the hearth, and the language of religion, be that which God apportioned to the Welsh, and while they keep it, they need not fear to be without protection or a shield against Satan and his ploys. Form in the minds of your children, and encourage in your husbands, a decision to defend the language of Wales. Do not be lead astray by vain glory, and do not encourage them to imitate the English. Appreciate that which is good in your English neighbours and defend yourself from the bad. But keep your undeniable right to be that which God made you – to speak the language which was taught to you by God – and above all to worship him in your own language, which, next to that, is to you and your children a bulwark of strength against bad habits and corruptions.

Apart from that, use your NATIONAL FLANNELS which have been since time immemorial the garb of our nation. No doubt their usage has been retained because of their many excellencies. They protect the body from the harmful influences of dampness and rain. And what is more, they protect the wearer from fire. We never hear of an infant in flannel clothing burning to death, but how many mothers have allowed their children to die, because of their foolish vanity, dressing them in poor quality cotton – the cotton of rheumatism, as the venerable Carnhuanawc called it,[2] which is only suitable for the inhabitants of India – because they thought it more fashionably grand. In this way mothers have paid for their foolishness on their own hearths with the lives of the innocent babes entrusted to their care.

---

[2] Reverend Thomas Price (Carnhuanawc, 1787-1848), a member of the Welsh antiquarian movement whose influence on Lady Llanover and her circle was profound.

Before leaving this topic, I wish to say a word about the WELSH HAT to my compatriots. I wish to urge you now and for ever to use (or revive) this suitable covering for the head, which is appropriate with a good flannel gown, and does not require either straw or ribbons. Let the Welsh woman APPEAR WHAT SHE IS, let her appear like herself, instead of wearing a *mask*, and she can depend upon it that she will feel it is much easier, as well as much more respectable, to appear in her own character, and be what she is, and what she should always want to be, rather than adopting English garb and pretending to be what she is not, as God has made her a Welsh woman. Rather than dressing herself in a garb unsuitable for those energetic and industrious exertions that should be the boast of every Welsh woman, she should wear Welsh garments even if they were more expensive, but that is not the case. In this way, rear your sons and daughters and while their minds are flexible make an impression upon them. Teach them to value everything which is good in their own country, and teach them in *what place*, in *what way*, and *why* many things in Wales are better than in other countries, and also how and why good things in other countries may be damaging in this one. Teach them to contemplate the ancient history of Wales, and to understand and appreciate the productions of their country. May they recognize the virtues of its native herbs and flowers, the particular sweetness of its lamb, and the warmth of its wool. Teach them to trace the paths of our rivers and the nature of our fountains, the variety and use of our metals, along with the best way to cultivate their own land. Fill their minds with the wonders of nature, and teach them to lift up their hearts towards the God of nature. Instruct them in all those arts of living which belong particularly to their own country, and which are most necessary in it.

All this is within your reach, Welsh women, and when your minds and those of your children are filled with love for your language and your country, then and not before then you can consider yourself *patriotic*, and then you will well understand that patriotism is a defence and a blessing, a sweetener in success and a comfort in adversity. Its adoption will prove a rampart against evil, filling all the empty corners of the mind, of which passions might otherwise quickly take possession, making their owner wretched. WELSH WOMEN OF WALES! May you study and truly understand patriotism; make much of it and nurture it in every way you can throughout your life. This is the warm wish of one who knows through experience that it is a great good, and not an empty noise. So sincerely desires your friend,

GWENLLÏAN GWENT

Part II

Feminist Dissent in the Pulpit, in Education and in the Temperance Movement

Sarah Jane Rees (Cranogwen), photographed by John Thomas and reproduced with the permission of the National Library of Wales.

INTRODUCTION
BY JANE AARON

Dissenting chapel culture dominated the social and political, as well as religious, life of nineteenth-century Wales and provided the context for Welsh women's struggle towards greater gender equality. Though the Calvinist Methodists started to ordain women as missionaries in 1887, the pulpits of Welsh chapels remained usually a male-only preserve, but not without protest. Two of the strongest voices to speak out on the topic published their attacks in the Welsh-language press of two continents: Cranogwen, or Sarah Jane Rees, in the periodical for women she edited from her home in Llangrannog from 1879 to 1891, *Y Frythones*, and Margaret Evans Roberts in the American weekly newspaper *Y Drych*. Representative examples of their protesting contributions are included here, in the original language and in translation.

From the late 1870s until she left the USA in 1911, Margaret Roberts was a regular contributor to *Y Drych*, the leading Welsh-language paper in the States during the years of her involvement with it. Born in 1833 in Llanfair-ar-y-bryn, Carmarthenshire, Roberts, née Evans, emigrated to the United States with her husband William in 1862, initially to farm in Iowa, before later settling in Scranton, Pennsylvania, where she ran a bookshop. She also took the opportunity to further her education, attending university lectures, and familiarizing herself with the new scientific ideas of the period. Her articles in *Y Drych* cover an impressive range of topics, including geology, astronomy, and phrenology, as well as religion, temperance and feminism.[1] Though she remained an active

[1] For further biographical information on Margaret Roberts, see Bill Jones, 'Margaret E. Roberts' in Elliott Barkan (ed.), *Making it in America: a Sourcebook of Eminent Ethnic Americans* (Santa Barbara, 2001), 315-16; and

member of the Calvinist Methodist sect, her frustration with
the limits it imposed upon women's participation in chapel
leadership is evident in the two articles by her included in this
section. Her stance is courageous: she accepts her isolated
position as one of the very few women objecting to the male
monopoly of power in the nonconformist sects, but keeps
asking other women to join her in asserting their shared
humanity and potential, and achieving new levels of equality.

In January 1879 Margaret Roberts welcomed in *Y Drych*
the first appearance of Cranogwen's periodical *Y Frythones*,
remarking with characteristic directness, 'da gennyf weled
fod fy anwyl [sic] chwiorydd yn Nghymru yn penderfynu
amlygu i'r byd fod ganddynt yn weddill eto ddigon o nerth
er profi eu bod yn fyw' ('I'm glad to see that my dear sisters
in Wales have decided to show the world that they still have
enough force to prove that they are alive').[2] Few women did
more than Cranogwen (1839-1916) to exemplify the forceful
potential of Welsh women during the second half of the
nineteenth century. She rose to fame during the aftermath
of the *Blue Books*, when the fact that she was a woman – a
talented, articulate, and profoundly religious Welsh woman
– appealed to audiences who saw in her further proof of the
iniquity of the 1847 Report's damnation of Welsh women
as characteristically ignorant and immoral.   Reared in
Llangrannog, a small fishing village on Cardigan Bay across
which her father sailed his ketch, she herself had worked
as a sailor initially, before acquiring further education and
becoming a teacher at the village school. She shot into the
Welsh limelight through winning a poetry competition in the
1865 National Eisteddfod at Aberystwyth; the glory of the win
was increased by the fact that two of the leading male poets

Aled Jones and Bill Jones, *Welsh Reflections: Y Drych & America 1851-2001*
(Llandysul, 2001), 74-75.
[2] Margaret E. Roberts, 'Y Frythones', *Y Drych*, xxix, 9 January 1879.

of the day, Islwyn and Ceiriog, were amongst the defeated contestants. Cranogwen started on her career as a lecturer immediately after this victory, and by 1866, when she was twenty-seven years of age, she was making enough money from public speaking to give up teaching, and turn to full-time lecturing, preaching and writing. In the pages of *Y Frythones* she created a network of Welsh-language women writers who knew one another, wrote about and for one another, and received inspiration and encouragement from one another, and particularly from 'the Ed.' ('Yr Ol.'), as Cranogwen liked to refer to herself. Cranogwen was a strong supporter of female suffrage, confidently predicting in 1886 that 'we know it is only a question of time before it becomes a fact.' ('Gwyddom nad yw ond cwestiwn o amser iddo ddyfod yn ffaith').[3]

An abridged version of the work for which she was by many most esteemed during her lifetime, the essay series 'Esther Judith', which appeared in *Y Frythones* between October 1880 and July 1881, is reproduced here in the original Welsh and in translation. Esther Judith, a neighbour of Cranogwen's during her childhood in Llangrannog, had worked throughout her life as farm labourer, and in old age was dependent upon the parish. But Cranogwen solicits respect for her memory as a profoundly religious woman, who had exceptional talents of intellect and eloquence, and would have made a great preacher. For all her poverty, had Esther Judith been male she might well have been afforded the opportunity to train for the ministry; within her chapel community her talents would not have gone unnoticed, and could well have gained her a community-funded place at a Calvinist Methodist theological college. But the talents of young women as opposed to men were not promoted by their chapel communities in the same way. Cranogwen's portrayal of Esther Judith emphasizes the manner in which women's abilities were wasted, and their

---

[3] Cranogwen, 'Dyrchafiad Merched', *Y Frythones,* 8 (1886), 236.

potential underdeveloped, much to their culture's loss, and to their personal frustration. The series 'Esther Judith' is a lament for the lost women preachers and writers of Wales.

However, in certain areas Welsh women made very rapid progress in the second half of the century; in particular the success of a movement to further the education of Welsh women was to a large extent responsible for their swift rise to a greater level of equality with men. In 1864 only 48 per cent of women in north Wales and 43 per cent in the south could sign their names, compared to 64 per cent of males in Wales as a whole, and in 1881 only 2133 Welsh girls attended secondary school, compared to 3827 boys. But in 1889 the Welsh Intermediate Education Act ensured that girls were afforded the same secondary school opportunities as boys, and also that the education they were given at school was the same: this was long in advance of similar measures in English education. As a result, by the end of the century the numbers of boys and girls in Welsh secondary schools were more or less equal.[4] In higher education also Welsh women were in the vanguard of reform: newly opened colleges of the University of Wales – Cardiff when it opened in 1883 and Bangor in 1884 – accepted women as students from the outset, awarding them full degrees, and so, from 1884, did Aberystwyth. By 1888, 33 per cent of University of Wales students were women, a far higher percentage than in English universities at the time.

These achievements were the result of a long and strenuous campaign fought mainly by Welsh women themselves. In arriving at their progressive position with regard to gender equality, the founders of the University of Wales were influenced by such figures as Elizabeth Phillips Hughes (1850-1925), a doctor's daughter from Carmarthen who

---

[4] W. Gareth Evans, 'Addysgu Mwy na Hanner y Genedl': Yr Ymgyrch i Hyrwyddo Addysg y Ferch yng Nghymru', in Geraint H. Jenkins, (ed.), *Cof Cenedl IV: Ysgrifau ar Hanes Cymru* (Llandysul, 1989), 99 and 105.

became the first head of the Cambridge Training College for women teachers, later named Hughes College in her honour.[5] In 1884 in the Liverpool National Eisteddfod, her essay on 'The Higher Education of Girls in Wales, with practical suggestions as to the best means of promoting it', was judged by Lord Aberdare and William Gladstone's daughter Helen to be 'by far the ablest of the competing Essays', and was duly published;[6] an abridged version of it is reprinted here. It recommends the establishment of a committee to further women's education in Wales; co-education for the sexes in schools and at the University of Wales; hostels for women at the University's colleges; and the use of the Welsh language in Welsh education at all levels. Above all, the essay stresses that, 'our education must be national, and therefore must be in our own hands'.[7] Hughes delivered a similar message in the columns she wrote for *Young Wales* in the 1890s: 'I do not believe that there is any force strong enough to keep our nationality for us except the force of education,' she wrote: 'If we accept the education of England, in due time we should be Anglicised.'[8]

In accordance with Elizabeth Phillips Hughes' suggestions in her Eisteddfod essay, the Association for Promoting the Education of Girls in Wales was duly established in 1886. One of its first two honorary secretaries, and later its vice-president, was Dilys Lloyd Davies (1857–1932), a member

[5] For further information on Elizabeth Hughes' career, see W. Gareth Evans, 'Un o Ferched Britannia: Gyrfa yr Addysgwraig Elizabeth P. Hughes', in Geraint T. Jenkins (ed.), *Cof Cenedl XVI: Ysgrifau ar Hanes Cymru*, (Llandysul, 2001), 95-122.

[6] Lord Aberdare, 'Adjudications: The Higher Education of girls in Wales, with practical suggestions as to the best means of promoting it', *Transactions of the Liverpool National Eisteddfod 1884* (Liverpool, 1885), 38.

[7] Elizabeth Phillips Hughes, 'The Higher Education of girls in Wales', *Transactions of the Liverpool National Eisteddfod 1884* (Liverpool, 1885), 57.

[8] Elizabeth Phillips Hughes, 'A National Education for Wales', *Young Wales*, i, (1895), 105.

of the London Welsh, and at that time a teacher at the North London Collegiate School for Girls. She became a regular speaker for the Association, on National Eisteddfod platforms and those of the Welsh and London-Welsh learned societies, campaigning industriously for greater gender equality throughout the educational system. In particular the Association fought throughout the 1880s to fill the perceived gap between girls' elementary and higher education, and their aims reached fulfillment with the passing of the Welsh Intermediate Education Act in 1889. Now married to a Bangor solicitor, in 1894 Dilys Glynne Jones, as she had become, published a typically far-reaching and practical account of 'The Duty of Welsh Women in Relation to the Welsh Intermediate Education Act' as one of the Association's publications; it is reproduced here as a representative example of the exemplary work of that group of women who so effectively furthered gender equality in Wales during the last decades of the nineteenth century. New horizons were opening up before Welsh women, and many made much of their extended opportunities, rising to professional, middle-class positions often from working-class backgrounds.

Other movements also contributed to their increased self-respect and confidence. From 1892 to the outbreak of World War I, the Welsh women's temperance movement inspired many of its members to take a far more public role than hitherto in their society. Although the North Wales Women's Temperance Association did not as an association officially support the suffragist cause,[9] many of its individual members did so, and the campaign for the vote was positively represented on the pages of its mouthpiece, the periodical *Y Gymraes*. In a seminal article on the history of Welsh women's temperance campaigns, Ceridwen Lloyd-Morgan recorded

---

[9] Ceridwen Lloyd-Morgan, 'From Temperance to Suffrage?' in Angela V. John (ed.), *Our Mothers' Land: Chapters in Welsh Women's History 1830-1939* (Cardiff, 1991), 152-3.

how quickly the North Wales Women's Temperance Union
grew from its formation in 1892: by 1896 it had 106 branches
and 11,821 members.[10] Throughout the towns and villages of
Wales, women strengthened one another in the cause in public
meetings; marched through their local streets under temperance
banners to picket popular taverns; established refuges to
save and succour weaker sisters in danger of succumbing to
alcoholism; attended law courts to try and prevent new public
house licences being granted, and invaded taverns en masse to
sing temperance hymns and harangue the customers directly.
Because of the rapid and unregulated growth of the coal, iron
and steel industries in south and north-east Wales, leading to
work stress, overcrowding, and social upheaval, alcoholism
had indeed become a pressing concern by the second half
of the nineteenth century. As it was also connected with the
stereotype of the Welsh as barbaric – the 1847 Report had
listed drunkenness amongst the sins of the Principality – to
regulate the consumption of alcohol became one of the first
priorities for those who wished to 'raise' Wales. Attacking
the great 'Seductress', that lured their men into disgrace
and poverty, was seen as a particularly appropriate role for
those pillars of familial and religious good order in Wales, its
dissenting women. 'Let us temperance women vow to point
our arrows at her,' wrote Buddug (Catherine Jane Prichard,
1842-1909) of the 'temptress' alcohol. A diligent worker for
the North Wales Women's Temperance Union, Buddug was its
Anglesey secretary.[11] Two of her assertive articles are included
in this section of the anthology, in the original language and in
translation, the first published in Cranogwen's *Y Frythones* in

---

[10] Ibid., 138 and 144.

[11] For further information on the life and work of Buddug, see R. Môn Williams,
'Buddug', *Cymru*, 39 (1909), 221-4; Mair Ogwen [Mary Griffith], *Chwiorydd
Enwog y Cyfundeb* (Caernarfon: Llyfrfa'r Methodistiaid Calfinaidd, n. d.
[1925]), 79-82; and Iorwen Myfanwy Jones, 'Merched Llên Cymru o 1850 i
1914', University of Wales, Bangor, MA thesis (1935), 114-17.

1880 and the second a decade later in *Y Gymraes*.

The influence of such writers depended to a great extent on the connection between their literary productions and what their readers knew about them: their personal story, as women who had given their lives to fight the demon drink and save its victims, was an important aspect of the effectiveness and popularity of their writings. The last woman to be included in this section was another of the same stamp, who also saw herself, like Buddug, as one of Cranogwen's disciples and success stories. In the lengthy series of articles entitled 'In the company of Cranogwen' which appeared in *Y Gymraes* from 1923-5, Ellen Hughes of Llanengan (1862-1927) provides a vivid picture of what Cranogwen meant to a young embryo writer like herself. She describes herself, at eighteen years of age, dropping and breaking a bowl of sugar in her happy confusion on hearing that her first attempts at poetic composition were to be published in *Y Frythones*.[12] In 1900, Cranogwen, as she looked back on Ellen Hughes' successful career, took pride in her early discovery: 'I felt like one who had gained much booty when, years ago...Ellen Hughes came into view,' she wrote in the second *Y Gymraes*, adding, 'I did not know, I might as well confess, that the interesting correspondent from Llanengan was to develop before very much time had passed to become one of the intellectual heroes of her age, and that, if it is of any significance to say so, without counting gender.' ('Teimlwn fel un wedi cael ysglyfaeth lawer pan, flynyddoedd yn ôl...daeth Ellen Hughes i'r golwg...Ni wyddwn, waeth i mi gyfaddef, fod yr ohebyddes ddyddorol o Lanengan i dyfu cyn y byddai hir o amser, i fod yn un o wroniaid meddyliol ei hoes, a hyny, pe y byddai bwys i'w ddweyd, heb gyfrif rhyw').[13] Through enthusiastically providing a platform for female talent and supporting its development in this way, Cranogwen

---

[12] Ellen Hughes, 'Yng Nghymdeithas Cranogwen', *Y Gymraes*, xxvii (1923), 134.

[13] Cranogwen, 'Miss Ellen Hughes, Llanengan', *Y Gymraes*, iv (1900), 7.

helped to bring into being a new type of Welsh woman, of whom Ellen Hughes is a worthy example.

Ellen Hughes is arguably the Welsh-language author of the period who comes closest to being a feminist in the modern sense. An autodidact who received very little formal education, she was well acquainted with both Welsh and English literatures and had also taught herself Greek and Hebrew. For thirty years she was a regular columnist in *Y Gymraes*, and her monthly contributions added substantially to the journal's progressiveness. A strong advocate of women's suffrage, she asks in a 1910 article, 'Women and Representation' ('Merched a Chynrychiolaeth'), 'if a woman is a reasoning and moral being, with the waves of eternity beating in her nature, how can she lack the qualifications to take part in governing her country?' ('Os ydyw dynes yn fod rhesymol a moesol, a thonau tragwyddoldeb yn curo yn ei natur, tybed ei bod islaw meddu y cymhwysder i gael rhan yn neddfwriaeth ei gwlad').[14] Her work is represented in this collection by two of her earlier contributions to the 'New Woman' debate in Wales, arguing against the ideal of womanhood as nothing other than a domestic angel, and trying to awaken in her female readers a consciousness of their independent identity and potential. Given that her forthright insistence on women's rights marks her out as the most obvious successor in Wales to Margaret Roberts in the Welsh communities of the States, her voice provides a suitable closing note to this section.

---

[14] Ellen Hughes, 'Merched a Chynrychiolaeth', *Y Gymraes*, xiv (1910), 148

4. Margaret Evans Roberts

Diystyru y Merched (Ignoring the Women)

Y Drych, 11 Gorffennaf 1878

Dywed Lecky[1] fod moesoldeb cenedl yn adnabyddus wrth y modd yr ymddygir at y merched; ac mai ymddygiad cenedl at ei merched yw un o'r pethau anhawdda i'w gwybod. A gwiriwyd y ddwy frawddeg yna yng Nghynhadledd y Presbyteriaid yn Pittsburg yn Mai diweddaf. Mae un dosbarth o'r gweinidogion Presbyteraidd, a dosbarth helaeth o'r byd crefyddol, yn barod i dynnu gorchudd dros eu hwynebau, rhag bod yn dystion o'r olygfa – gwaith dau gant ac un o weinidogion yn pleidleisio yn erbyn i ddynes (am ei bod yn ddynes) ddywedyd un gair o glod nac anghlod i'w Chreawdwr a'i chynhaliwr. Ai tybed fod iddi Greawdwr a chynhaliwr heblaw dyn? Ni alwaf y cyfryw rai yn "Barchedigion", ni oddefaf i'm gwefusau na'm pen lunio geiriau croes i'm calon; ac ni alwaf hwy yn frodyr chwaith, o herwydd y maent hwy wedi gwadu y berthynas, ac o'm rhan fy hun, yr ydwyf yn berffaith foddlawn. Yn wir, os yw y nefoedd yn cael ei gwneud i fyny o'r fath bersonau â hwy, yr ydwyf yn foddlawn iddynt wneud y gorau o honni [sic]. Yn nos dywyll Pabyddiaeth, ni oddefid i ddynes dderbyn y cymundeb heb faneg am ei llaw, gan ei bod hi yn rhy aflan, meddai y Pabau; ond yr oedd gwisgo y faneg yn drugaredd yn ymyl creulondeb Presbyteriaid y bedwaredd ganrif ar

---

[1] Yr hanesydd Eingl-Gwyddelig Edward Hartpole Lecky (1838–1903).

bymtheg! O! fel y gwna y syniad o uwchafiaeth ladd y bywyd mwyaf annwyl a nefol! Pe buasai y dynion yna yn ymddwyn yr un fath at rai o'r rhyw wrywaidd o'r eglwysi, buasai digon o uchelgais yn y rhai hynny i droi allan fel un gŵr; ond am y merched druain, y maent hwy wedi cael eu cadw cyhyd dan y cysgod, fel nad oes ganddynt ewyllys na gallu i symud oddi yno.

Mae yn syn meddwl fod y Presbyteriaid mor ffôl â chadw cymaint o sŵn, a threulio cymaint o'u hamser yn ofer er rhwystro y mudan i lefaru. Nid oes braidd fwy o debygolrwydd i'r merched a fegir yn eglwysi yr enwad uchod, lefaru (gyda'r eithriad o M. E. R.) nag oedd i asen [sic] Balaam wneud hynny; ond rhag i'r angel ddyfod a chynhyrfu yr asen [sic], yr oedd yn rhaid cael y magwyr. Ai tybed nas gellir gwneud gwelliant ar y ddynes, gyda golwg ar ei pheiriant llefaru? Ai tybed na all Mr Darwin trwy ryw *good selection*, wneud gwelliant yn y peth hwn, fel na fydd angen colli amser gyda hi yn y dyfodol. Do, yn Pittsburgh, dedfrydwyd y creadur mud byth i barhau felly; ac ni chaniatawyd iddi yr hun a ganiataodd y pagan i Paul, sef ateb drosti ei hun. Ond gwnawn ni yr un fath ag y mae pawb arall wedi gorfod wneud, sef ymladd dros ein rhyddid, a gwnawn hynny nes ei gael. Mae llawer bywyd wedi ei aberthu dros y gwirioneddau a fwynheir gennym; ac nid yw yr eiddom ninnau yn fwy gwerthfawr. Gallwn fforddio colli gwên siriol llawer brawd a chwaer; gallwn fforddio cael ein galw yn greaduriaid penboeth ac *od*; ond ni fedrwn roddi i fyny gwyno pan yr ymdrechir ein newynu i farwolaeth! Pa nifer, tybed, o ferched Cymreig, sydd yn feddiannol ar ddigon o fywyd i deimlo fod yr hyn a wnaed yn yr Assembly yn gynigiad at ein newynu? Byddai yn dda gennyf wybod. A fyddai yn ormod o beth i mi ofyn gan bob merch ag sydd yn teimlo rhywbeth dros y gwirioneddau a amddiffynnir ganddynt, ddanfon i mi *bostal card*, neu lythyr, fel y gallwyf weled a yw merched y Cymry yn teimlo diddordeb yn y pwnc. Rhodder yr enw personol, ac enw y lle, ynghyd â'r enwad crefyddol i'r hwn y perthynir;

ac os na byddys yn perthyn i un enwad crefyddol, dyweder hynny. Nac esgeulused yr un ferch na gwraig wneud hyn. Os na allant ysgrifennu eu hunain, gall un arall wneud yn eu lle; Cymraeg neu Saesneg, nid oes wahaniaeth. Yr hyn sydd gennyf mewn golwg wrth wneud hyn, yw deffroi meddwl y merched ieuainc at y gwirionedd, eu bod wedi cael eu gosod yn y byd er gwneud rhywbeth dros y byd, ac er symud pob rhwystr o'u meddwl hwy, yn gystal ag o feddwl y rhyw arall gyda golwg ar hyn – symud y rhwystrau fel y gall natur gyflymu ym mlaen yn gyson a mawreddog. Cyfeirir fel hyn: Margaret E. Roberts, Iowa City, Iowa.

Ignoring the Women

Lecky[1] says that the morality of a nation is to be known from the way in which it treats its women, and that the way in which a nation treats its women is one of the most difficult things to know. Both those sentences were shown to be true in the Presbyterian conference in Pittsburg in May. One class of Presbyterian ministers, and the largest class amongst the religious world, is willing to draw a veil over its face, so as not to witness the sight – the sight of two hundred and one ministers voting against a woman (because she is a woman) having the right to say one word of praise or detraction to her Creator and upholder. Can it be that she has no Creator or upholder except man? I will not call such as these 'Reverends', I will not permit my lips or my mind to form words contrary to my heart; and I will not call them brothers either, because they have denied the relationship, and for my own part, I am quite content. Indeed, if heaven is made up of such persons as they, I am willing for them to make what they can of it. In the dark night of Popery, no woman was permitted to take communion

---

[1] The Anglo-Irish historian Edward Hartpole Lecky (1838-1903).

without a glove on her hand, because she was too impure, said the Papists; but wearing the glove was merciful compared to the cruelty of nineteenth-century Presbyterians! O! how the idea of superiority kills the dearest and most heavenly life! If those men behaved in the same way towards some of the male church members, there would be enough ambition in them to rebel as one man; but as for the poor women, they have been kept for so long in the shade they do not have the will or ability to move out of it.

It is strange to think that the Presbyterians are so foolish as to make so much noise, and waste so much of their time, forbidding the mute to speak. There is scarcely less likelihood that the women who are muted in the churches of the above sect should speak out (with the exception of M. E. R.) than that Balaam's ass should have done so; but lest the angel should come and disturb the ass, they had to have the silencers. Cannot some improvement be made in woman, with regard to her speaking mechanism? Cannot Mr Darwin through some good selection, make an improvement in it, so that time need not be lost with her in future? Yes, in Pittsburgh, the mute creature was decreed always to remain so; and that was not permitted to her which the pagan permitted to Paul, that is, to speak for herself. But let us do as all others have had to do, fight for our freedom, and do so till we have it. Many lives have been sacrificed for the sake of the truths which we enjoy, and our own lives are not more precious. We can afford to lose the affable smile of many brothers and sisters, we can afford to be called hot-headed and odd creatures; but we cannot afford to give up protesting when the attempt is being made to starve us to death! How many Welsh women, I wonder, possess enough life to feel that what was done in the Assembly was an attempt to starve us? I would be glad to know. Would it be too much to ask of every woman who feels something for the truths which they defend to send me a postcard, or a letter, so that I can see whether the women of Wales feel an interest in the subject. Give your personal name, and location, and the name of the religious sect to which you belong; and if you are not a member of a sect, say so. No woman or girl should neglect to do this. If you cannot yourself write, another can do so for you; English or Welsh, it makes no difference. What I have in mind is to awaken the consciousness of young women to the truth, that they have been placed in the world in order to do something for the world, and to remove every obstacle from their minds, as well as from the minds of the other sex in this respect – removing the obstacles so that nature can hasten on consistently and grandly. Write to : Margaret E. Roberts, Iowa City, Iowa.

Merched yn y Pwlpud (Women in the Pulpit)

Y Drych, 4 Ionawr 1894

Adolygiad ar ysgrif y Parch. R. H. Evans, Cambria – *Dysgeidiaeth yr Iesu*.

Yr oedd yn dda gennyf ddarllen sylwadau caredig y Parch. R. H. Evans ar Miss Rosina Davies fel efengyles yn *Y Drych*, a deall ei fod yn rhydd oddi wrth ragfarn yn erbyn merched i ddweud stori y Groes wrth bechaduriaid, pan fo llawer fel arall.[1] Gobeithio na theimla Mr Evans, na neb arall o'r frawdoliaeth, fy mod yn angharedig atynt wrth wneud y sylwadau a ganlyn ar yr ysgrif, gan fod y maes o amddiffyn iawnderau y rhyw fenywaidd yn y wlad hon ym mhlith y Cymry yn cael ei adael bron yn hollol i mi. Yr wyf yn penderfynu mawrhau y fraint hon, er bod llawer chwaer yn codi ei ffroen mewn diystyrwch arnaf am wneud – i'r rhai y maddeuaf yn rhwydd, fel y gwnaf i blentyn am gamsyniadau angenrheidiol ei natur blentynnaidd. Mae oesau di-rif o ddiystyrwch a chreulondeb, oesau o gario a magu babanod y ddynoliaeth, ac ar yr un pryd gario ei beichiau, wedi gwneud y ddynes fel peth cyffredin yn hollol foddlawn ar ei sefyllfa israddol. Yr arwydd cyntaf ei bod yn ymryddhau oddi wrth rwymau ei gwddf yw, ei gwaith yn gofyn am ychwaneg o le; a phan bydd yn gofyn am le i wneud daioni, profa ei bod yn edrych ym myw llygad ei Gwaredwr, yr hwn 'sydd yn myned oddi amgylch i chwilio am le i drugarhau'.

Mae y ffaith fod y rhyw arall trwy oesau paganaidd ac anwaraidd y byd wedi cael edrych arnynt fel yn uwchraddol, o herwydd y cyfrifid fod gorchfygu llwythau a chenhedloedd cylchynol trwy ryfel yn dwyn mwy anrhydedd na maethu a gofalu am y rhai oedd gartref, wedi bod ac yn parhau yn anfantais er lleoli y rhywiau yn iawn, pan mewn amgylchiadau

---

[1] Rosina Davies (1863-1949), efengylwraig, y gyntaf o dair, boblogaidd yng Nghymru a'r Unol Daleithiau; yr oedd ar daith bregethu yn yr Unol Daleithiau yn ystod 1893-4.

gwahanol. Mae yn ffaith hefyd fod y gwroniaid rhyfelgar a gorchfygol hyn yn cael eu duweiddio tra yn fyw, ac wedi iddynt feirw, y bobl yn eu haddoli, yn cadw urddas neilltuol ar y rhyw wrywaidd. Hefyd, gwneid pob gwasanaeth a ystyrid yn angenrheidiol ar y duwiau hyn gan eu rhyw eu hunain, felly mae addoliad wedi ei gadw trwy yr oesau braidd yn hollol i'r un rhyw; hwy sydd yn ffafr y duwiau.

Dysgodd yr Arglwydd Iesu egwyddor hollol wahanol; eto myn y bobl gario ym mlaen egwyddorion paganiaeth ac Iddewiaeth er rhwystr a thlodi dygn i'r ddynoliaeth. Mae yn amhosibl deall beth all fod rheswm y bobl sydd yn proffesu awyddu am achub y byd, dros i hynny gael ei wneud yn rhannol gan ddynes. Nid wyf yn gwybod am un enwad crefyddol sydd wedi gwrthod i'r merched fyned i blith paganiaid ac anwariaid y byd i ddweud am Waredwr wrthynt; yn hytrach ymorfoleddant yn y syniad eu bod yn myned; ond maent yn bur amheus a ydyw merched yn gymwys i wneud hynny gartref. Paham? Gwyddom fod yn ofynnol gwneud llawer mwy o aberth er myned i China, India, neu Affrica i bregethu yr efengyl nag i wneud hynny gartref. Ai dyna y paham? Gwna y syniad yna y tro i baganiaeth, ond nid i Gristionogaeth.

Dyfynnwn ychydig o lythyr Mr Evans, er mwyn gwneud chwarae teg â'r syniadau: 'Mae gan ferch ddoniol am dro neu ddau fantais i gael gwrandawyr, ac anfantais i wneud argraffiad priodol, oblegid fod dynion yn dod i'w gwrando er porthi chwilfrydedd,' &c. Gwn fod hynyna yn eithaf gwir, ond ai tybed y dylai fod yn wir yn yr oes hon? Yr ydym yn gyfrifol, nid yn unig am yr hyn a wyddom, ond am yr hyn y cawsom fantais i'w wybod. Os oes efengyl arall ar gyfer y ddynes heblaw yr hon a osodwyd gan yr Iesu, byddai yn dda gennym ddeall beth yw, fel y gallo y brodyr a'r chwiorydd addoli eu gwahanol dduwiau ar wahân. Os mai efengyl rhyw yw efengyl Crist, gadawer hi i'r brodyr; neu os yw yn efengyl i'r ddynoliaeth, tewch â'ch rhyw am byth, a dewch allan fel dynion gonest mewn unrhyw fasnach arall, gan amlygu fod perygl i ddynes weithio dan bris, a thrwy hynny eich niweidio.

Proffesir credu mai trwy y ddynes, ar wahân i ddyn, y rhoddodd Duw y Mab i'r ddynoliaeth; os felly, ai tybed fod rhywbeth yn anweddus i'r ddynes ddweud am dano wrth y byd? Ai nid yw yn rhesymol meddwl fod ganddi hi lawn cymaint o hawl a chymhwyster i hynny ag sydd gan y dyn? 'Dynion da,' medd Mr Evans, 'yn credu nad yw Duw yn galw merched i bregethu, a llawer o wragedd yn credu yr un peth.' Dynion a gwragedd 'da'; da i beth? Dichon eu bod yn barod i farw, ond nid yw yn debyg y gallant wneud llawer o dda i'r byw, gan, yn ôl tystiolaeth Mr Evans ei hun, nad yw eu cred yn unol â dysgeidiaeth y Beibl ar bwnc pwysicaf y dydd.

Dywed Mr Evans nad yw yn gwybod pa un a yw Miss Davies yn dduwiol ai peidio; a'i fod yn gobeithio na chymer dim le yn ei hanes fydd yn achos i ddwyn anfri ar yr efengyl, a darostwng y rhyw fenywaidd fel siaradwyr cyhoeddus. Gobeithiwn ninnau hynny o'n calon, fod Miss Davies yn dduwiol, a bod Duw wedi ei galw i bregethu yr efengyl. Gwyddom fod cannoedd, os nad miloedd, yng Nghymru yn proffesu eu bod wedi cael eu dwyn at yr Iesu trwy ddylanwad yr efengyles o Dreherbert. Mae Miss Davies wedi bod yn efengylu bellach am dros bedair blynedd ar ddeg, a dechreuodd y gwaith cyn ei bod yn 15 oed. Pa un a ddigwydd rhywbeth annymunol i Miss Davies yng nghwrs ei bywyd, nid oes neb yn gwybod, o herwydd 'Edryched yr hwn sydd yn sefyll na syrthio' yw hi gyda phawb. Ond paham y gosoda Mr Evans y fath bwys ar ei bod hi yn sefyll yn fwy nag ar y rhyw arall, nid wyf yn deall! Ai tybed ei fod yn fwy o ddirmyg ar yr efengyl i ddynes gwympo nag i ddyn wneud hynny? Os felly, mae yn rhaid fod dynes yn uwch na dyn, o herwydd po uchaf y safle, dyfnaf y cwymp. Wel, credwn nad yw yn anfantais i Miss Davies ei bod yn ferch er dal profedigaethau bywyd. Mae dwy ferch yn grefyddol am bob mab, ac mae un ferch yn y carchar am bob deg ar hugain o feibion!

Meddai Mr Evans ym mhellach: 'Nid oes un prawf wedi bod, mae yn debyg, ar ei hunanymwadiad.' Mr Evans, yr ydych wedi ceryddu cryn lawer ar eich brodyr yng Nghymru, am eu bod wedi ymddwyn mor oer atoch; ond mae Miss Davies wedi bod o dan belennau tanllyd yr unrhyw frawdoliaeth fwy nag unwaith, fel y deallais pan ar dro yng Nghymru. Mae brodyr yn y weinidogaeth a Chymanfaoedd wedi bod yn brwydro llawer o'i phlegid. Ai tybed nad oedd hi yn teimlo am yr oll o hyn! Mae hi yn gwybod beth yw bod ym mhlith brodyr gau am flynyddau yn ei gwlad ei hun.

Dywed Mr Evans 'fod Miss Davies yn derbyn llawer o arian ar hyd y wlad,' a 'bod perygl i arian ladrata ei chalon a lladd ei dylanwad. Dylai gysegru rhan o'r hyn a dderbynia i'r Arglwydd.' Mae y cyngor yn eithaf priodol; ond a oes mwy o ddyletswydd ar ddynes i gysegru i'r Arglwydd nag sydd ar ddyn? Nid wyf yn cofio i mi weled na chlywed fod y cyngor yn cael ei roddi i'r llu brodyr pregethwrol sydd wedi bod ar ymweliad â'n gwlad, er bod llawer ohonynt wedi cario codaid go drom dros y Werydd! Y rhyw wrywaidd yn gyffredin sydd yn cario *pocket book*, a hwy sydd yn cyfrannu yn y casgliad; ac os ydynt yn cyfrannu yn y casgliad i ddynes, ar yr un egwyddor ag y maent yn cyfrannu iddi ym mhob cysylltiad arall, sef o haner [sic] i ddwy ran o dair o'r hyn a roddir i ddyn am yr un gwaith, nid oes achos i Mr. Evans fod yn bryderus iawn am galon Miss Davies!

Mae yn dda gennyf weled fod pregethwyr ac arweinwyr ym mhlith y Cymry yn America mor garedig i'r efengyles, ac hefyd eu bod yn awyddus i ferched gymeryd y rhan fwy blaenllaw yn holl wasanaeth y cysegr. Nid y brodyr yn unig sydd i'w beio am lesgedd y chwiorydd gyda chrefydd; gorwedda llawer o'r diffyg wrth eu drws hwy eu hunain. Deddf natur, corff ac enaid yw, os am gynyddu a datblygu, mae yn rhaid gosod y dalent yn y farchnad, ac os na wneir hynny, y ni sydd yn gyfrifol, a byddwn yn sicr o ddioddef o'r herwydd.

Mae achos i ofni fod llawer o chwiorydd crefyddol yn credu

mai y brodyr yn unig sydd i weddïo yn y dirgel, yn y teulu, ac
yn y capel; eu bod hwy yn hollol esgusodol. Clywais adrodd
am ddynes grefyddol yn ddiweddar pan yn ymyl angau yn
dweud, 'Pe buasai fy nhad yn fyw, buasai efe yn gweddïo
droswyf.' Yr oedd y tad yna wedi marw ers pum mlynedd, a'r
fam yn fyw, ac yn yr ystafell ar y pryd, ac yn fam rinweddol;
ond tebyg na ddaeth i feddwl y ferch oedd yn marw alw arni
hi i weddïo. Paham? Credaf fod Cymdeithas y *Christian
Endeavour* ym mhlith yr ieuainc yn myned i greu chwyldroad
yn y cyfeiriad hwn. Gobeithio mai felly y bydd.

Women in the Pulpit

Review of the essay by the Reverend R. H. Evans, Cambria
– *Teachings of Jesus*.

I was gratified to read the kind comments of the Rev. R. H.
Evans in *Y Drych* on Miss Rosina Davies as an evangelist,
and to understand that he was free of the prejudice against
women telling the story of the Cross to sinners, when many
are otherwise.[1] I hope that neither Mr Evans, nor any other
member of the fraternity, will feel I am unkind towards them
when I make the comments which follow in this essay, as the
field of defending the rights of the female sex in this country
amongst the Welsh has been left nearly wholly to me. I have
decided to make much of this privilege, though many a sister
looks down her nose at me in disdain for doing so – which
type I forgive freely, as I would a child for errors necessary
to its childlike nature. Countless ages of neglect and cruelty,
ages of carrying and nurturing the babes of humankind, and at
the same time carrying its burdens, have made the female in
general perfectly satisfied with her subordinated position. The
first sign that she is freeing herself from the fetters about her

---

[1] Rosina Davies (1863–1949) was a popular evangelist in Wales and the
USA; the first of her three preaching tours of the USA took place in 1893-4.

neck is, her act of asking for more space, and when she asks for more space in which to do good, she proves that she is looking into the eye of her Creator, who 'goes about searching for a space from which to be merciful'.

The fact that through the pagan and barbaric ages of the world the other sex have been seen as superior, (because overcoming neighbouring tribes and nations through war brought more honour than nourishing and looking after those at home) has been and remains a disadvantage when it comes to placing the sexes appropriately, under different circumstances. It is also a fact that these warmongering and conquering heroes were deified whilst alive, and worshipped after their deaths, thus preserving a special pomp for the male sex. Also, all necessary services to these gods were performed by members of their own sex, so that worship has been retained through the ages as specific to the one sex; it is they who are in the favour of the gods.

The Lord Jesus taught an entirely different value-structure; yet the people insist on maintaining the values of the barbarians and the Jewish patriarchs, in the face of the frustration and dire poverty of humanity. It is impossible to understand how those who profess a desire to save the world can reason against the notion that this should be done in part by women. I know of no religious sect which has prevented women from going amongst the heathens and barbarians of the world to speak to them of the Saviour; rather, they glory in the fact that they do so; but they are very doubtful as to whether it is appropriate for women to do so at home. Why? We know that it is necessary to sacrifice much more in order to go to China, India or Africa to preach the gospel than to do so at home. Is that why? That idea might do for paganism, but not for Christianity.

We will quote a little from Mr Evans' letter, in order to do justice to his ideas: 'Once or twice, an amusing woman will have an advantage in securing listeners, though a disadvantage in making an appropriate impression, because men will come to listen to feed their curiosity,' &c. I know that is true enough, but should it be true in this day and age? We are responsible, not only for that which we know, but for that which we have the opportunity of knowing. If there is a different gospel for women other than that which was established by Jesus, we would be glad to know what it is, so that the brothers and sisters can worship their different gods separately. If Christ's gospel is sexed, the brothers can have it; but if it is a gospel for humankind, shut up about your sex for ever, and come clean like honest men in any other business, making it clear that there is a danger that women may work for money, and through doing so injure you.

We profess to believe that God gave his Son to humankind by means of the female, not the male; if that is so, how can there be something unsuitable about a woman speaking of him to the world? Is it not reasonable to think that she has the right and the attributes with which to do so, just as much as man? 'Good men,' says Mr Evans, 'believe that God does not call women to preach, and many women believe the same.' 'Good' men and women: good for what? No doubt they are good enough to die, but it's not likely they can do much good to the living, because, according to the testimony of Mr Evans himself, their belief is not one with the teaching of the Bible on the most important subject of the day.

Mr Evans says that he does not know whether Miss Davies is godly or not, and that he hopes nothing will take place in her history which will disgrace the gospel, and discredit the female sex as public speakers. We also hope from our heart that Miss Davies is godly, and that God has called her to preach the gospel. We know that hundreds, if not thousands, in Wales profess to have been brought to Jesus by the influence of the female evangelist from Treherbert. Miss Davies has now been preaching the gospel for over fourteen years, and she began on the work before she was fifteen years of age. Whether or not something undesirable will happen to Miss Davies during her life's course, no-one knows, because it's a matter of 'Let he who stands look that he does not fall' for everyone. But why Mr Evans lays such emphasis on the importance of her standing as opposed to the other sex, I fail to understand! Can it be that it brings more discredit on the gospel for a woman to fall than for a man to do so? If so, then the female must be higher than the male, for the higher the position the deeper the fall. Well, we think it's no disadvantage to Miss Davies that she is a woman when it comes to withstanding the troubles of the world. Two women are religious for every male, and one woman is in prison for thirty men!

Mr Evans says again, 'No test has been made, presumably, of her selflessness.' Mr Evans, you have often scolded your brothers in Wales because they have behaved so coldly towards you; but Miss Davies has been under the fiery bullets of the same brotherhood more than once, or so I understood while on a visit to Wales. The brethren in the ministry and general assemblies have often quarrelled about her. Can it be that she felt nothing about all this! She knows what it is to live amongst false brothers for years in her own country.

Mr Evans says that 'Miss Davies receives much money throughout the country' and 'that there is a danger that money will steal her heart and kill her influence. She should consecrate part of that which she receives to the Lord.' The advice is seemly enough; but is there more call on woman to consecrate to the Lord than on man? I do not remember seeing or hearing this advice given to the host of brother preachers who have visited our country, though many of them carried a heavy enough swag back over the Atlantic! It is the male sex which usually carries the pocket book, and it is they who contribute to the collection, and if they contribute to the collection for a woman according to the same principle as they contribute to her in every other connection, that is, at the rate of a half to two-thirds of that which is given to men for the same work, there is no need for Mr Evans to be too anxious for Miss Davies' heart!

I am glad to see that preachers and leaders amongst the Welsh in America are welcoming to the female evangelist, and also that they are eager to see women taking a more prominent part in all the sacred services. It is not the brothers only who are to be blamed for the feebleness of the sisters with regard to religion; much of the fault lies with themselves. Nature's law, for souls as well as bodies, is that if we wish to increase and prosper we must take our talents to the market-place, and if we do not do so, it is we who are responsible, and we will be certain to suffer as a consequence.

There is reason to fear that many religious sisters believe that it is the brothers only who are to pray in private, amongst the family, and in chapel; that they are entirely excused. Recently I heard tell of a religious woman who, on nearing death, said, 'If my father were alive, he would have prayed for me.' That father had been dead for five years, but the mother was alive, and in the room at the time, and a virtuous mother; but it would appear that it did not occur to the dying daughter to call upon her to pray. Why not? I believe that the Christian Endeavour Society is going to create a revolution amongst young people in this direction. Let us hope that will be the case.

5. Cranogwen
(Sarah Jane Rees)

Esther Judith (Cymraeg)

Y Frythones, ii-iii (Hydref 1880 – Gorffennaf 1881)
Diwrnod oer o'r gaeaf ydoedd, a'r ddaear dan fantell
esmwyth o eira glân dilychwin, pan ganlynai cwmni go gryf o
gymdogion 'arch blwyf' syml, a gynhwysai ynddi 'ddaearol
dŷ' hen chwaer dlawd, o fwthyn bychan to gwellt ar waelod
cwm, i fynwent P___.[1] Nid oedd yno neb wedi ei wneuthur yn
amddifad drwy y farwolaeth hon – neb yn galaru rhyw lawer,
oddieithr efallai un neu ddau o'r cymdogion agosaf […] ac eto
teimlai pawb fesur o barch i goffadwriaeth yr un yr oeddid yn
awr yn ei hebrwng i 'dŷ ei hir gartref,'[2] ac yr oedd tafod pob
un yn rhydd a chyflym i fynegi a chydnabod neilltuolrwydd
ei chymeriad […] Yr oedd Esther Judith ar ei phen ei hun ym
mhlith holl ferched a gwragedd yr ardaloedd […] Nid hi oedd
yr unig 'hen ferch' yn y gymdogaeth, y pryd hwnnw, yn fwy
nag yn awr, ond hi oedd yr unig un yn ei dosbarth hi. Nid hi
oedd yr unig hen greadur ar y plwyf yn yr ardal, ond yr oedd
ar ei phen ei hun yn hynny hefyd; yr oedd hi ar y plwyf yn
rhywfodd heb fod un radd o ddarostyngiad hynny yn glynu
wrthi […]
   Un o neilltuolion yr hen chwaer y mynnem barhau a pharchu
ei choffadwriaeth ar y tudalennau hyn, ydoedd ei *dawn*

---

[1] Penmorfa, capel y Calfiniaid Methodistaidd yn Llangrannog.
[2] Ecclesiastes, xii, 5.

ymadrodd nodedig. Medrai siarad yn gryf, yn rheolaidd, yn hylithr, ac awdurdodol iawn. Nid oedd pall ar ei chyflawnder o eiriau; yr oeddynt at ei galwad yn hollol; nid oedd raid iddi ond agor ei genau ar unrhyw fater, na fyddai ffrydlifoedd o ymadroddion yn rhedeg oddi wrthi ar unwaith. Ac nid rhyw fath o eiriau a ddefnyddiai, megis y geiriau cyffredin, afluniaidd, a haner Seisnigaidd ar lafar pobl y cymdogaethau, ond y geiriau gorau, cryfaf, a mwyaf detholedig. Yr oedd ei genau megis wedi ei llunio i siarad; yr oedd ymadrodd mor naturiol iddo ag yw i lygad y ffynnon roddi dŵr allan. Nid geiriau gweigion hefyd oedd ei geiriau, ond geiriau llawn o sylwedd, synnwyr a barn; fel gan fynychaf, yr oedd y gweddusrwydd a'r cymhwyster llwyraf yn nodweddu yr holl achos. Yr oedd cael clywed Esther Judith yn gofyn bendith ar bryd o fwyd yn – o'r bron na fu i ni ddweud – gystal â'r bwyd ei hun; wel, mewn gwirionedd, yr oedd yn well na hynny, a bydded y bwyd mor dda ag y byddai; yr oedd yn 'ras' yn wir, i'r neb a feddai galon rasol i dderbyn a rhynu [sic] iddi […]

Cyfrifai rhai y byddai ein hen chwaer dan sylw hytrach yn arw yn ei siarad weithiau, ac y byddai yn defnyddio rhai geiriau nad oeddynt yn gweddu un yn proffesu duwioldeb. Enwi yr un drwg yn bur anghamsyniol y byddai, gan ei alw weithiau yn ôl ei enw byrraf a mwyaf anghymeradwy. Yn awr, dealler i gychwyn, mai un o bobl yr oes o'r blaen oedd Esther Judith – un o'r *hen* bobl blaen a ffraeth, nad oeddynt wedi eu dysgu am ledneisrwydd fel yr ydym ni yn y dyddiau hyn wedi ein dysgu. Ond heblaw hynny, yr oedd yn bwnc o farn ganddi hi, nad oedd raid bod yn rhyw ochelgar a llednais iawn wrth enwi y gelynddyn; yr oedd ei enw gwaethaf yn ddigon da iddo meddai, a'r dull mwyaf dibarch o'i yngan yn gystal â gwell. Sut bynnag, gwnâi wahaniaeth pwysig bob amser wrth enwi y Gwaredwr, 'Yr Arglwydd Iesu Grist' fyddai ei gair amdano gan fynychaf, neu 'y Gwaredwr Mawr,' gan roddi sain hwy i rai o'r silliau nag a fydd arferol gan bobl y Deheudir yma, a chan ddweud y geiriau gyda phwyslais o barch ac edmygedd addoliadol […]

Un arall o neilltuolion cymeriad ein hen chwaer hynod oedd *cryfder deall*. Meddai gyneddfau meddyliol cryfion, cof a dealltwriaeth yn arbennig felly […] Yn oes Esther Judith - yr oes o'r blaen, gwirionedd y Beibl oedd prif fater astudiaeth pawb, o'r rhai hefyd astudient o gwbl, o fewn y cylch y troai hi ynddo, ac fel yr ystyrid bod yn hyddysg yn yr Ysgrythurau yn gyfystyr a bod yn ddeallgar a gwybodus…Wel, yr oedd ein hen chwaer yn berchen synnwyr cryf […] ac nid oedd odid adnod o blith y rhai tywyll ac aneglur eu hystyr, nad oedd ganddi hi ryw eglurhad go foddhaol arni. Yr oedd dinodedd tlodi ei hamgylchiadau yn peri na wneid cyfrif mawr o honni yn yr ystyr yma - ddim o'r cyfrif a wnelsid pe buasai yn sefyll ar fryn amgylchiadau gwell a mwy golygus; ac eto, cydnabyddai pawb a'i hadwaenent, fod Esther Judith yn berchen meddwl cryf, a'i bod yn gadarn iawn yn yr Ysgrythurau. Gan nad pwy oedd ehud, a gwamal, ac yn bwhwman, nid oedd hi felly. Ar brif faterion, neu athrawiaethau sylfaenol rheswm a datguddiad, yr oedd yn ansigledig fel y graig; ynfydrwydd fyddai ceisio ymosod arni […] Gwirionedd manwl, diaddurn, ydyw fod geiriau y Beibl ar flaen bysedd ein hen chwaer dan sylw; yr oedd yr adnodau yn hollol at ei galwad. Deuent yn union fel y mynnai; nid yn afrosgo, yn anystwyth neu lapriog hefyd, ond megis o'u gwirfodd, dan redeg a chan ymddangos ar eu gorau […]

Un o'i hynodion yn y cysylltiad hwn, priodol yn unig iddi ei hun, ydoedd ei dull hynod artrefol [sic] a di-ofn o *wrandaw* mewn cyfarfodydd crefyddol pa un bynnag ai ar weddi ai ar bregeth. Wrth hyn – ei dull hytrach yn ddigrifol o wrandaw, yr adwaenid hi gan lawer na feddent adnabyddiaeth fanylach o honni [sic]. Pan gâi'i [sic] hi rywbeth a fyddai yn o bwrpasol at ei harchwaeth, a chyda llaw gallwn ddweud y byddai raid iddo fod yn bur dda tuag at fod felly, byddai yn fuan yn effro a bywiog iawn, ar ei thraed yn syth, pwys un law ar y 'ffon fach' (fel ei galwai) a'r llall i fyny, ac yn o aflonydd

ond odid, a'r amenau, y 'felly yn wir;' 'gwir iawn;' 'dyna hi;'
'mawr dda i ti;' a rhyw ymadroddion plaen felly, yn swnio
dros yr holl gapel. Mewn ambell oedfa gynnes *iawn*, byddai
yn anhawdd penderfynu pa un ai llais y pregethwr ai eiddo
E. Judith a fyddai yn uchaf. Gall hyn swnio yn rhyfedd, os
nad yn anghymeradwy ar bapur fel hyn, - yn fwy na digon o
ddigrifwch, ac o aflonyddwch ar gyfarfod o addoliad, ond yn
ei le ei hun, yn y dyddiau hynny, ydynt erbyn hyn dipyn yn
ôl, ac oddi wrth E. Judith, un o'r hen bobl blaen a chynnes,
yr oedd gan fynychaf yn arddunol. Dyna ein teimlad ni. Oddi
wrth unrhyw un cywir a gonest, byddai yn dda gennym ei
glywed eto. Priodol i'r Cymry crefyddol ydyw, ni a wyddom;
ond Cymry ydym ni, a heb ddewis bod yn ddim arall. […]

Go sych a fyddai ambell oedfa i'n hen chwaer; go ddistaw
a fyddai hithau y pryd hwnnw […] Golygai ei gwedd yn
anghamsyniol ei bod yn hiraethu am y terfyn[…] Cofiwn am
dani rai troeon (yn ei dyddiau olaf o ddirywiad iechyd) yn
methu dal y brofedigaeth, ac yn troi allan o gam i gam *cyn
y terfyn* […] Ond pan gai hi flas, 'hyfryd a llon' a fyddai yr
olwg arni. Gwelsom hi yn symud y pryd hwnnw hefyd, o flaen
awelon yr hwyl – yn symud lathenni yn ôl a blaen, a'r 'wlanen
goch' – y fantell ysgarlad wedi ei throi yn gyfleus dan y fraich
yn lle oddi arni, fel y gellid dyrchafu y llaw yn ôl yr ewyllys
a'r teimlad […]

Adeg ein cof cyntaf o Esther Judith, yr oedd yn byw yn ei
bwthyn bychan to gwellt, wrthi ei hun, ac yr oedd yn dioddef
oddi wrth gyfyngdra diffyg anadl *(asthma)*, fel mai anaml, ar
hyd y blynyddoedd, y byddai yn *gorwedd* yn ei gwely, hyd
rywbryd yn y bore, pan ymysgafnhäi yr awyr, ac y câi hithau
ychydig seibiant. Ar ei lled-eistedd y byddai gan hynny o'r
bron drwy y nos, yn effro bid sicr, a'i difyrrwch a fyddai,
rhyw draethganu adnodau a phenillion, weithiau yn uwch,
ac weithiau yn is. Treuliai oriau cyfain felly, a hyfryd iawn
a fyddai y sain a ddeuai oddi wrthi allan, megis swn ymson
pererin wrtho ei hun, un a fyddai yn tynnu tua'r wlad, a thŷ

ei dad. Yr hen greadures annwyl! Llawer dengwaith y buom yn tynnu at ei ffenestr fechan, weithiau yng ngoleuni tyner y lloer, megis yn wylaidd ac yn ochelgar, bryd arall drwy'r tywyllwch du, megis yn hyf a chalonnog; weithiau drwy fyned allan o bwrpas i hynny a phrydiau eraill wrth ddyfod o honnom adref heibio i 'dŷ Esther,' a phasio i'n tŷ ein hunain; mynych, mynych y buom yn gwrando arni yn peraidd ganu, neu yn peraidd ymson ar ei heistedd yn y gwely, heb fod y pryd hwnnw, yr ydym yn ofni, yn gallu gwerthfawrogi ei theimlad, a chydymdeimlo â'i hunigedd (yn y byd hwn) fel y dylem, ac eto yn teimlo swyn y felodedd dyner oddi wrthi. Llawer o sôn a fyddai hefyd, ym mhlith plant a phobl yr ardal, am glywed Esther yn 'dweud wrthi ei hun;' ond y mae yn chwith gennym y funud hon, ac yn alarus, mor ychydig a ddeallent wir ystyr a chyfeiriad ei hunan-ymgom o fawl a gweddi [...]

Tymher gynhyrfus a thanllyd ydoedd eiddo Esther Judith; yr oedd ei hysbryd gan fynychaf yn cynwys ynddo lawer o wefrdân; pe y buasai yr amgylchiadau yn wahanol, *lawer* o honynt, a hi yn hollol yr un, gwnaethai areithiwr o'r bron digymar; gallwn ddychymygu y rhoddasai y byd ar dân gan nerth huawdledd, brwdfrydedd ysbryd, a sêl dros y gwirionedd, ond nid oedd hyn i fod yn ei hachos hi, yr *ochr* yma; ni gyfrifwn fod yr holl rwystrau wedi eu symud o'r ffordd yn y 'wlad well, 'a hithau yn nofio yn nwyfus yn ei helfen ei hun, gan nad p'un a pha fath yw hono [sic]. Sut bynag [sic], llawer o beth ydoedd i ysbryd fel yr eiddo Esther Judith – i fôr fel hwnw [sic] ymlonyddu ac ymorphwys yn dawel ar ei dywod. Ni wnai yr eiddo hithau ond ar amodau neillduol o gyd-gyfarfyddiad rhwng y naturiol a'r ysbrydol, a'r *nos*, ar ei heistedd yn y gwely, y byddai hyny [sic] yn aml iawn [...]

Byddai Esther Judith yn chwannog iawn ar adegau o hin deg, i ddyfod allan o'i bwthyn, naill ai i'r drws, neu i fwlch yr ardd o flaen y tŷ, a'r Beibl mawr ganddi, a'r gwydrau ar ei llygaid, a darllen yno yn uchel, fel, os y mynnai rhywun, y gellid ei chlywed o gryn bellter. A darllen yn ardderchog a wnâi yr hen chwaer. Byddai o'r bron gystal â phregeth ei chlywed yn darllen, pan fyddai yn yr hwyl iawn i hynny; yr oedd ei hynganiad o eiriau mor gyflawn, a hyglyw, a digoll, a'i pharabl mor weddus – mor ryw barchedig a defosiynol, a'r synnwyr yn cael ei osod allan mor dda ganddi, fel y byddai yn wir amheuthun cael gwrando arni […]

Byddai rhai yn chwannog i feddwl mai rhyw Phariseaeth yn yr hen chwaer fyddai y darllen allan hynny - fel y gwelid ac y clywid gan ddynion ei bod yn darllen, ac yn cydnabod y gair; ond pell ydym ni o feddwl hynny am dani. Nage fawr, barddoniaeth ei nhatur [sic] ydoedd; huawdledd naturiol ei hysbryd yn mynnu ei ffordd allan yn rhywfodd. Yr oedd ei bwthyn yn fychan, yn isel, a hytrach yn dywyll; yr oedd yr hen chwaer yn hoff iawn o dipyn o *scope* i bob amcan, yr oedd ei llais llawn a threiddgar yn gofyn am dipyn o eangder i chware ynddo, ac i'w doi; ac yr ydym yn hollol foddlawn i dybied, y byddai yn ryw esmwythâd iddi gael ei arfer weithiau – ei ollwng allan megis am draws y greadigaeth, i ganol cynulleidfa anian, yn gymaint ag na chai un gynulleidfa arall yn astud i wrando arni. Yr ydym ni yn ei ddeall yn dda fel yn hollol gydweddol ag arddunedd teimlad ac uchelgais Esther Judith, fod yn rhaid iddi, er mwyn cael tywallt allan gronfeydd yr huawdledd naturiol o'i mewn, gael darllen allan weithiau ar garreg y drws, weithiau ar y grisiau i'r ardd (felly yr oedd y fynedfa i'r ardd) rai o'r Salmau barddonol, ac o'r prophwydoliaethau mwyaf arddunol, gan roddi iddynt megis o gyflawnder ynni a nwyfiant ei hysbryd ei hun, eu llonaid o ystyr a nerth.

Ysmotyn paradwysaidd i ni ydoedd gardd Esther Judith, y mwyaf felly, yn ein *fancy* blentynnaidd, o holl erddi a llanerchau prydferth y meddwl. Hyd ei llwybrau y gwelem Adda ac Efa yn mwynhau dyddiau eu diniweidrwydd, a'u cymdeithas ddirwystr â'r ysbrydol; iddi hi dros y 'sticil' fel y galwem y grisiau ar i fyny a arweinient iddi, y gwelem y sarff gyfrwys yn ymlusgo at Efa, a rhwng ei llwyni eirin Mair ac

arall, a than y pren afalau yn y gwaelod, y gwelem Adda euog
a darostyngol yn ymguddio ar ôl y cwymp colledus; a thros
y grisiau bychain drylliog – y 'sticil' eto, y gwelem y ddau
droseddwr cwynfanus yn gorfod troi allan, heibio i ddrws
bwthyn Esther, a drws y bwthyn arall ar ei bwys, ac allan i'r
byd diaddurn a digydymdeimlad; ac ar y bwlch bychan yma
y dychmygem weled y cerubiaid wedi eu gosod, a chanddynt
gleddyfau tanllyd ysgwydedig i gadw ffordd pren y bywyd.
Gardd Esther yw gardd Eden i ni hyd y dydd hwn; nis gallwn
gofio am Baradwys ein rhieni cyntaf ond drwyddi hi. A hyn
i gyd, nid am fod gardd yr hen chwaer daclus yn y byd, na
chelfyddgar o wedd, yn cael ei thrin yn dda, nac yn cynnwys
fawr o flodau a phrydferthion; ond am fod rhywbeth yn ei
sefyllfa fel allan o'r byd, ac yn dra chyfeillgar a'r nefoedd o
haul a lleuad a sêr, ac am fod Esther, y perchennog, i'n meddwl
plentynnaidd ni, yn fwy na neb arall, yn cynrychioli yr Hen
Destament – yr hen amser i gyd megis hyd ddechrau y byd.
O'r braidd, yn wir, na thybiem nad oedd Esther yn bod megis
o'r dechrau; ac nad oedd rhywbeth a fynnai â'r ardd honno
o flaen ei drws, hyd yn nod [sic] pan ydoedd yn Ardd Eden.
Nid hefyd oblegid y cyfrifem hi mor hen â hynny, ond yr oedd
mor gyflawn o wybodaeth, fel y tybiem, ac mor gynefin â'r
ysbrydol, mor artrefol [sic] yn yr holl wirionedd, fel yr ydym
yn tybied yn sicr yr ymddangosai i ni fod Esther Judith, mewn
rhyw fodd neu gilydd, yn bod erioed [...]

Yn rhywfodd neu gilydd, nid oes amheuaeth yn ein meddwl
nad oedd Esther o dylwyth y proffwydi; golwg broffwydol
oedd arni; ymddangosiad proffwydes oedd iddi; a bywyd
ddiddeddf, di-drefn, ac annibynnol proffwyd i fesur helaeth a
arweiniai. Gresyn na ddeallodd hi na neb arall ar y ddaear yr
hyn a fuasai yr alwedigaeth briodol iddi. Meddai ddull un a
allasai wneuthur argraff ar ddynion, a chyflawni neges o bwys
megis rhwng y byd hwn a'r byd a ddaw; ond ni ddeallodd
neb o hynny. Gan nad pwy a alwyd i 'gadw tŷ' a thrin teulu
(ac yn ddiddadl, y mae y rhan amlaf o lawer o ferched wedi

eu galw a'u donio i hynny, ac yn ateb i'r alwad), *ni* alwyd
Esther; ni feddai fawr fwy o gymhwyster a gallu i hynny
nag a feddai Ioan Fedyddiwr, neu un o'r proffwydi cyntaf;
yr oedd yr ardduneadd a berthynai i'w hysbryd yn golygu
angof o'r byd i fesur helaeth. Y mae barddoniaeth *trefn* ni a
wyddom; y mae beirdd a phroffwydi a ganant yn orau mewn
gerddi prydferth a rheolaidd, ac ystafelloedd glân a threfnus.
Y mae beirdd rhif a mesur, beirdd llafariaid a chytseiniaid,
beirdd rheol, beirdd wrth y llathen a'r pwys; ond nid o honynt
hwy yr oedd Esther Judith; nid o blith proffwydi y coleg, a'r
ddesg, yr esmwyth-fainc, a dillad esmwyth, yr ydoedd hi; un
o feirdd y bryniau a llethrau y mynyddoedd ydoedd Esther,
un o broffwydi yr anialwch; a buasai yn hollol gydweddol â'i
natur, pe y deallasai hi hynny ar y cyntaf, fod 'ei dillad o flew
camel, a'i bwyd yn locustiaid a mêl gwyllt.'[3] Y golled ydoedd
na ddeallodd Esther, na neb arall ydoedd yn fyw ar unwaith
â hi, y neges arbennig y gallasai y ddawn ydoedd ynddi hi
ei chyflawni yn y byd [...] Nid oedd fawr fwy o briodoldeb i
Esther geisio 'cadw tŷ,' nag a fuasai i eryr wneud nyth a magu
cywion dan fondo ei bwthyn.

Golwg o *lymder* oedd un gyntaf Esther Judith wrth iddi
ddyfod tuag at un, golwg megis eiddo un wedi ymgynefino
â'r anialwch, â neillduedd; golwg *hen* iawn, fel y dywedasom,
megis pe buasai oes Elias, neu un o'r proffwydi cyntaf, yn
rhythu arnom eto, a golwg lem annibynnol, ddi-ildio. Tybiwn
y funud hon ei gweled o flaen ein llygaid, yn tynnu at y tŷ,
ar ôl bod i fynnu [sic] neu i lawr hyd y gymdogaeth, yn ôl ei
harfer gyson. Byddai yn pwyso yn drwm ar ei ffon, a'r war yn
crymu yn benderfynol. Het a alwn yn un wrywaidd a fyddai
ar ei phen gan fynychaf (fel hefyd a fyddai yr arfer gan lawer
hen wraig y dyddiau hynny) [...]

Golwg o *wroldeb* hefyd ydoedd eiddo yr hen chwaer, megis
pe na wyddai am ofn, yn ystyr gyffredin y gair. Ac felly mewn

---

[3] Mathew, 3, 4.

gwirionedd yr ydoedd – mor llawn o ryw oleuni ynddi ei hun –
mor hunanddibynol, fel y byddai cwmni Esther yn nhywyllwch
y nos, neu mewn ystorm o fellt a tharanau, yn cael ei gyfrif a'i
deimlo gennym ni y plant, yn ddinas noddfa hollol ddiogel,
megis amddiffyn castell cadarn. Rhedem at Esther hyd yn
nod o'n tŷ ein hunain, ac oddi wrth ein mam, pan tybiem fod
argoel perygl o bwys. Mewn ystorm o fellt a tharanau, hi
ydoedd ein 'twr a'n gwaredydd.' Yr oedd cael bod ar bwys
Esther yn gyfystyr a bod yn hollol ddiogel, canys ni theimlai
hi un ofn. Mor gofus gennym ei gweled yn troi allan ar bwys
y ffon fach, ryw brydnawn o fellt a tharanau hollol frawychus
– yn troi allan, ac yn esgyn y rhiw oddi wrth y tŷ i ben ychydig
o fryn gerllaw, i gael golwg gyflawn ar y gogoniant arddunol,
yn myned felly mor sionc a hunanfeddiannol, tra yr ymdorai y
daran ddychrynllyd uwch ei phen; ac meddai yn dawel, 'Llais
ein Tad yw hwn; llais ein Tad'.

Felly, creadures ryfedd y bu fyw; o 'don i don' o ran
amgylchiadau y bywyd hwn, heb ofalu fawr dros drannoeth,
ond gan gyfrif fod yn 'ddigon i'r diwrnod ei ddrwg ei hun;'
ac o 'nerth i nerth' o ran cynhaliaeth ysbrydol, gan ymddifyru
yn bennaf bob amser ym mhethau Duw a'r nefoedd - felly y
bu fyw ei thaith is y nen […] Y mae ei bedd wedi ei anghofio;
y mae yn amheus gennym a ellid hyd yn nod eisoes gael
hyd iddo. 'Twmpath gwyrddlas' ydyw yn awr ym mhlith
lliaws o rai eraill tebyg; ond yr ydym yn tybied y clywn lais
yr Atgyfodiad a'r Bywyd yn dywedyd, 'Myfi a'i hatgyfodaf
hi yn y dydd diweddaf.' Saif heddyw ar fynydd Sïon, 'yng
nghymanfa a chynulleidfa y rhai cyntaf-anedig'.[4]

---

[4] Hebreaid, 12, 23.

Esther Judith

It was a cold winter day, the earth under a soft cloak of spotless snow, when quite a sizable company of neighbours followed the simple parish coffin which made up the 'earthly home' of a poor sister, from a thatch-roofed cottage at the bottom of the valley to P – cemetery.[1] No-one had been orphaned by this death – nobody was grieving much, apart perhaps from one or two of the closest neighbours […] and yet everybody felt a measure of respect for the one whom they were now accompanying 'to her long home',[2] and every tongue was quick and free to express and recognize the distinction of her character […] Esther Judith stood alone amongst the women and wives of the area […] She was not the only spinster in the neighbourhood, at that time any more than today, but she was the only one of her type. She was not the only old creature on the parish in the area, but she stood alone in that as well; somehow she lived off the parish without a modicum of the humiliation of that state attaching itself to her […]

One of the peculiarities of the old woman whose memory we want to record and respect in these pages was her striking *eloquence*. She could speak strongly, in a measured mode, lucidly and with great authority. There was no end to her abundance of words; they were entirely at her disposal; she had but to open her mouth on any subject and a flood of phrases would stream from her at once. And she did not use any old words, like the ordinary, unshapely and half-anglicized words spoken by much of the neighbourhood, but the best, strongest and choicest words. Her mouth was, as it were, made for speech; utterance was as natural to her as it is for a fountainhead to give out water. Nor were they empty words, but words full of substance, sense and reason; so that

---

[1] Penymorfa, the Calvinist Methodist chapel in Llangrannog

[2] Ecclesiastes, xii, 5.

usually propriety and an entire suitability characterized the whole case. Hearing Esther Judith asking a blessing on a meal was – we nearly said – as good as the food itself; well, in fact, it was better than that, let the food be as good as it could be; it was a 'grace', indeed, to all with a heart gracious enough to accept it [...]

Some felt that the old sister we speak of was somewhat rough in her conversation at times, and that she used certain words which were unsuitable for one professing godliness. She tended to name the devil pretty unmistakably, calling him sometimes according to his shortest and least recommended appellation. Now, it must be understood to begin with, that Esther Judith was one of the previous generation – one of the old plain and outspoken people, who had not learnt politeness as we in these days have learnt it. But quite apart from that, it was a matter of belief with her that there was no need to be careful and polite when naming the enemy of man; the worst name was quite good enough for him, she said, and the least respectful way of uttering it was better or best. At any rate, she spoke quite differently always when naming the Saviour, 'the Lord Jesus Christ' was her usual name for him, or 'the Great Redeemer', giving a longer sound to some of the syllables than is usual amongst these Southerners, and saying the words with a worshipful emphasis of respect and admiration [...]

Another of the peculiarities of this curious old sister was her *intellectual strength.* She possessed strong mental abilities, and an unusual memory and understanding [...] In Esther Judith's age – that age gone by, the truths of the Bible were everybody's chief study within her circle, amongst those who did study at all, and to be learned in the Scriptures was considered the equivalent of being intelligent and well-informed [...] Well, our old friend had a sound intelligence [...] and there was not a verse from amongst the most dark and obscure passages of which she could not give a satisfactory explanation. The insignificance and poverty of her circumstances meant that she was not seen as of any *great* account for this – she was given none of that attention that she would have received had she stood on the eminence of better circumstances and fairer prospects; and yet all her acquaintance recognized that Esther Judith had a strong mind, and was very thoroughly versed in the Scriptures. Whoever else was rash, or frivolous, or wavering, she was not. On primary matters, or on the basic teachings of reason or revelation, she was as unshakeable as the rock; it would have been madness to try to attack her [...] The exact, unpainted truth is that the words of the Bible were at her fingertips; its verses came instantly to her call. They came exactly as she wished them to: neither awkwardly nor stiffly nor distortedly either, but as if of their own free will, hastening and appearing at their best [...]

Another of her eccentricities in this context, specific to herself, was her strangely unselfconscious and fearless way of *listening* in religious meetings, whether at a sermon or a prayer. By this – her in some ways comical manner of listening – she was known by many who had no other detailed knowledge of her. When she got hold of something which was very much to her taste, and by the way one can say that it had to be pretty good if it was to please her, she would soon be very stirred up and lively, on her feet straight away, one hand leaning on the 'little stick' (as she called it) and the other held up, and quite restless, more than likely, with the amens, 'it is so, truly', 'very true', 'that's it', 'great good to you', and other such plain phrases, to be heard all over the chapel. In some very heated meetings, it would be difficult to make out whether it was the preacher's voice or that of E. Judith which was loudest. This might sound strange, if not unadvisable, put down on paper like this – more than enough entertainment, and a disturbance for a meeting of worship, but in its place, in those days, which by now are some time gone, it was generally sublime. We thought so, at any rate, and would be glad to hear the like again, from a true and honest person. It is a peculiarity characteristic of the religious Welsh, we know; but then we are Welsh and do not wish to be anything other [...]

Some services were considerably less to her taste; she would be pretty quiet then [...] Her face conveyed clearly enough that she was longing for the close [...] On some occasions (during her final days of deteriorating health) we remember her being unable to bear the experience, and exiting slowly step by step *before the end* [...] But when she was pleased, she looked 'delightful and joyous'. We saw her moving at such times too, swaying before the breezes of fervour – moving yards to and fro, with the red cloak folded back conveniently under her arm instead of over it, so that the hand could be lifted according to the will and feeling.

At the time of our first recollection of Esther Judith, she was living in her little thatched cottage, by herself, and suffering from asthma, so that only rarely throughout those years would she *lie down* on her bed until the early morning hours, when the air was lighter and she had a little rest. For most of the night she would be half-sitting, very much awake, entertaining herself by chanting verses and hymns, sometimes loudly, sometimes more quietly. She would spend hours on end in so doing, and very beautiful was the sound she made, like the murmuring meditations of a pilgrim as he approached the land and house of his father [...] Dozens of times we were drawn to her little window, sometimes in tender moonlight, humbly and warily, at other times through black darkness, more quickly and confidently, sometimes going out deliberately to it, at other times walking home past 'Esther's house' as we passed on to our own; many, many times we listened to her sweetly singing, or sweetly soliloquizing, sitting up on her bed, without being able at that time, we fear, to understand her feeling or sympathize as we should with her loneliness (in this world), and yet charmed by her tender music. Amongst the children and adults of the neighbourhood there was much talk of hearing Esther 'talking to herself', but it grieves and

pains us at this moment to think how little was understood of
the true meaning and direction of her solitary communion of
worship and prayer […]

Esther Judith's temper was lively and fiery; her spirit
generally contained much electric fire; if the circumstances
had been different, *many* of them, and she exactly the same,
she would have made an incomparable orator; she would
have set the world on fire with powerful eloquence, spirited
enthusiasm, and the zeal for truth, but this was not to be in
her case, *this side*; we will believe that all the obstacles have
been moved away in the 'better world', and that she is now
floating blissfully in her own element, whatever that may be.
At any rate it was a big thing for a nature like that of Esther
Judith – for a sea like that one, to quieten and rest gently on its
sand. Hers did not do so except under special circumstances,
marking the coming together of the natural and spiritual, and
it was often at night, sitting on the bed, that such a moment
occurred […]

On sunny days, Esther Judith liked to come out of her
cottage, either to the door, or to the garden gap at the front of
the house, with the big bible, and the spectacles on her eyes,
and read out loud there, so that, if you wished, you could hear
her from some distance. And she would read excellently. It
would be as good as a sermon to hear her reading, when she
was in the right mood for it; her pronunciation was so full,
and clear, and faultless, and her discourse so appropriate, so
respectful and devotional, with the meaning laid out so well
by her, that it was truly a treat to hear her.

Some might like to think that it was a sort of Pharisaism in
her to read like that – so that people could hear and see that she
was reading and acknowledging the word, but we are far from
thinking so of her. By no means – it was the poetry of her
nature; the natural eloquence of her spirit insisting on finding
its way out somehow. Her cottage was small, low and a little
dark; the old sister very much liked some scope for all her

intentions; her full and penetrating utterance demanded some space to play in; and we are happy with the notion that it gave her some ease to give it its head at times – to throw her voice out as if across the creation, into the middle of the audience of nature, in so far as she had no other attentive audience to listen to her. We understand very well that it was entirely in conformity with the sublimity of Esther Judith's sentiment and ambition, that, in order to pour out the sources of the natural eloquence within her, she had to read out loud, sometimes on her doorstep, sometimes on the garden steps, some of the poetical Psalms, and the more sublime prophecies, giving them, as if from the abundance of the energy and liveliness of her own spirit, their full sense and strength.

Esther Judith's garden was a paradisiacal spot for us, the most so, in our childlike fancy, of all the beautiful gardens and glades of the mind. Along its paths we saw Adam and Eve enjoying the days of their innocence, and their unrestricted and companionship with the spiritual; into it, over the '*sticil*' as we called the stile steps that led up to it, we saw the devious snake slithering to Eve, through its gooseberry bushes; under the apple tree at the bottom we saw the guilty and fallen Adam hiding after his fall into loss; and over the little broken stairs – the '*sticil*' again – we saw the two transgressors forced to exit, past the door of Esther's cottage, and the door of the cottage next door,[3] and out to the unadorned and unsympathetic world; and on this little stile in the gap we saw the cherubim stand, with flaming swords to guard the way to the tree of life. Esther's garden is still to this day the Garden of Eden for us; we cannot remember the Paradise of our first parents except through her. And that not because the old sister's garden was the tidiest in the world, or the most artistic in appearance, or well cared for, or containing many flowers and beautiful plants; but because there was something in its position as out

---

[3] That is, Cranogwen's own childhood home.

of this world, and very friendly with the heavens of sun and moon and stars; and because Esther, its owner, to our childish mind, more than any other represented the Old Testament – all the old time as if since the beginning of the world. We were near to thinking that Esther had existed from the first; and that she had something to do with that garden before her door, even when it was the Garden of Eden. Not that we thought she was as old as all that, but she was so full of knowledge, so familiar with the spiritual, so much at home in all its truths, that somehow it seemed to us as if Esther Judith had always existed […]

Somehow or other, we doubt not that Esther belonged to the family of the prophets; she had a prophetic look; her appearance was that of a prophetess; and she largely followed the lawless, methodless and independent life of a prophet. What a shame it was that neither she herself nor anybody else on this earth realised what would have been her appropriate calling. She had the manner of one who could have made an impression on people, and accomplished a mission of importance between this world and the next, as it were, but no-one understood that. Whoever else was called to 'keep house' and look after a family (and unarguably many women are called upon and given the talent to so do, and respond to the call) Esther was *not*; she possessed as little aptitude and ability in that direction as did John the Baptist, or one of the early prophets; the sublimity which belonged to her spirit meant that she forgot the world to a great extent. There is a poetry of *order*, we know; there are bards and prophets who sing best in regular and pretty gardens, and in clean and tidy rooms. There are bards of number and measure, bards of vowels and consonants – bards of rule – bards by the yard and measure; but Esther was not of their kind; she was not of the prophets of the college, and the desk, the easy chair and the fine clothes; one of the bards of the hills and mountain ranges was Esther, one of the desert prophets; and it would have been entirely compatible with her nature, had she understood it from the first, that her 'raiment' was 'of camel's hair' and her 'meat of locusts and wild honey'.[4] The loss was that neither Esther nor any of her contemporaries understood the special work that the talent which was hers could have accomplished in the world […] It was not more appropriate to expect Esther to 'keep house' than it would have been to expect an eagle to make its nest and rear chicks under the eaves of her cottage.

A look of *severity* was Esther Judith's as she first approached one, a look as of one accustomed to the desert, and to isolation; a very old look, as we say, as if the age of Elias or one of the first prophets was staring out at us, and a stern, independent, unyielding look. It seems as if just this minute we saw her in front of our eyes, coming towards the house, after having been up and down the neighbourhood, in her usual manner. She would be leaning heavily on her stick, bent forward determinedly. On her head she usually wore what we would call a masculine hat (such as many old women wore in those days) [...]

A look of *courage* was hers as well, as if she knew not fear, in the ordinary sense of the word. And that was indeed the case – she was so full of some light within herself – so self-dependent, that her company in the darkness of the night, or in a storm of thunder and lightning, was recognised and felt by us children as a perfectly safe sanctuary, like the defence of a strong castle. When we had forebodings of a serious danger, we ran to Esther in preference even to our own home and our mother. In a storm of thunder and lightning, she was the 'tower which saves us'. To be allowed to be close to Esther was to be perfectly safe, because she felt no fear. How well we remember seeing her coming out leaning on her little stick, some afternoon of really frightening thunder and lightning – coming out, and climbing the slope from the house to the top of a nearby hill, to have a full view of the sublime scene, climbing in so brisk and self-possessed a fashion, while the

---

[4] Matthew, 3, 4. The reference is to John the Baptist.

frightful thunder broke over her head, and she said quietly, 'This is the voice of our Father; our Father's voice' [...]

In such a way she lived, a strange creature; tossed from wave to wave with regard to her circumstances in this world, with little care for the morrow, except the belief that 'sufficient unto the day the evil thereof', and going from strength to strength in terms of spiritual sustenance, always taking most interest in God's concerns and in heaven – so she underwent her journey [...] Her grave has been forgotten; we doubt whether anyone by now could find it. It is a green mound among a myriad identical ones, yet we hear the voice of the Resurrection and the Life saying, 'I will resurrect her on the last day'. She stands today on mount Sion, in 'the general assembly and church of the firstborn.'[5]

---

[5] Hebrews, 12, 23.

6. Elizabeth Phillips Hughes

The Higher Education of Girls in Wales (1884)

It is undesirable and impossible to discuss the Higher
Education[1] of Girls in Wales, and ignore the wider question
of the higher education of women, and the still wider one of
higher education itself. We are continually being reminded
that we cannot examine anything as an isolated fact […] There
is yet a further difficulty which threatens to make our subject
unmanageably large. How far are we to allow the ideal to be
included? Are we to build up an ideal education, as we think it
ought to be, possibly as we may hope it will be in the future,
or are we to confine ourselves to the immediate present and
the severely practical? An ideal, rightly used, is of immense
practical value…With an ideal before us – a theory which we
have thought out – we feel we are not patching, but making;
we distinguish between the permanent and the temporary,
and give the former its true place. We can never truly see the
meaning or glory of the present until the future cast some light
upon it […] Evolution in education, as in everything else, has
been in the past to a great extent unconscious, that is, the result
of experience. Surely the time has now arrived, when we can
have conscious evolution […] It seems clear, that the rate of
the future progress of the world will depend chiefly on the

---

[1] By 'higher education' Elizabeth Phillips Hughes would appear to mean
what would today be termed 'secondary' or 'further' education, rather than
degree level studies.

wisdom of the theories which man evolves. A theory of higher education is essential to every rational teacher, and, if possible, more so to anyone who ventures to plan out a practical system of education. I maintain, therefore, that it is of great practical moment that everyone who is keenly interested in Welsh education, should attempt to forecast the future to some extent, and, as we begin to build up our national education, we should have some rough idea of the structure we want to erect […] Having briefly examined the present state of the Principality, educationally considered, I shall attempt – guided on the one hand by my theory of higher education, and on the other by the actual state of affairs at the moment – to give a few practical suggestions as to the best method of gaining the priceless chance of a higher education for Welsh Girls.

In discussing higher education, it is of extreme importance to distinguish two questions frequently confounded. What is the aim of such an education? What are the most appropriate means to obtain it? A liberal education is sometimes defined as an education in classics, but this merely gives us the means employed, and sheds no light on the fundamental point as to what is the essence of a liberal education. Concerning the first question there is a general agreement; concerning the second, there is at present no consensus of opinion.

A distinction may be drawn between a liberal education, and a technical or professional one. In the former case, man is considered as an individual – an end in himself; its great aim is to develop his faculties, to turn his potential powers, whatever they may be, into actual powers. In the second case, man is regarded rather as a means to an end, not so much as an individual, but as a doctor, lawyer, or artisan, as the case may be. It is only a certain portion of his potential powers which are developed. Unless the man becomes that for which he is trained, much of his technical and professional education is wasted. It is true that a higher education, by developing the individual, prepares him to some extent for any occupation in the future; but this is not its primary aim. A distinction is likewise drawn between a higher education on the one hand, and a primary and secondary or intermediate education on the other. The last two have the double aim of developing the faculties to some extent, and giving the information necessary for future life, and also for a technical or a higher education. It seems agreed, therefore, that the object of a higher education is the development of man, considered as an individual. When we come to consider what are the most appropriate means to attain this end, we find ourselves plunged into one of the keenest controversies of the day.

The most common opinion is still that a study of classics gives an intellectual culture which is pre-eminently a part of a liberal education. The means employed, the material used, is considered of great importance: 'Without classics, no higher education', is the opinion of many educated men. I venture to suggest, on the contrary, that the material is of comparatively little moment; and that it is the manner in which that material is used which is the vital point. In other words it is not so much what we teach, but how we teach it, that decides whether it shall cultivate the minds of our scholars […] Any subject, if properly studied, can form the nutriment of a higher intellectual life – the gateway from the narrow and straightened pathway of the uneducated to the fuller, freer, life of the developed and cultured man […] It is not the knowledge which the teacher gives, but the aspect of knowledge which he imparts, which is cultivating […]

When we turn to the question as to whether the education of girls shall be differentiated from that of men, and the education of Wales from that of England, it seems to me clear that in both cases the answer should be in the affirmative. Education can be viewed under two aspects; it develops the individual, and it fits him for future life. In so far as women and men are different, and also in all probability their future work in life will be dissimilar, their education will not be exactly alike, whichever view we adopt. I do not consider that we have sufficient data at present to decide wherein that difference will be shown. The only course which seems open to us is to give girls and women the same education as boys and men, and to leave to the educated women of the future the work of deciding where their course of study shall branch off from that provided for men [...]

An ideal Welsh education must be national. It must differ from an ideal English education primarily because of the difference of race. I cannot help thinking that this difference of race is not realized nearly so much by the English as it is by ourselves. This is possibly explained by the fact that many of us get our education in England; and living among English people, unconsciously we lose some of our more superficial differences. This does not, however, in any way remove our fundamental characteristics. History is silent as to any satisfactory explanation of the difference between races. The gulf between Teuton and Kelt was fixed in pre-historic times by mighty influences of which we know nothing; we can but judge of their strength by the permanence of their effects. As far as we know, type characteristics are not being obliterated. Judging from analogy, an appropriate and thorough education will only deepen and develop them. It is among the uneducated that we find a monotonous similarity, among the most highly educated we come across refreshing differences. Education must be national, however, before it can fully develop the national type of character. Differences of race, far from being a subject for regret, as far as possible should be deepened and perpetuated. We value individuality of character in an individual, so should we value it in a race [...] Integration is not possible without differentiation...

There is also the difference of language. In 1871, it was computed that out of a population of 1,426,504, in Wales and Monmouthshire, no less than 1,000,000 habitually spoke Welsh. Our nationality does not depend on our language, but it seems probable that Welsh will remain a spoken language for some time. It has become a matter of patriotism, there is a Welsh literature to preserve it, and it is at present inseparably connected with the religion of Wales. It must be noted also that religion in the Principality is almost the same social power as it was in Greece. Much of Welsh social life is centred in religious and semi-religious meetings. It is certainly a question which requires careful consideration whether under these circumstances the Welsh language should not form at any rate an optional subject in a scheme of Welsh Higher Education. There are few things which would appeal more to Welshmen than this recognition of their language, and I believe it would form a powerful inducement to them to a more prolonged and careful course of study. Emerson says, 'Nothing great was ever achieved without enthusiasm.' The establishment of a Higher Education in Wales is great both in itself and in the efforts which it must call forth. It appears to me that a recognition in our educational scheme of the Welsh language would be one easy method of arousing that enthusiasm which we shall so greatly need in order to carry out any complete and thorough scheme.

There is also some difference of religion. Three-quarters of the population are Nonconformists, and the Established Church is here the church of the minority. Hence, all Welsh national education must be unsectarian. This is almost universally acknowledged in Wales to be the only way out of sectarian difficulties.

Wales is for the most part a poor country, and her people cannot afford high fees. There are scarcely any Welsh endowments, and, because of difference in language, and an almost complete absence of good intermediate and higher education in the Principality, Welshmen are very seldom able to obtain by competition any advantage from the English educational endowments. The population in Wales is scattered, and we have few large towns. As we have already pointed out, good cheap schools, if unendowed, must be large; hence, this is a serious difficulty.

There is great ignorance in Wales as to the true nature of education. We have passed from our ideal education to a consideration of the actual state of affairs in Wales at present, and it must be confessed that the outlook seems dreary. It is not surprising that the committee appointed for considering the Higher Education in Wales should have made the remark that they found considerable difficulty in offering suggestions as to the higher education of girls in Wales: 'Our difficulty lies in the fact that the unsatisfied requirements are so great, and the available resources apparently so meagre.' The difficulties in Wales are unique. In England, the chief work has been to enable women to share the educational advantages of men; but in Wales, we have to create a higher education for both sexes. Dr. Johnson considered it was worth more than a thousand a year to an individual to possess the habit of looking at the bright side of things. Kelts are supposed to have this habit, and it is well that at this point in our national history Welshmen and Welshwomen have an income of this sort to draw upon.

In spite of great difficulties, there are many causes for hopefulness. Those of us who know something of Welsh character, and what it is without education, are inspirited by the thought of the effect on Wales of a good Higher Education. We believe profoundly that Welsh girls are very well worth educating [...]

There is also one cause for hope outside Wales. From the comparative poverty of the country, and its utter want of good educational establishments, there is great need just at present for special Government assistance; and this seems likely to be granted. I think it is a very significant and hopeful fact, that in the Welsh Sunday Closing Bill the present Government recognised that a certain difference does exist between England and Wales, which made it advisable that the case of Wales should be considered separately.

I will now venture to make some practical suggestions. I am fully aware of the profound difficulty of doing so, especially at the present moment when we do not know as yet what Government intends, or will be able, to do for us. Likewise the amount of Government assistance, and its manner of bestowal, must, from the special circumstances of the case, modify to a great extent any educational scheme.

The work to be done is enormous, and the material is very unprepared. We must therefore take advantage of every modern contrivance for saving labour and making what we possess as effective as possible. Association, cooperation, is one of the mighty forces of today, and should be used. Local feeling is strongly developed in Wales, as well as Patriotism, and this should also be recognised. The advantages of centralisation are immense, but they are quite compatible with giving local bodies considerable power. What do we really want in Wales for the promotion of higher education?

> I. A highly efficient staff of teachers. I mention this first because I believe it is the most important. The best and most rapid way to educate a nation is to educate its teachers. I would also urge that the cheapest way of promoting Higher Education is to pay good salaries to the best teachers that can be obtained. I would point out that a first class teacher is not only a man or woman who thoroughly knows his subject, but one who is trained to teach, and who knows thoroughly how to impart knowledge in such a manner as to lead to the mental development and culture of his pupils.
>
> II. We want to spread in Wales a true knowledge of what education really is, and to arouse enthusiasm about it.
>
> III. There must be established throughout Wales efficient High Schools for girls, and arrangements for women students must be made at our provincial colleges.
>
> IV. We require, unfortunately, a considerable amount of

money to effect these reforms.

I venture to propose that a Union be formed for the Promotion of the Higher Education in Wales, and that a committee of that Union specially undertakes the Higher Education of girls […] I suggest that this committee be formed of teachers from the colleges and schools of Wales, Welshmen interested in education, and English educationalists. I suggest that half the committee be women. I have already spoken of the advantages of centralisation. Anything less than a united national effort can do but little.

A committee so formed would be able to sketch out a scheme of education far better than any individual can; but I will venture to indicate some of the directions in which I think such a committee would find appropriate work.

(A) Such a committee would be admirably suited to start a Welsh Girls' Public Day School Company. That Company should be regarded as a business concern, and half the managing council be business men. It might be worked somewhat on the same lines as the English Company; and, like that, undertake to start a High School in any town which would buy a certain proportion of the necessary shares; and then a local committee could be appointed. It seems to me very desirable that the central council should have far less actual work to do than it has in England. In Wales, especially, probably the central council would know far more about education than the local committee; but as long as it has the power of interfering in case of need, and especially in the appointment of teachers, it seems desirable that as much as possible should be done by the local committee, which will thus feel much more interested in the school. A man on the spot, deeply interested in the school, can frequently do far more for it than a man who lives elsewhere and has no local interest in it, however wise the latter may be. The central council would form a kind of court of appeal for all the teachers, and the local committees; and after the starting of a school, unless a case of emergency arises, the central council's work as regards an individual school should be little. The course of study should be roughly sketched out by the committee [...] In this case, as in all others, it seems very undesirable that we should be fettered by the English course of study [...]

All the Welsh High Schools need not be on exactly the same plan, but they should be sufficiently alike for children to pass easily from one to another and to give a certain uniform character to our national system. The Head Mistress should have considerable power; and, of course, both she and her assistant mistresses should have the power to appeal to the Central Committee in case of need. The fees must be low, not more than £8 a year. Such schools would, of course, have to be unsectarian. The question may be asked, why not take advantage of the English Company already existing? The requirements in Wales are so different that we cannot expect the operations of the English Company to be sufficiently elastic to meet them. It is also desirable, according to my view, that we ever keep in mind that in the future our education must be national, and therefore must be in our own hands. Two great difficulties remain to be removed. The High Schools which we have suggested can only exist in our large towns; for example, in Wrexham, Merthyr Tydfil, Cardiff, Swansea, and Bangor, all of these I should think would be able to support such schools in a very short time. Even in these large towns with low fees the greatest economy would be necessary [...] However economically we can manage our High Schools, in the smaller towns they are impossible on account of the necessary expense. Here I would suggest that a novel plan be adopted, and that we should try co- education of the sexes. In infant schools, boys and girls learn together, and in the University of Cambridge, Mason's College Birmingham, University College London, and elsewhere, men and women share the same lectures. Why must they be separated during the intervening years? The experiment of co-education has been tried in America and has succeeded; why should we not attempt it in Wales, where it is so vitally important that our schools should be as large as possible? The experiment should be tried with caution, and it may at first be made very partial. My suggestion is that we should have twin schools under one roof, and very largely under one management. Boys and girls could be educated together to the age of twelve with mutual gain. From that age, if found advisable, they could be educated separately by the same staff of teachers. Science and other lectures could easily be given to the *whole* school, and thus gradually the complete co-education of the sexes could be introduced. The head master would superintend both sides of the school, the second teacher would be a woman in charge of the girls' department, but not necessarily teaching exclusively in it. The advantage to the girls would be greater than to the boys, in so far as the standard of teaching and course of study would probably be far better than otherwise; but there would be some advantage to the boys, as the school would be at any rate nearly twice as large, there would be economy of building, teaching apparatus, and it would be possible to have a far better staff of teachers, and above all more specialists. Other advantages would follow; for example, better school libraries would be possible. If found advisable, the education of the girls could be easily differentiated to some extent, and I should suggest that much useful knowledge, specially suitable to girls, could be given in the school course. These twin High Schools could be established in most small towns, and have the same course of study as the separate High Schools in the larger towns [...]

It would be highly advisable to have scholarships from the elementary to the High Schools, and from these to our provincial colleges. The links would be complete if further scholarships could be obtained to the English Universities, until such times as we have an University of our own. It would be very advisable if the three endowed Grammar Schools for Girls could be put into the hands of such a Welsh Girls' Day School Company. The funds could then be administered far more economically. It is also extremely advisable that they should be made unsectarian. The Court of Chancery, in 1847, took an unsectarian fund, and established two Church Schools with it, in a country where the majority does not belong to that Church. This injustice surely need not be perpetuated. Many of the Grammar Schools in Wales are badly attended, and give a form of education not adapted to the local requirements. I should suggest that they be turned into High Schools, and where the endowments could not be shared by girls (if such is possible) that a girls' High School be started by public subscription, and attached to the boys' school.

(B) The Committee might undertake to get hostels attached to the three provincial colleges. The system of boarding out, if bad for men, is ten times worse for women. Hostels, economically arranged, simply paying their expenses, with no profits, provided a large number of students were obtainable, could charge very low fees. Of course, eventually they must be self-supporting; but I would suggest that the colleges should aid in starting them […]

(C) The Committee might help to spread through Wales a true knowledge of what education is, and arouse an enthusiasm for obtaining it, especially for girls. I have already referred to the fact that we can easily arouse Welsh enthusiasm for fitting objects, and I believe the chief work of the committee would be to direct it into useful channels. They might publish pamphlets on the subjects, and possibly hold public meetings […]

(D) The Committee should endeavour to aid the self-education of girls who have left school. I believe a vast field for usefulness is open in this direction. If a girl has attended a thoroughly good school, and on her return home has no encouragement to continue her education, we can scarcely expect her to do so in the majority of cases. A boy has his trade or profession, and a more public life, to widen his interests and keep up his mental vigour. A girl has none of these helps; frequently she has for some years after leaving school considerable leisure, but this valuable time is not made the most of […] The Committee could assist in the establishment of libraries, museums, and loan exhibitions, and arrange for lectures in connection with them, without which, as I venture to think, their usefulness would be very limited. Evening classes on popular subjects might also be established, and the love of the Welsh for music could be cultivated by lectures on music and singing classes. Debating societies, and societies for self-education, could be encouraged and helped […]

(E) A scholarship fund could be started to assist poor girls of unusual ability,

(F) One of the greatest difficulties will be how to obtain a competent staff of teachers […] The Committee could do much in promoting the education and training of Welsh women teachers. An association of Welsh teachers of all grades and both sexes, if skilfully managed, would do much to spread a love of learning, and a professional interest in the art of teaching. It is one of the great defects in the Higher Education of England that there is no adequate training for her women teachers of a higher grade. Wales is too poor to start a training college, but the Committee could, by lectures on education, a lending library of educational books, and scholarships for teachers to English Colleges, do much to promote professional knowledge. The Scholarships could be given on the understanding that the recipient should teach for a certain number of years in Wales. The Committee could encourage information being collected concerning education in the United States and on the Continent.

(G) In the future, the Committee could endeavour to form a Welsh technical College, in which there should be a woman's department. The Eisteddfodau could be reformed, or rather further developed, and made more educational.

We want for these educational reforms a most considerable amount of money. It is to be hoped that Government will give a grant to Aberystwyth College equal to those of Bangor and of Cardiff. There is no precedent, I believe, for a Government grant to intermediate education. But conditions are changing rapidly, and this fact is not an insuperable objection. If elementary and higher education receive Government aid, it seems strange that intermediate education should be left unaided. Money was granted to Ireland for the building of her Queen's Colleges, and to Scotland for the new College buildings at Glasgow. Government grants for the sites and buildings of the High Schools described previously would be very valuable aid. The English High School Company, which provides its own sites and buildings, is supposed to pay five per cent; but in Wales the fees would have to be much lower than in England, and probably would not meet initial expenses.

I would once more refer to the subject of centralization. We have in our Annual National Eisteddfod a very suitable centre for national concerns. Such an Education Union as I have suggested would find a very fitting place of meeting there, and the same remark would apply to a Welsh teachers' union, to which could be given over the educational section of the *Cymmrodorion.*

As regards the troubled question of a Welsh degree-giving University, it is apparently a question for the future. We have not at present the necessary educational substratum. Some might urge that it is best for a Welshman or Welshwoman to go to an English University, if possible. If they have no other choice, it practically means that the majority of them cannot go at all. Also, as I have endeavoured to point out, it is necessary that our education should be national; and for a perfect national education a University is an essential requirement.

7. Dilys Glynne Jones

The Duty of Welsh women in Relation to the Welsh Intermediate Education Act (1894)

Introductory

'There is a tide in the affairs of men which taken at the flood leads on to fortune.'[1] Never was there an epoch in the history of Wales more fully exemplifying this wise saying of the poet than the present time. Everywhere are signs of awakening, and of new life, and these are most strikingly seen in matters of education.

The University Colleges, the much coveted, newly acquired Welsh University, and the Welsh Intermediate Education Act, which is gradually spreading its benefits over the length and breadth of the land, as one County scheme after another passes into law, are all evidences of this new life in the Principality. Now, more than ever, the Welsh nation has an opportunity of showing to the world of what stuff it is made, and what it can do.

In these three institutions the work of administration is entrusted to a large number of men and women, to be chosen by the nation, so that in the election of representatives to serve on the governing authorities of the three University Colleges and the University, as well as on the various bodies of Governors constituted under the Intermediate Education Act,

---

[1] Shakespeare, *Julius Caesar*, III, iv, 217.

opportunity is afforded for an extensive exercise of judgment and discretion.

In all these, therefore, let the Welsh nation see to it that choice is wisely made, so that the bodies entrusted with our national education in all its branches, shall consist of the best, and most efficient men and women in the land. In these provisions for education, that which marks this epoch as especially noteworthy is the comparatively modern recognition of the rights and duties of women. In all three University Colleges women act on the Council and on the Court of Governors. At Cardiff two women are engaged in teaching in the Normal or Teachers' Training department, and are therefore members of the staff. In the Welsh University charter also, provision is made that 'every degree and every office of the University and membership of every body and authority in it are open to women equally with men.' The day may come when a woman shall be seen in the proud position of Chancellor of the University.

I do not propose now to dwell upon the University Colleges or the Welsh University, except to express my satisfaction at this recognition of the justice extended to women in the constitution of the University.

Women Representatives

The matter however with which I propose to deal more especially here is that of the duties and privileges of women in connection with the working of the Intermediate Education (Wales) Act.

As you already know, provision is expressly made that a considerable number of women shall take part in the working of that Act. An examination of the County schemes will show that to fill the minimum number of places accorded to women on the Governing Bodies constituted by the Act, one hundred and fifty-four women are required. This number is probably considerably below the actual number that will be needed, as there are some of the County schemes, such as those for Denbigh and Merioneth, where no express stipulation is made for women governors, and we call hardly suppose the electors of those counties will show themselves so unenlightened as to fail to elect a fair number of women.

It is of course perfectly obvious, and need not be here insisted upon, that wherever it is proposed that girls should be educated, women should of necessity have a place on the Governing Body, so as to have a share in the management of such education. I would go further, and say emphatically, that women should have a place on every Governing Body dealing with the education of children, whether girls or boys.

In some of the schemes, such as those for Brecknock, Swansea, Cardiff, and Monmouth, provision is made that where there are girls to be educated, there shall be some additional Governors who shall be women, to deal only with matters relating to girls' schools. This seems to imply that they cannot be trusted to deal with matters in which the education of boys is concerned. This is very absurd; surely mothers are the first educators of both boys and girls, and the education of their sons must be of equally vital importance to them as that of their daughters? For my own part, I think such distinctions in the constitution of those Governing Bodies are both ill-judged and unnecessary.

Duties of Welsh Women

Perhaps the most important aspect of the question for us just now, is that of the *duties* incumbent upon us as Welsh women, arising out of present circumstances. The *rights* for which we and those who have gone before us have long contended, have in a measure been accorded to us. Let us consider them as *privileges* and see what are our *duties* in relation to them.

There are, I believe, many women in our land who are ready and willing to help forward the good cause of education if they only knew how to set about it. There are many, I know, who plead want of time as an excuse for not taking their share in the nation's awakening. Far be it from me to judge any such, but I would point out a danger into which many of us are liable to fall. We fill our hands with work, of a kind, truly, but we do not set ourselves to consider what work is worth doing, and what had better be left undone, and so we often fritter away valuable time in a sort of busy idleness which finds no time for work of a permanent and really useful character.

Each one must judge for herself how far this is applicable to her individual case, but no woman, however busy, should fail to take at least an intelligent interest in the work that is so rapidly going forward in our land.

There are many and various ways in which we can help.

Sympathy
1. 'They also serve who only stand and wait.' Quite so – but such service would be considerably increased, if while standing, we would cheer on with friendly sympathy and encouragement, those who are pressing on up the steep hill, at the foot of which we are waiting.

Elementary Education
2. In elementary education we can ascertain in our own neighbourhood what is the present state of things. This may by done by visiting the schools, Board or National schools as the case may be, making friends of the teachers and the children. By such intercourse we can find out who are the promising pupils, and who may need help, either in money, or books, or in simple stimulating conversation.

Secondary Education
3. In secondary education again, we can make ourselves acquainted with the condition of the schools, find out what opportunities already exist for educating the young people of our own locality, and ascertain to what extent such

opportunities are grasped by them. It frequently happens that young people, especially girls, drift into a groove and sink into a dull monotonous life, for just the need of a friendly word of help and encouragement, that would have stimulated them to renewed intellectual vigour had it been given at the right moment.

That the state of secondary education in Wales is bad, we all know, and that the improved state of things will soon be made evident, we all hope – but unless apathy and indifference are conquered both in parents and girls, a great many opportunities will be missed whereby life may be made brighter, and more full of beauty and usefulness by the revelation of the wider horizon which a more extended education can secure.

Occupations for Women

4. Another way in which we can assist is by finding out, and helping others to see, the particular need of the time in the matter of employment for women.

At one time every woman who wished to earn an honest, and at the same time a so-called genteel livelihood, opened a school. For this, little or no experience or training was supposed to be necessary. The schools were often but too palpably inefficient, no light was thrown on them from without by means of anything approaching inspection by unbiased persons, and they went on their humdrum way, subjecting children to the dull, unintelligent, monotonous round of learning by rote, and parrot-like repetition, which was all that many of them knew of teaching. The day of such schools is now happily passing away. More rational methods of teaching are being introduced – more rational, because based upon fuller knowledge of children and child-nature.

No girl now has any excuse for entering the profession of a teacher without first qualifying herself for her work, not only by a full and extensive education, but also by passing through a 'course of training in the science and art of teaching itself'.

No doctor is allowed to practise, until he has qualified himself for his profession, by a course of hospital practice, or something equivalent, in addition to any University or other education he may have had. If a doctor is not allowed to experiment upon the bodies of people without training, still less should teachers be allowed to experiment upon the plastic minds of children without adequate previous training.

When, therefore, we are called upon for advice as to the best way in which a girl can be brought up so as to earn her own living, let us see that our advice is wise.

If she wishes to be a teacher, advise her to make every effort to secure special training as well as thorough education. Let us also be fully alive to the value of technical subjects as offering opportunities of useful work in teaching, such as cookery, needlework, and laundry work, which are now being specially emphasized in modern schemes of education. Gymnastics, or organized physical training, and the kindergarten method of teaching young children are departments in which there is an increasing demand for teachers. To be successful nowadays in teaching, as in other things, specialisation must be aimed at.

Avenues of useful work, other than teaching, are continually being revealed: Post Office clerkships, librarian work, gardening, nursing, designing, decorating and furnishing, and many others. Whatever special aptitude a girl may have, should be considered in advising her as to her future, but every girl of fair average ability should be induced to qualify herself thoroughly for at least one branch of useful work, that she may, if the need should arise, be able to support herself and stand alone.

Women's Duties as Governors
5. Again, should we be elected to serve on a Board of Managers, or the Governing Body of a school, let us hail the opportunity eagerly, recognising at the same time the fact that it involves a considerable measure of self-sacrifice.

You must have noticed how often it happens that in a committee of any size, the real work is done by a very few, the others being content to be merely present to record their votes, and to agree or disagree with propositions which have been thought out by the active members. This is not the sort of ideal for us: we must be workers in the hive, not drones.

If we set ourselves to work to fully acquaint ourselves with the problems before us, to devote time, thought, and energy to them, we shall be able to exert an influence, and our opinions will be of some value; while if we are merely indolent and apathetic our membership will be but an empty name.

Qualities Necessary for Governors

In order to fulfil these duties efficiently and effectively we need preparation; time and thought must be liberally expended; we must aim at fitting ourselves to be wise rulers, in order that we may take a useful and honourable part in the education of our country. We must acquire business capacity, cultivate tact, and the power of working with others, even when we do not wholly agree with them in matters of detail. We must learn to distinguish the *essential* and *lasting,* from the unimportant and transitory. We must learn to see when is the time for laying down merely general principles in the working out of a particular scheme, or in the management of any school, and when the time has *come* for the assertion of an individual opinion in reference to some particular detail. We sometimes fail in this, and diminish our usefulness by worrying ourselves and those working with us over details when our attention should be devoted to broad principles. A little exercise of imagination and tact, with a spirit of unselfish forbearance, will remove this danger.

Necessity for Studying the Schemes

6. One very obvious and straightforward task which we should each one undertake, whether a member of a Governing Body

or not, is to study the Intermediate Education Act and the County schemes as they are published, to master the details so as to understand how the provisions will affect each particular district. This task I urge most earnestly upon all Welsh women of intelligence. Copies may be obtained at small cost on application to D. Fearon, Esq., Charity Commission, Whitehall, or through local booksellers.

It frequently happens that a casual reading of a document of this kind may lead one to suppose that certain things are intended, which upon a more careful study of the several clauses are found to be quite otherwise. A most important example of this has just occurred in the interpretation given to the County scheme of Caernarfon by the Charity Commissioners. The matter is the more important as in the absence of anything to the contrary, the interpretation given of the scheme for Caernarvonshire will hold good for all the other County schemes of Wales.

Subordinate Position of Mistresses of Dual Schools

In most of the County schemes formulated under the Welsh Intermediate Education Act, provision is made for the establishment of Dual schools. Such schools are defined as schools in which there are two departments – one for boys and one for girls, with separate entrances, class rooms, cloak rooms and play grounds for each department, but in which boys and girls may be taught together in some or all of the classes.

One such school has already been opened in Caernarfon. Bottwnog has added a girls' side to the existing school for boys.

Now in the Caernarvonshire scheme, as in those for several other counties, are certain clauses bearing upon the appointment of teachers.

1. In the introductory clauses there is 'headmaster includes headmistress, and master includes mistress.'

2. The headmaster shall be appointed by the County Governing Body.

3. All assistant masters shall be appointed by the headmaster, subject to the approval of the Local Governing Body.

When the appointment of headmaster to the Caernarfon school had been made, the question arose as to the appointment of the headmistress. Some members of the County Governing Body naturally supposed that they had the right of appointment, seeing that 'headmaster includes headmistress'. But the question appears to have been disputed and was therefore submitted to the Charity Commissioners for settlement.

To my intense surprise and disappointment, and I may add to the great surprise of some of our leading educationalists, the Charity Commissioners gave their decision in favour of the appointment being made by the *headmaster*.

That is, they said, the scheme only contemplated *one head*, which might be headmaster or headmistress. In the present state of public opinion it is not to be expected that a woman will, in this generation at any rate, be appointed head of a boys' school. So consider what this decision means, and consider it especially as applying to the first *dual* school ever established under precisely present conditions, and therefore it is the establishment of a precedent for all the other dual schools of the Principality.

A Dual School has no Headmistress

It means that the headmistress of the girls' department of a dual school is an *assistant-mistress* simply. She takes her authority from, and is in all points subservient to, the headmaster. Moreover, by refusing to her the status of *headmistress,* all the capitation fees of the girls go to the headmaster, the headmistress having thus no more direct interest in the success of the school than any of the other assistants. Let it be clearly understood, I do not complain of insufficient payment to the headmistress, but surely it would be more in keeping with justice and expediency that the headmistress' salary should be made up of a fixed sum and capitation fees, than that it should be a fixed sum without the personal responsibility of the numerical success of the school which attaches to the right to capitation fees. If the principle of capitation grants is believed to be a stimulus to the headmaster, should it not also be so to the headmistress?

In the County schemes of Flint, Denbigh, Merioneth and Cardigan the right of appointing assistants and the apportioning of their salaries is given to the Local Governing Bodies. Let me urge every woman in those counties at least, to induce the various Local Governing Bodies to exercise their power with full recognition of the claims of headmistresses, so as to give to them all the authority possible as well as a share in the capitation fees.

In every other County scheme under the Act the right of appointments and apportioning of salaries is in the hands of the headmaster.

What is a Dual School?

The fact is, the Charity Commissioners have interpreted the term *dual* school as having the same signification as *mixed* school, so far as its teachers are concerned. I maintain that an ideal *dual* school should be something more than a mixed school, in that it should have its two departments under heads appointed by the same body, of equal authority in their several departments, not necessarily on equality as regards amount of salary, but equal as regards the manner in which that salary is made up, and equal also in so far that the responsibility for the success of each department should rest upon each head-teacher. If necessary for simplicity of government, let the headmaster have a larger measure of authority than the headmistress over the whole school, but as regards matters of discipline and management in the girls' department let the headmistress be supreme. In this particular a Dual School resembles a Board

School with separate departments for girls, boys and infants, the heads of each individually responsible to the School Board which appoints them. It differs from a Board School in that the heads of the boys' and girls' departments respectively may confer together to utilise the whole staff for purposes of both departments.

It should be clearly understood that in dual schools classes composed of girls and boys may be taken together by a teacher of either sex. Thus; when, for example, a master takes the classical teaching throughout the school, for girls as well as boys – for modern languages, a mistress would probably be found to do the work most satisfactorily for boys as well as girls. All this is matter for arrangement in individual schools and by individual Governing Bodies. The important matter before us is to see that no fatal blunder is made at the start, such as will inevitably be the case if the headmistress is in all senses made subordinate to the headmaster, for where that is so the chances are very strongly against the best qualified women being appointed, particularly as the most experienced and best qualified women will not care to seek appointments under such conditions, and the success of girls' education in such schools will thus be hampered from the beginning. I have dwelt with some detail on this subject, because I feel it to be a matter of vital importance that now, before any more dual schools are established, the right principle should be laid down as a precedent for future guidance.

With a strong conviction of the importance of action in this matter, I have drawn up a series of resolutions embodying the points I have referred to. These resolutions were passed unanimously at the Annual Meeting of the Welsh Union of Women's Liberal Associations held at Rhyl in March, 1894.

It would be of great value if resolutions of similar import, differently worded, were passed at the various Women's Liberal Associations throughout the country, and sent in due course to the Charity Commissioners, and to Welsh Members of Parliament.

A strong representation of its views on the subject coming from the Liberal women of the Principality cannot but have weight with the authorities in whose hands the settlement of this matter finally rests.

I have endeavoured to show you a few of the ways in which, as I think, the women of Wales have before them opportunities of usefulness never before so fully enjoyed. The way in which we in this generation acquit ourselves of our responsibilities will affect in large measure the future history of our country:-

> Then while the soul its way with sound can cleave
> And while the arm is strong to strike and heave,
> Let soul and arm give shape that will abide
> And rule above our graves.
> Come, let us fashion acts that are to be
> When we shall lie in darkness silently.

Association for Promoting the Education of Girls in Wales

Resolutions passed at the Third Annual Meeting of the Welsh Union of Women's Liberal Associations, at Rhyl, March 29th 1894.

'That this Meeting is of the opinion that in all Dual Schools established under the Welsh Intermediate Education Act:-

1. The title and status of Headmistress should be given to the principal female Teacher in the Girls' Department.

2. The Headmistress should be appointed by the authority which appoints the Headmaster.

3. The Headmistress should have a pecuniary interest in the success of the school by receiving the capitation fees in respect

of the girls, while the Headmaster should receive similar fees in respect of the boys only.

4. The Headmistress, like the Headmaster, should be a member of, and be entitled to be present at all meetings of the Local Governing Body.

5. In all cases where the Headmaster has the appointment of Assistant-masters, the Headmistress should have a similar right with regard to Assistant-mistresses.

8. Buddug
(Catherine Jane Pritchard)

Paham yn arbenig [sic] y dylai merched bleidio dirwest
(Why in particular women should plead temperance)

Y Frythones, ii, Rhagfyr 1880, 369-71.

Nid anghyffredin yn y dyddiau hyn ydyw clywed y cwestiwn yma yn cael ei ofyn a'i ddadleu – paham y dylai merched lwyr ymwrthod â diodydd meddwol? Pa angenrheidrwydd y sydd ar fod i ferched ymuno â chymdeithasau dirwestol? Aml un a ystyrir yn dda ar lawer o gyfrifon, pan welant ferched a gwragedd yn gwneuthur proffes gyhoeddus o'r egwyddor, ac yn ei chefnogi, a glywir yn dywedyd yng ngeiriau arch-ormeswr yr Israeliaid gynt, 'Gwelwch mai ar ddrwg y mae eich bryd; nid felly, ewch yn awr y gwŷr, a gwasanaethwch yr Arglwydd.' Ond dysg yr Arglwydd ni trwy ei air heddyw, mai 'â'n llanciau ac â'n henafgwyr yr awn ni, â'n meibion hefyd ac â'n merched, â'n defaid ac â'n gwartheg yr awn ni,'[1] oblegid y mae y locust meddwol hwn yn toi o'r bron yr holl dir, yn ysu llysiau cysuron teuluaidd, yn gwywo gwyrddlesni cymdeithas, yn mallu gogoniant gwlad a chenedl, yn bwyta bara y plant, yn newynu mamau tyner, ac yn ymyrraeth â chysegr Duw. Y mae yn blino pob ardal, a rhaid yw i ninnau wasanaethu yr Arglwydd trwy ymarfogi â phob moddion cyfreithlawn yn ôl gair y Goruchaf, i ymlid y gelyn difäol hwn o'n gwlad – ein llanciau a'n henafwyr, ein meibion a'n merched, ein defaid

---

[1] Ecsodus, x, 9-11: Pharo yw'r arch-ormeswr.

a'n gwartheg, ie, ein holl dda. Nis gwyddom â pha beth y gwasanaethwn yr Arglwydd hyd oni ddelom yno, sef at ein dyletswydd. Dyletswydd pob un y sydd yn proffesu dylyn [sic] yr Arglwydd Iesu Grist ydyw caru cyfiawnder, ac nid oes neb, ni dybiwn, nad addef yn rhwydd, fod y gorthrwm a nodwyd ac a achosir gan y fasnach feddwol yn anghyfiawnder moesol, a dweud y lleiaf am dano. Pa hyd y gwrthodir neu yr esgeulusir gwneuthur barn? Pa hyd y noddir ac y cefnogir y cyfryw draha gan lywodraeth Gristionogol? Pa hyd y cyfreithlonir y fath fasnach gan deyrnas, rheol yr hon yw y Beibl? Yn y cyfamser, tra byddo byd ac eglwys megis yn hepian, ac yn cydblethu dwylaw i gysgu, a thra nad oes odid dŷ heb un marw ynddo o haint meddwdod, ai tybed mai yn llaw gwraig y dyry yr Arglwydd y gorthrymydd hwn? Gan fod pethau mawrion a grymus wedi eu cwblhau trwy offerynoliaeth merched a gwragedd, y mae hynny yn gosod arbenigrwydd ar y paham y dylai merched yn neilltuol bleidio dirwest; a chan fod meddwdod yn elyn mor aruthrol, ei lywodraeth mor eang, a'i afael mor gref, gelwir ar bob dyngarwr i ymfyddino yn ei erbyn a rhoddi ei holl egnïon ar lawn waith i atal ei rwysg. Dywedyd a ddylai pob benyw fel y dywedodd Deborah wrth Barac, "Gan fyned yr af gyda thi;"[2] gan geisio ei gorau i ymestyn at y fraint o gael gosod hoel yn arlais y gelyn.

Why women in particular women should plead temperance

It's not unusual these days to hear this question being asked and debated: why should women totally abstain from alcohol? Why is it necessary for women to join teetotal societies? Many a one who's considered worthy on many counts, when

---

[2] Barnwyr, iv, 9.

they hear women and girls making a public profession of the principle, and supporting it, are to be heard saying in the words of the old arch-oppressor of the Israelites, 'Look to it; for evil is before you. Not so: go now ye that are men, and serve the Lord'. But the Lord teaches us through his word today that 'we will go with our young and with our old, with our sons and with our daughters, with our flocks and with our herds,'[1] because this locust of drunkenness is covering nearly all the land, destroying the comforting hearths of the family, decaying the green freshness of society, smashing the glory of country and nation, eating the children's bread, starving vulnerable mothers, and interfering with God's sacrament. It troubles every area, and we must serve the Lord by arming ourselves with every legal means according the word of the Most High, to rout this deadly enemy from our land – with our young and our old, our sons and our daughters, our sheep and our goats, yea, all our cattle. We do not know what will serve the Lord until we get there, that is, to our duty. It is the duty of every one who professes to follow the Lord Jesus Christ to love righteousness, and there is no-one, we believe, who would not admit freely that the oppression which is nourished and caused by the market in alcohol is a moral injustice, to say the least. For how long will we refuse or neglect to exert judgment? For how long will such a desecration be nurtured and supported by a Christian government? For how long will such a trade be legalized by a kingdom whose rule is the Bible? In the meantime, while the world and the church are as if slumbering, and folding their hands to sleep, and while there is barely one house without one dead in it of the plague of drunkenness, may it not be that the Lord will deliver this oppressor into the hands of woman? Because great and powerful things have been completed through the instrumentation of girls and women, they in particular should pledge temperance; and

---

[1] Exodus, x, 9-11. Pharaoh is the arch-oppressor.

because drunkenness is so terrible an enemy, its government so wide-spread, and its grip so strong, every philanthropist is called upon to do battle against it and put all his energies fully to work to stop its pomp. All women should say as Deborah said to Barak, 'I will surely go with thee,'[2] doing her best to arrive at the privilege of being allowed to smite the nail into the enemy's temple.

---

[2] Judges, iv, 9.

Na Chaffed Hudoles Fyw (Let Not an Enchantress Live)

Y Gymraes, Mehefin 1900, 78-9.

Hudoles fwyaf peryglus ein hoes ni ydyw y ddiod feddwol. Ymdynghedwn ninnau ferched dirwestol i anelu ein saethau ati. Dichon y dywed ambell un nad gweddus i ferched saethu, ond y mae ein dwfn argyhoeddiad yn yr ymgyrch bresennol yn erbyn yr 'Hudoles' yn ein gwneud yn ystyriol o'n rhwymedigaeth i osod ein llaw ar y bwa, a saethu. Nid unwaith, na dwywaith, na theirgwaith. 'Dylesit daro bump neu chwech o weithiau,' ebe gwr Duw wrth Joas brenin Israel, 'yna y tarewsit Syria nes ei difa.'[1] Rhaid taro nes difa. Nid lladd y bragwyr na'r distyllwr, na'r tafarnwr, na'r meddwyn, ond lladd y ddiod […]

Eiddo yr Arglwydd y rhyfel hwn, a gelyn pennaf ei deyrnas Ef ydyw yr 'Hudoles'. Ni ellir ei difetha ar unwaith, ond bob yn ychydig ac ychydig. Nid maes y gwaed ydyw maes ein rhyfel. Ein harfau ni nid ydynt gnawdol […] Gallwn ninnau wneud llawer tuag at ladd yr 'Hudoles' trwy ei hanwybyddu. Nac ymgyfathrachwn â hi; na chredwn ynddi dan unrhyw amgylchiad. Nid ydyw yn feddyginiaeth ddiogel hyd yn nod dan gyfarwyddyd meddyg. Mae y swyn sydd ynddi yn rhy gydnaws â natur lygredig, wan, fel mai ei hanwybyddu ydyw yr unig sicrwydd am ddiogelwch. Mae ei gwenwyn mor angheuol fel y mae y rhif o dri ugain mil a leddir ganddi yn flynyddol lawer yn rhy isel erbyn hyn […]

Mae y cynydd yn amlwg yng Nghymru hefyd. Mae rhai o ferched Ysgolion Sabothol Cymru dan draed yr Hudoles. O, deffrown, gydag eiddigedd sanctaidd i anfon yr Hudoles o'n gwlad. Wyryfon, byddwch yn esiamplau i'r llanciau. Wragedd ieuanc, na lithier [sic] chwi gan yr Hudoles ar ddechrau eich gyrfa. Famau oedrannus, deliwch y faner ddirwestol i fyny. 'Yn enw ein Duw y banerwn'.[2]

---

[1] 2 Brenhinoedd, xiii, 19.

[2] Salmau, xx, 5.

Let not an enchantress live

The most dangerous enchantress of our age is alcohol. Let us temperance women pledge ourselves to aim our arrows at her. No doubt some will say it is not seemly for women to shoot, but our deep convictions in the present struggle against the 'Enchantress' makes us aware of the necessity to lay our hands on the bow, and shoot. Not once, or twice, or three times. 'Thou shouldst have smitten five or six times', said the man of God to Joash, king of Israel, 'then hadst thou smitten Syria till thou hadst consumed it.'[1] We must smite to kill. Not to kill the brewer or the distiller, or the tavern-keeper, or the drunkard, but to kill the drink [...]

This war is the Lord's, and the greatest enemy of His kingdom is the 'Enchantress'. She cannot be defeated at once, but little by little. The field of blood is not our battle-field. Our arms are not material [...] We can do much towards killing the Enchantress by ignoring her. Let us have no connection with her; let us not believe in her under any circumstances. She is not a safe medicine, not even under doctor's orders. The charm which is hers is too compatible with corrupt, weak nature, so that to ignore her is the only certainty of safety. Her poison is so deadly that the number of sixty thousand a year said to be killed by her is too low by now [...]

The increase is apparent in Wales too. Some of the girls of the Welsh Sunday Schools are under the feet of the Enchantress. O, let us awake, with sacred jealousy to drive the Enchantress from our land. Maidens, be an example to the lads. Young wives, do not be seduced by the Enchantress at the beginning of your careers. Aged mothers, hold up on high the banner of temperance. 'In the name of our God we will set up our banners.'[2]

---

[1] 2 Kings, xiii, 19. The prophet Elisha is the 'man of God'.

[2] Psalms, xx, 5.

9. Ellen Hughes

Merch – ei Hawliau a'i Hiawnderau (Woman – Her Claims and Her Rights)

Cyfaill yr Aelwyd a'r Frythones, i (1892), 251-4.

Tra yr oeddem yn myfyrio ar y testun uchod, enynnodd tân, ond barnasom yn ddoethach i ymatal oddi wrth yr ysgrifbin nes i'r ystorm o'n mewn dawelu ychydig, gan gredu fod mwy o ddylanwad a nerth mewn pwyll nag mewn angerddoldeb. Can belled ag y mae ein profiad personol a'n sylwadaeth yn myned, y mae enaid ar dân yn fynych yn anfantais i un i ddadleu dros ei bwnc [...]

Nid ydyw yr hyn a ddywedasom yn gwneud i ffwrdd â dyletswydd dyn neu ddynes i ddadleu dros ei hawliau, ac i'w mynnu os bydd modd, ond yn unig yn profi y gall un fforddio cymeryd pwyll ac aros cyfle wrth fyned o gwmpas y gwaith. Ni fu erioed les o frysio gormod. Y mae yn ddyletswydd arnom fynnu ein hawliau rhag i ni fod yn 'gyfrannog o bechodau rhai eraill.' Y mae y rhai a ataliant ein hawliau oddi wrthym yn euog o ladrad; ac ni ddylem ar un cyfrif gefnogi eu lladrad trwy ei oddef. Heblaw hynny, oni roddir i ni ein hawliau, nis gallwn wneud y gorau o'n bywydau ein hunain, ac yr ydym trwy esgeuluso gwneud a allom i fynnu ein hiawnderau yn amddifadu ein hunain o gyfleusterau i wella ein hunain a gwasanaethu cymdeithas; a thrwy fod yn ddiofal iawn am ein hawliau, gallwn analluogi ein hunain i gyflawni y dyletswyddau mwyaf amlwg. Nid ydym yn meddwl fod yn bosibl i ni fod yn rhy ofalus am ein hawliau, ond i ni fod yn gyfartal ofalus am hawliau rhai eraill, ac yn bwyllog wrth symud ym mlaen. Y mae digon o le i bawb yn yr anfeidroldeb yr ydym ynddo; ac y mae yn resynol, yn dra gresynol, fod neb yn gwrthod cydnabod hyn, ond yn eiddigeddu dros ei eiddo ei hun, neu yn hytrach yn ceisio gwneud yn eiddo iddo ei hun yr hyn sydd o ran ei hanfod yn gyffredinol; ac er na lwydda byth yn ei ymgais, eto gall fod yn achos llawer o chwerwder i'w gyd-ddynion.

Gyda golwg ar hawliau Merch, buasem yn disgwyl na cheid yn 'yr oes oleu hon' yr un dyn o synnwyr cyffredin yn meddwl am eu hamau. Ac y mae y syniad fod hynafgwr o ddoethineb Mr Gladstone yn amau cymhwyster y cyffredin o ferched i gael pleidlais mewn etholiad, yn ymddangos i ni yn rhywbeth i saith rhyfeddu ato! Yn wir, y mae yn dwyn ar gof i ni y dicter a deimlem flynyddau lawer yn ôl wrth wrando ar ddoethwyr o'r rhyw arwaf yn siarad a'u [sic] gilydd am y 'Cyfarfod Brodyr,' ac yn beio un brawd am hysbysu ei wraig o'r ymdrafodaethau pwysig a gerid ym mlaen yno! Paham, yn enw y nefoedd, gofynnai ein calon ieuanc glwyfedig, y rhoddwyd i ferch syched diderfyn am wybodaeth, ac am y fath fwyaf aruchel a gogoneddus o wybodaeth, os yw hi yn y diwedd yn anghymwys i gael gwybod mân, fân gyfrinachau y 'Cyfarfod Brodyr'? Pe y dywedasid nad ydyw y rhai hyn fel rheol ond prin yn ddigon pwysig i fod yn werth i ddyn eu hailadrodd wrth y rhan fenywaidd o'i deulu, buasai rhyw gymaint o synnwyr yn hynny. Nid ydyw y gwŷr hynny a soniant am anghymwysder merch i gyflawni unrhyw orchwyl neu lenwi unrhyw swydd, pa mor bwysig bynnag – nid ydyw y cyfryw erioed wedi astudio y natur fenywaidd. Yr ydym wedi dechrau synnu er yn blant mor lleied o athroniaeth a ymddangosai fod yn y meddwl gwrywaidd, a deuai y diffyg hwn fwyaf i'r golwg pan ddeuai rhyw gwestiwn o berthynas i ferch i mewn ar unrhyw adeg. Y mae un Americaniad doeth wedi sylwi fod yn ymennydd y Sais fath o gaead, yn agor ac yn cau wrth ei ewyllys, ac na fedd y Saeson callaf y gallu i feddwl yn ddim pellach na'r Esgob ar faterion eglwysig, ac na'r Trysorlys ar faterion gwladol! Fel yna y mae lliaws o'r Cymry – call yn eu ffordd – yn colli y gallu i ymresymu can [sic]gynted ag y cyflwynir i'w sylw y cwestiwn o safle a hawliau Merch. Y maent wedi cymeryd yn ganiataol, rywfodd, o'u mebyd, fod merched yn israddol iddynt hwy, ac y mae y syniad hwn yn boddio yr hen ddyn o'u mewn yn ormod iddynt ei gollwng o'u gafael ar frys. Ac eto, os ydynt yn boddio eu hunanoldeb, y maent yn colledu eu hunain yn ddiderfyn. Y mae Tennyson wedi cyfansoddi chwareugan, gyda'r teitl, 'Y Dywysoges', gyda'r amcan o wneud ychydig o wawd o ferched uchelgeisiol. Yn y coleg a grea ei ddychymyg ef y mae llu o 'Enethod mwyn, graddedig, gyda melyn-wallt'. A ydym i'n beio yn fawr am deimlo megis rhyw oruchafiaeth ar y bardd, wrth feddwl iddo gael byw i weled ei freuddwyd wedi ei sylweddoli? Credwn y bydd y cenethod graddedig' wedi dyfod mor gyffredin yn fuan, fel na fydd i'r syniad am danynt gynhyrfu y wên ar wyneb y mwyaf gwamal. Ond y mae Tennyson yn dechrau dweud ei farn yn ddifrifol cyn y diwedd, ac meddai:-

> Woman's cause is man's,
> They rise or sink together.

Nid ydym yn amau hyn am funud, ond credwn y byddai mor gywir pe y newidid ef ychydig, a dweud :-

> Man's cause is woman's,
> They rise or sink together.

Wrth gadw Merch i lawr, y mae dyn mewn effaith yn cadw ei hun i lawr […]

Nid oes dim sydd yn bradychu amddifadrwydd o bob athroniaeth yn fwy na gwaith dynion yn ymresymu israddoldeb y rhyw fenywaidd oddi wrth y ffaith mai lled weiniaid yr ymddengys galluoedd meddyliol lliaws o ferched *yn eu cyflwr presennol*, heb fod neb erioed wedi 'ymofyn am eu henaid' rhyw lawer; wedi eu hamgylchynu gan foch a gwartheg, cryciau a phiserau, heb nemawr funud o'r bore hyd y nos i gasglu eu meddyliau yng nghyd; a'u gorchwylion beunyddiol yn gofyn llwyr ymgyflwyniad o'u holl ymadferthoedd. Onid ydyw yn afresymol i'r eithaf i gasglu fod y merched, druain, yn ddwl o angenrheidrwydd? ac mai felly y buasent o dan unrhyw amgylchiadau, tra mae yn hawdd gweled pe y cadwynid Benjamin Franklin a'i gyffelyb yn sefyllfa y merched hyn, y buasai y cwbl drosodd arnynt gyda golwg ar ddyfod yn enwogion mewn doethineb? Beth fedrai Socrates wneud, pe na chai bum' munud o amser i *feddwl*? Os ydyw y merched ar hyd yr oesau wedi ysgubo y lloriau yn lle y dynion (ac y mae ysgubo yn burion yn ei le), onid gwael yn yr olaf ydyw eu dibrisio am eu bod yn gwneud, a haeru na fedrant wneud dim arall? Yr ydym yn cywilyddio dros y ddynoliaeth am na fuasai hi wedi agoryd ei llygaid yn fwy ar 'y posibl', ac wedi dangos mwy o ffydd yn yr Anweledig gyda golwg ar alluoedd ei phlant. Dilys gennym fod y merched galluocaf fu yn ein byd yn cynrychioli ein rhyw yn llawer tecach (yn dangos yn well, mewn geiriau eraill, beth a fuasai merched pe y cawsent chware teg i ymddadblygu) na miloedd merched anwybodus ein gwlad. Gwyddom na cheir llawer o ymddadblygu yn y fuchedd hon ar y gorau, a bod yn rhaid wrth awelon rhydd byd arall cyn y bydd yr *ideal* o hawliau merched wedi ei sylweddoli; ond gellir cymeryd cam bychan ym mlaen yn barhaus, a gwneud rhyw gymaint i ddwyn y ddaear yn fwy ar ddelw y Nefoedd.

Woman – Her Claims and Her Rights

As we mused on the above topic, it lit a fire, but we deemed it wiser to refrain from writing until the storm within had quietened somewhat, believing that there is more influence and power in self-restraint than vehemence. According to our personal experience and observation, a soul on fire is often at a disadvantage when debating a point [...]

But what we have said does not do away with the duty of men and women to argue for their claims, and to insist on having them if at all possible, but only proves that one can afford to be wise and await the right opportunity while going about the work. No good ever came of rushing too much. It is our duty to insist on our claims lest we 'collude with the sins of others'. Those who keep our claims from us are guilty of theft, and we should by no means support their theft through putting up with it. Further, if we are not given our claims we cannot make the best of our own lives; through neglecting to do what we can to insist upon our claims we deny ourselves the opportunity of improving ourselves and serving our society, and through being very careless of our claims we leave ourselves incapable of fulfilling the most obvious duties. We do not think it possible for us to be too careful of our claims, as long as we are equally careful of the claims of others, and move on steadily. There is room enough for everybody in the immensity in which we are placed, and it is regrettable, very regrettable, that anybody should refuse to recognise this, but should be jealous of what they own, or rather should try to make their own that which is essentially common to all; though they will never succeed yet they can be the cause of much bitterness to their fellows.

With regard to Woman's claims, we would have expected that in this 'enlightened age' no man of common sense could think of doubting them. And the idea that an elder of the wisdom of Mr Gladstone should doubt the capacity of the majority of women to vote in an election strikes us as wondrously astonishing![1] Indeed, it reminds us of the anger we felt many years ago on hearing some wiseacres of the rougher sex talking to one another of the 'Brothers' Meeting' and blaming one brother for telling his wife of the important debates which went on there! Why, in the name of heaven, asked our youthful wounded heart, was woman given a boundless thirst for knowledge, and for the highest and most glorious type of knowledge, if in the end she is unfit to know the petty, petty secrets of the 'Brothers' Meeting'? If it had been said that these were not usually of sufficient importance to be worth a man repeating them to the female part of his family, there would be some kind of sense in that. Those men who speak of women's unfitness to complete some task or fill some post, however important – have never studied female nature. We started wondering in childhood at how little philosophy there appeared to be in the male mind, and this lack became most apparent when some question to do with women came up at any time. One wise American has noted that in the mind of the Englishman there seems to be a kind of shutter, opening and closing at will, and that the cleverest Englishman does not have the ability to think further than the Bishop on religious matters, or further than the Treasury on secular ones! That is how it is with the majority of Welshmen – wise in their way – but losing the capacity to reason as soon as the question of the position and claims of Woman is brought to their attention. They have taken it for granted, somehow, from childhood that women are inferior to them, and that idea pleases the old devil inside them too much for them to drop it from their clutches quickly. And yet, if they thus satisfy their selfishness, they deprive themselves endlessly. Tennyson has composed a verse-play, entitled 'The Princess', aimed at mocking ambitious women. In the college

---

[1] The reference is to the Liberal leader William Gladstone's opposition to a women's suffrage bill of 1892.

his imagination creates, there are hordes of 'Sweet yellow-haired girl graduates'. Are we much to be blamed for feeling a sense of victory over the poet, in that he has lived to see his dream realised? We believe that 'girl graduates' will soon have become so commonplace that the idea of them will not raise a smile on the silliest face. But Tennyson begins to state his opinion seriously before the close and says:-

> Woman's cause is man's,
> They rise or sink together.

We do not doubt this for a moment, but think it would be equally true were it changed a little, and read:-

> Man's cause is woman's,
> They rise or sink together.

By subordinating woman, man in effect subordinates himself [...]

Nothing betrays an entire privation of all philosophy more than the work of men in arguing for the inferiority of women from the fact that the mental powers of women in their present condition appear relatively weak, when no-one has ever bothered much after their souls; surrounded by pigs and cattle, crocks and pots, with barely a minute from dawn to dusk to collect their thoughts, with their daily tasks demanding the full involvement of all their energies. Is it not excessively unreasonable to deduce that these women, poor things, are of necessity stupid, and would be so under any circumstances, while it is easy to see that if Benjamin Franklin and his like were in these women's positions, it would all be over for them with regard to becoming famous for wisdom? What could Socrates have done if he had not had five minutes in which to *think*? If women throughout the ages have swept the floors instead of men (though sweeping is fine in its place), is it not shoddy of men to devalue them because they have done so, and insist that they can do nothing else? We feel ashamed for humanity that it has not opened its eyes further to 'the possible', and shown more faith in the Unseeable with regard to the capacities of its children. We are convinced that the ablest women who have ever existed represent their sex far more fairly (show more truly, in other words, what women could be if they had fair play to develop themselves) than the myriad uneducated women of our country. We know that at best this world does not allow for much development, and that the free breezes of another world must blow about us before the ideal of women's claims is realised, but we can take small steps on perpetually, and make some progress in bringing the earth closer to the image of Heaven.

Angylion yr Aelwyd (Angels in the House)

1899; *Murmur y Gragen* (Dolgellau: Swyddfa'r 'Goleuad', 1907), 37-40.

Defnyddiwyd yr ymadrodd uchod yn Nhŷ y Cyffredin yr wythnos o'r blaen pan yn ymdrin â'r cwestiwn o ethol swyddogion ar fwrdd Llywodraeth Leol Llundain. Cafodd y Seneddwyr parchus eu hunain mewn cryn benbleth wrth geisio penderfynu pa faint o ryddid i'w ganiatáu i ferched, heb eu cau allan yn llwyr o swyddau [sic] cyhoeddus ag yr oeddynt eisoes wedi eu llenwi er bodlonrwydd cyffredinol. Rhywbeth lled anystwyth ydyw egwyddor, ac wedi ni ddechrau gweithredu yn ei hôl, gall ein harwain i leoedd newyddion a dieithr na feddyliasom erioed am gael ein hunain o fewn 'pellter mesurol' iddynt. Pwy na chydymdeimlai â'r gwŷr da yn Nhŷ y Cyffredin yn eu petruster rhag ofn eu bod yn agor y drws i chwyldroad yn llywodraethiad eu gwlad? Wedi unwaith gydnabod cymhwyster merched i eistedd ar Fyrddau Ysgolion, i fod yn Gynghorwyr a Henaduriaethwyr ar Fwrdd Llywodraethol y Brifddinas, yn sicr y mae yn gofyn cryn fedrusrwydd i brofi eu hanghymhwyster i fod yn Faerod neu yn Aelodau Seneddol! [...]

Feallai mai Mr Labouchère oedd y mwyaf cyson ag ef ei hun o holl aelodau y Tŷ.[1] Aroglai chwyldroad yn yr holl ymdrafodaeth, a hiraethai am fyned yn ôl i'r hen ffordd oedd bob amser mor ddiogel ac esmwyth. Ni fynnai gael ei ystyried yn ôl i neb mewn edmygedd at ferched ond edmygai hwynt yn eu lle priodol – fel 'angylion yr aelwyd' [...]

Naturiol ydyw meddwl y gallai 'angylion yr aelwyd' brofi yn angylion y tu allan i'r aelwyd. Ac yn ôl a glywn, nid ydyw yr aelwyd, mewn un modd, yr unig le ag y mae gofyn am ei angeleiddio. Ond dywed Mr Labouchère nad ydyw yr angylion

---

[1] Henry Du Pré Labouchère (1831-1912), AS Rhydfrydol dros Northampton o 1880-1906, a gwrthwynebydd yr etholfreintwragedd.

hyn yn awyddus am helaethu cylch eu gweithgarwch, 'ag eithrio nifer fechan o honynt, ag ydynt, oblegid aflwyddo fel merched yn ceisio gwneud eu hunain yn ddynion' […] Tybed ynte fod byd merch mor gyfyng fel y mae yn rhaid iddi ystyried ei hun yn aflwyddiant am nad oes galw am ei gwasanaeth yng nghylch yr aelwyd? Os felly, y mae yn hen bryd i'r Seneddwyr i agor y drws. Y mae rhywbeth allan o le, os y rhaid i unrhyw fod dynol fodloni ar fod yn aflwyddiannus. I lwyddo y crëwyd ni oll, nid i aflwyddo. Dyna yr hyn y dylem fod yn ei gylch bob dydd o'n bywyd – rhwystro ein hunain ac eraill rhag myned yn fethiant. Bid sicr, os oes rhyw ferch mewn gwirionedd wedi aflwyddo fel merch, byddai yn gystal iddi blethu dwylaw a rhoddi y byd i fyny, gan ei fod allan o'r cwestiwn iddi lwyddo fel dim arall. Os ydyw pysgodyn wedi methu â dysgu nofio, oferedd iddo godi ei olwg yng nghyfeiriad ehedeg. Ac y mae pobl yn siarad fel pe na byddai merch y tu allan i'r cylch teuluaidd ond fel pysgodyn yn yr awyr. Ond dywed synnwyr cyffredin yn gystal â phrofiad fod hyn yn gamgymeriad pwysig. Y mae yn amhosibl i ferch lwyddo ond fel merch, ond nid ydyw hynny yn dweud nas gall lwyddo mewn llawer cylch a llawer gwaith ag y mae y byd wedi arfer eu gwahardd iddi. Hefyd, tybier fod merch wedi cychwyn ym myd y rubanau, y ffasiynau, y *parties*, a'r *bouquets*, ac wedi aflwyddo yno, onid clod iddi ydyw ei bod wedi derbyn ei haflwyddiant gyda gwroldeb, ac yn troi ei hynni i gyfeiriad rhagorach? Gellir ystyried methu mewn un cyfeiriad yn alwad arnom i geisio mewn cyfeiriad arall. Ac y mae yn amhosibl i unrhyw ddynes aflwyddo fel dynes tra yn dilyn yn onest lwybr dyletswydd, hyd yn nod [sic] pe yr arweiniai hi i binacl neu i gwter na bu yr un ddynes erioed o'r blaen.

Wedi y cwbl, os ydyw dynes i raddau yn angel, ni fyn aflwyddo […] Ac yr ydym yn ddiolchgar am fod cynifer o ferched na fynnant gydnabod eu hunain yn orchfygedig. Sicr gennym na wnaethai yr angylion ychwaith mo hynny, canys y maent yn rhy hoff o sibrwd gobaith wrthym ni fodau israddol,

ac o ddweud wrthym gydag awdurdod yn ein munudau o
anobaith: 'Gelli, ti elli!'

Nid ydym yn sicr nad oes amryw o'r merched ydynt
'wedi aflwyddo fel merched ac yn ceisio gwneud eu hunain
yn ddynion' yn bur gynefin â chymdeithas angylion wedi'r
cwbl. Y mae yr 'ysbrydion gwasanaethgar' yn ymweled
â llawer man heblaw â'r aelwyd, a gadawant bob amser eu
dylanwad ar eu holau. Lle y byddo eu hymweliadau fynychaf,
ceir eangder golygiad, dyfnder cydymdeimlad, cryfder ffydd,
ac ysbrydolrwydd syniad […] Hoffant angylion bychain yr
aelwyd, a chynorthwyant hwy lawer pryd gyda'r pleser mwyaf
diffuant, ond nid oes neb yn apelio at eu cydymdeimlad fel y
chwiorydd hynny a deithiant lwybrau anhygyrch a geirwon,
trwy froydd diffrwyth o gefnogaeth […] Pan fo cnawd a chalon
yn pallu, ceir un o'r bodau gwynion, chwim, ar unwaith ar
ei aden, ac nid ydyw yn hir heb ddyfod yn ddigon agos i'w
leferydd i fod yn glywadwy. Gwrandewch! Beth a ddywed?
'Na hidiwch, anwyliaid; yr wyf yn eich deall.'

Angels in the House

The above phrase was used in the House of Commons last
week when discussing the question of electing officers on
to the London Local Government Board. The Honourable
Members found themselves in some perplexity as they tried
to decide how much freedom to allow women, without cutting
them off completely from public roles they had previously
filled to general satisfaction. A principle is a rather rigid
thing, and once we have started working with it, it can lead
us to new and strange places of which we never thought to
find ourselves within 'measurable distance'. Who would not
sympathise with the good fellows of the House of Commons in
their perturbation in case they should be opening the door to a
revolution in the government of their country? Once they had

recognised the suitability of women to sit on School Boards, to be Councillors and Aldermen on the Governing Board of the Capital, certainly it demanded much ingenuity to prove their unsuitability to be Mayors or Members of Parliament! [...]

Perhaps it was Mr Labouchère[2] who was most self-consistent of all the Members of the House. He discerned revolution in the whole discussion, and yearned to return to the old ways which were always so safe and comfortable. He did not wish to be considered behind any in his admiration for women, but he admired them in their appropriate place – as 'angels in the house' [...]

It is only natural to think that 'angels in the house' would still be angels away from the house. And from what we hear, the house is by no means the only place that needs angelizing. But Mr Labouchère says that these angels are not eager to extend the circle of their activities, 'apart from a few who, because they have failed as women, try to make themselves men' [...] Surely it cannot be that a woman's world is so narrow that she must consider herself a failure because there is no call for her services in the house? If that is the case, then it is high time the Members opened the door. There is something out of place if any human being has to be resigned to be a failure. We were all created to succeed, not to fail. That is what we should be about every day of our lives – preventing ourselves and others from becoming failures. Certainly if any woman has indeed failed as a woman, she might as well fold her hands and give up the world, as it is out of the question that she should ever succeed as anything else. If a fish has failed to learn to swim, it is pointless for it to hope to fly. And people talk as if a woman outside the family circle is but a fish in the air. But common sense as well as experience says that this is a serious mistake. It is impossible for a woman

[2] Henry Du Pré Labouchère (1831-1912), Liberal MP for Northampton from 1880 to 1906, was renowned for his anti-suffragist views.

to succeed except as a woman, but that does not mean she cannot succeed in many circles and on many occasions from which the world has been accustomed to debar her. Further, if a female has begun in the world of ribbons, fashions, parties and bouquets, and has failed in it, is it not to her credit that she has accepted her failure with courage, and has turned her energies to a worthier direction? It could be thought that to fail in one direction was a summons to us to try in another. And it is impossible for any woman to fail as a woman while honestly following the path of duty, though it may lead her to a pinnacle or to a gutter where no previous woman has ever ventured.

After all, if a woman is to some degree an angel, she will not wish to fail [...] And we are thankful that there are so many women who refuse to consider themselves conquered. We're certain that angels too refuse to do so, for they are too fond of whispering hope to us subordinate creatures, and telling us with authority in our moments of hopelessness: 'You can do it, you can!'

It may be that not a few of those women who 'have failed as women and try to make themselves men' are pretty familiar with the company of angels after all. The 'attendant spirits' visit many places apart from the house, and always leave their influence behind them. Where their visitations are most frequent, we find largeness of vision, depth of sympathy, strength of faith, and inspired ideas [...] They like the little angels in the house, and help them many times with the humblest pleasures, but nobody appeals to their sympathy like those sisters who take rough and inaccessible routes, through areas barren of support [...] When flesh and heart fail, one of those swift white beings is at once on the wing, and it is not long before it is close enough for its speech to be heard. Listen! What does it say? 'Never mind, my dears; I understand you.'

Part III

Gender, Class and Party:
Liberal and Labour Movement Writings

Mr. Lloyd George: "My conviction is that you will never get really good effective measures for housing, for temperance, or for other social reforms, until you get the millions of the women of the land to co-operate in such legislation." (Albert Hall, Dec. 5th, 1908.)

Miss Wales: "I am ready, David. I have helped you. When are you going to help me?"

This cartoon by Mrs D. Meeson Coates, was first published in *The Common Cause*, the paper of the National Union of Women's Suffrage Societies, in September 1909, on the occasion of a women's suffrage meeting in Cardiff addressed by the society president, Millicent Fawcett. The original caption said simply: 'Miss Wales; Do justice to the women, David'. The paper used it again in November 1910, when Welsh Liberal women were threatening to withdraw their help from party election candidates who did not support women's suffrage. The later caption quoted Lloyd George's own words in support of women's suffrage, linking temperance legislation and women's citizenship, and Miss Wales asks 'I am ready David. I have helped you. When are you going to help me?' As Chancellor of the Exchequer, Lloyd George was a key member of the Liberal government led by the anti-suffragist Prime minister, Asquith.

INTRODUCTION
BY URSULA MASSON

The writings in this section represent new possibilities in the political and associational life of women in the late nineteenth century, when, despite their disenfranchisement, they began to enter party organisations in great numbers. For Conservative women, the mixed-sex Primrose League, and for Liberal women, the local Women's Liberal Associations (WLA) and their federal bodies the Women's Liberal Federation (WLF) and the Welsh Union of Women's Liberal Associations (the Welsh Union) were expanding in the 1880s and 1890s. From the 1890s, Labour movement women could be active in the Cooperative Women's Guild (WCG), Independent Labour Party (ILP), the Social Democratic Federation (SDF), the Fabian Society, and, from 1906, the Women's Labour League (WLL), which became affiliated to the Labour Party. The new political structures provided new opportunities and outlets for women's writings, and a burgeoning variety of forms. Minutes, reports, statements and manifestos, letters, lengthy polemic, propaganda, printed speeches and addresses were published by the women's organisations themselves, in the commercial press, and in the newspapers and periodicals of the parties.

There was a much greater volume of writing from Liberal women in the 1890s than in the next decade from Labour women. There is not the space here to explore the reasons, but it must have had something to do with the nature and size of the respective organisations: Liberal women's organisation was big, strong and independent in the mid-1890s, while Labour women's organisation in the next decade was fragile, patchy, and incorporated into the party. In the 1890s, the fervour, if short lived, of the Welsh national vision interacted with vigorous Liberal feminist organisation. The class-based analysis of the 1900s contained within it an assumption of comradely support for the equality of the sexes within the Labour movement; the liveliest writings from the Labour movement women in this period were provided when that complacency was being punctured, as in some of the writings reprinted here.

Liberal women: gender and nation.
The section begins with 'An Appeal to Welsh Women', by Nora Philipps (Mrs. Wynford Philipps). The declamatory style of the pamphlet, published by the Welsh Union in Welsh and English, is untypical of Philipps's writing. However, its clear outline of a political programme, combined with a construction of women's politics as essentially altruistic, make the 'Appeal' a good guide to Welsh women's Liberalism in this period. The rhetorical sentences and bold typography are intended to grab the attention, and perhaps to imitate a platform speech, though an extremely theatrical one. Its antecedent was Olympe de Gouges' *Declaration of the Rights of Woman and the Citizen* (1791), an attempt to insert women's rights into the French Revolutionary constitution. Comparisons are instructive. De Gouges began her postscript: 'Women awake! ...Discover your rights!' and Philipps's, 'Women awake! You have a political duty to perform' demonstrates her strong historicism, displayed in all her writings, and at the same time, the different terms of the call being made on women in late 19th century Wales. Philipps and de Gouges were at one on the right to representation of all those who paid taxes and were subject to the law, and on the necessity of women's incorporation into the State for national, social and moral progress; but where the French feminist's emphasis was on the 'natural, inalienable, and sacred rights of woman' (language applied to men only in the 1789 'Declaration of the Rights of Man and the Citizen'), Philipps's emphasis is on the duties of women in relation to the causes of Liberalism, and on behalf of other (working-

class and poor) women.

The 'rules and objects' produced by local WLAs were an attempt to embody the politics outlined by Philipps in a way which would also enable the creation of local collective identities. Again, comparisons and contrasts are suggestive; variations from the model produced by the Welsh Union indicate that it was debated by local groups, and changed to express their own sense of their political values. The pattern provided a general statement of the field of women's Liberal politics in this period, stressing the principles of female Liberalism rather than party electoral needs. Differences of emphasis between the associations indicated some social and political diversity of membership in different localities: one association might show a concern for women workers, in others the explicitness of references to women's enfranchisement varied. As well as sensitivity to local cultures and conditions, women were mindful of the broader context of prescriptive discourses about women's role and women's nature. In this light, the language of the Aberdare WLA is interesting. Their promise of 'quiet work' signalled that there was to be no shrill or competitive activity, that most of the work would be safely out of the public gaze - a promise they did not keep. The post-script, with its encouraging words for women inexperienced in, but drawn to, politics, acknowledged that for many of the women now being mobilized, this was new ground.

The statement represents an exercise in self-representation by women mostly unknown outside their own locality. Women of the middle and lower-middle classes, they had the same range of concerns as women with more exalted connections: the temperance movement, women's rights, religious questions, women's role in local government, and the moral transformation of public life. Their membership of the Welsh Union and the WLF, and of temperance and other societies, and their usefulness to their MPs, allowed them to project those concerns at a national and Parliamentary level. Maria Richards

(Mrs. D. M. Richards, d. 1930), author of the pamphlet on parish councils, is an example: her influence in the Aberdare district, in party politics, local government, temperance organisation and a range of civic activities, continued to the end of the 1920s.[1] Women's ambitions in local government are presented in the practicalities of parish council and Poor Law work, supported by a statement about the freedom and progress of women, of women's suitability for such work, and the moral and religious duty to embrace it. It would also be a step towards 'greater things' in the governance of the kingdom – in other words, the Parliamentary vote. Richards's reference to the Italian writer Mantegazza is a reminder that it was not only the educated upper-class women of the movement who had access to, and eagerly utilised, the writings of European thinkers; and that the political culture of women was far from being narrowly bounded by locality.

The remaining items from the Liberal women's movement were originally published in the monthly *Young Wales* (1895-1903), the journal of 'Cymru Fydd', the term used to express rising national feeling amongst Liberal Nonconformists, and the unsuccessful attempt to create a unified Welsh party. In the journal, meanings of Wales and Welshness were debated, often in relation to 19th century European nationalist philosophies. No other Welsh journal of the period gave as much space to the women's position, status and politics. The journal's decade of publication, through the changing fortunes and mood of Welsh Liberalism, suggests that nationhood was a shifting, gendered ideal. Born in optimism, *Young Wales* was to be the expression of a growing sense of national unity, and its writers endorsed the equality of men and women in the new Wales, as a sign of national progress and progressiveness. However, the early optimism waned as the Liberals lost power at Westminster,

---

[1] Ursula Masson, *Women's Rights and 'Womanly Duties': Aberdare Women's Liberal Association 1891-1910* (Cardiff, 2005), Introduction.

and divisions emerged in the Welsh party. How did this affect representations of women in the nation?[2]

Women contributed to the journal in a number of ways, publishing fiction, polemic, news and commentary. Under the editorship of Philipps and her sister-in law, the column 'The progress of women in Wales' discussed the work of organised Liberal women, the suffrage movement, and the relationship of women to national aims. Other women also wrote, on WLA activities, on women as Poor Law Guardians, on educational and religious matters. Philipps's last column appeared in January 1897, after which the irregular nature of the coverage, and the authorship and content of articles, reflected the loss of the political feminist edge she had provided, and a weakening of the journal's commitment to women's emancipation.

The English-born daughter of European Jewish parents, who had married into the Welsh squirearchy, Philipps (née Gerstenberg, 1862-1915) was 'a committed feminist who reflected the movement's late Victorian preoccupations'.[3] She was the founding president of the Welsh Union and was active at the British level in the suffrage societies of the 1880s and 1890s, and in temperance organisations. As a supporter of the suffragist faction in the WLF, Philipps and others worked, in 1891-2, to create WLAs in Wales to bolster the cause. The history of Welsh women's organisation which Philipps provides in these articles is its connection to a broader British feminism as well as to the nationalist developments. She shared the optimism of the founding moment of the journal,

---

[2] For background to these writings, see Ursula Masson, ' "Hand in hand with the women, forward we will go": Welsh nationalism and feminism in the 1890s', *Women's History Review*, vol. 12, no. 3, 357-86; Jane Aaron, *Nineteenth Century Women's Writing in Wales: Nation, Gender and Identity* (Cardiff, 2007), ch. 6.

[3] See Linda Walker, 'Philipps [née Gerstenberg] Leonora' (1852-1915), *Oxford Dictionary of National Biography* (*ODNB*) (Oxford, 2003), an account which indicates the breadth of Philipps's involvement in many aspects of the women's movement of the late nineteenth century.

the sense that Wales was 'a rising nation' creating its own laws and institutions, and taking its women along with it, although it would be women of the middle class who would benefit most.

Philipps was a key figure of the 1890s; her speeches and writings both reflected and shaped the ethos of Welsh women's Liberalism; hence several pieces by her are reprinted here. Inevitably, less is known about some of our other writers. Little is currently known about Anna Jones, author of 'Women and Religious Freedom'. This brief but effective re-insertion of women into the story of the making of the Nonconformist nation, was surely a reply to Philipps's lack of a history for Welsh women between the Romans and the 1890s. Jones was a London-based member of the committee of the Welsh Union, and had been a delegate for Dolgellau WLA. This is another example of the extent to which the political culture of the period opened up the possibilities for writings by relatively unknown women. By contrast, Gwyneth Vaughan (Annie Harriet Hughes, 1852-1910), had some fame as a novelist, Welsh nationalist and Celticist. A temperance campaigner prominent in the British Women's Temperance Association (BWTA), Vaughan was also an active suffragist, one of the Welsh Union's best known speakers outside Wales as well as within, and an indefatigable worker for the causes she believed in, at some cost to herself. Vaughan, and Alis Mallt Williams (Alice Matilda Langland, 1867-1950), writer of fiction and polemic, writing here as 'Un o'r ddau Wynne', were founders together of 'Undeb y Ddraig Goch', the aims of which are reflected in Williams's article: safeguarding the language, promoting 'native' arts, crafts and industries, with a special responsibility for this cultural reproduction of the nation placed on women. Almost all of the pieces, reflecting the historical awareness of Philipps's 'Appeal', are concerned with history and its connection to nationhood; with women's history, and women's relationship to nation building. They represent different approaches to the questions of women, feminism, and national identity, from the full-blooded feminism of Nora Philipps, to the ethnic nationalism of Mallt Williams.

Labour Women: sex and class.

Politics was brought very close to home by labour movement women in the early twentieth century, addressing family, household and locality, the position within them of working-class women, and the realities of life for women in industrial and urban Wales. This is a location which is barely visible in the *Young Wales* writings. Conversely, it will be noticed how rarely 'Wales' appears in writings by the women of the left. The imagining of communities was shaped by the very different political ideologies and languages. However, to compare the statement of the WLL 'Object and Method' (page 237) with the objects of the WLAs of twenty years before is reminder of how little, politically, had changed for women.

The articles here come from three sources. The confident account of the year's activities by the Cardiff WLL comes from the *League Leaflet* (later *Labour Woman*), the central WLL newsletter. Local organisation of the League was always fragile, but Cardiff was its strongest centre in Wales. In such reports, activists portrayed their associations as vigorous and effective, as a spur to further efforts. The Swansea WLL articles, mostly unsigned, appeared in 'Our Women's Column' in the *Swansea and District Workers' Journal* (1899-1914), published by the Swansea ILP. The articles by 'Matron' come from an important body of writing in 'Our Women's Column' in the *Rhondda Socialist*, published in Pontypridd (1911-1913) with an all-male editorial board from Rhondda ILP branches. The use of the same title, 'Our Women's Column', reflects the extent to which editorial decisions were taken by like-minded networks of men: it acknowledges separate women's organisation and interests, while the possessive pronoun, with its familial connotations, safely encompasses them within the class movement.

The *Rhondda Socialist* had no 'women's column' until December 1911. Until then, the paper concentrated on local labour movement and coal industry news, conducting a war of words with Liberalism and Nonconformity, showing no consciousness of the existence of women amongst the Rhondda working class. The change came in the autumn of 1911, when Penygraig ILP announced that it had booked visiting speakers on socialism and votes for women. The absence of women from ILP activities in Rhondda before this date, and the party's perception of their lack of autonomy, is revealed by the announcement: 'The women folk must be induced to attend these meetings. Married men, bring your wives, Single men, bring your sweethearts.'[4] Clearly, the movement and the paper's readership were understood to be male, but at least there was a recognition of 'women's interests', at a time when the labour movement and the constitutional suffrage movement drew closer, forming an electoral pact. As suffrage activity in the valley increased, the *Rhondda Socialist* ran supportive items on the movement. Prompted by this new interest in women, the first 'Our Women's Column', authored by 'Matron', appeared in December 1911. It addressed, not women's political rights, but the communal and familial tragedy of infant mortality played out daily in the Rhondda. After this, Matron produced a column for almost every issue of the paper until its merger with the Merthyr based *South Wales Worker* in 1913, on health, housing, poverty, maternal and infant welfare, and women's suffrage. Her piece on 'Women and the Liberal Party' was timely: Liberal women in south Wales were increasingly disillusioned with their party in government, for its refusal to introduce women's suffrage. Matron's analysis of inequality under Liberalism included the 'tortures' inflicted on imprisoned suffragettes, in contrast to

[4] *Rhondda Socialist,* no. 4, Nov. 1911.

the treatment of male political prisoners, unequal provision under the National Insurance Act, and unequal pay in the job market. Two articles on women's suffrage in January and March 1912 provided the opportunity to promote the Labour position, comparing the struggle for citizenship of 'women of all classes' with the class struggle, the 'sex/class analogy' which informed Labour thinking on the 'woman question'.

However, Matron did not perceive that all was well in the sexual politics of the labour movement, or amongst the working class. In 'Women in the Labour Movement' she acutely analysed the exclusion of women from working-class politics in the Rhondda. Here she felt that class solidarity should overcome the gender divide: working-class women needed solidarity from working-class men, not well-meaning condescension, as she saw it, from middle-class women. She was unsentimental about domesticity, motherhood and marriage in the conditions of working-class life as she saw them, subjecting the domestic work of women to the kind of analysis more usually applied to the male worker; women's health, self-respect and humanity were at stake. The much-praised 'tidy wives' of the Rhondda did not fill her with pride: where, she asked, 'does the dignity and glory of womanhood come in here?'

The contrasts with the writings of Liberal women are striking. The latter tackled the 'headline' issues of politics – disestablishment, temperance, Home Rule, education, the nation, women's suffrage – and when they talked about women in the family, exalted domesticity and motherhood and household skills as a foundation of women's claims to the public sphere, or as the arena within which they reproduced the nation. Matron saw marriage and family, in conditions of a harsh capitalism, as sites of inequality and oppression. Instead of blaming the victims of these conditions, she looked to social and material explanations, and for collective solutions, through housing, health care, a clean milk supply, education and support for mothers. The problems could 'only be completely overcome by a Socialist state', but meanwhile the district and county councils, still Liberal dominated, could be chivvied to awaken their humanitarian conscience, and the male working-class movement must learn to include women.

So who was Matron? The editorial announcing her arrival in the *Rhondda Socialist*, described her as 'one of the ablest and best known women in the Rhondda'. The pseudonym claims the authority of a mature married woman – experience, knowledge of the world, and of women's concerns. That might be a disguise, but the columns do have maturity, breadth and depth. What was her class identity? The writing is clear and accomplished, and suggests a good level of education. She might have been one of the teachers becoming active in Rhondda Labour politics at this time, like Gwen Ray, later Gwen Ray Evans, a trade union activist, and in the 1920s a member of the Labour Party and the Communist Party. The other woman active at this time in Rhondda Labour politics, who left behind a body of very effective writing, was Elizabeth Andrews, active in the ILP and the WCG, who was to become the party's women's organiser for Wales in 1919. But Matron was critical of the labour movement and working-class men as Andrews never was in her solidaristic writings of the 1920s and 1930s. However, Andrews's later role as a party employee must have shaped her approach to propaganda in the inter-war years. Andrews and Matron shared characteristics as writers: a liking for quotation, especially from the bible; a positive relish for statistics and hard data to support arguments. Their subject matter was often the same, but so it would be, since both addressed social conditions affecting working-class women which only deteriorated in the period when Andrews was writing, through the strikes and lock-outs of the 1920s and the depression of the 1930s.[5] For the moment, the identity

[5] Elizabeth Andrews, *A Woman's Work is Never Done and Other Writings* (ed. Ursula Masson, Dinas Powys 2006).

of Matron remains a mystery.

The adoption of a pseudonymous persona is rather different from the modest anonymity of the writer or writers of 'Our Women's Column' in the *Workers' Journal*. The last column printed here was signed 'R.C.', which can be confidently be identified as Mrs. R. Chalk, the secretary of the Swansea branch of the WLL at this time. Much of it was a repetition of an earlier unsigned article, suggesting that Mrs. Chalk was also the author of the anonymous pieces. The column was used to promote the League, and was therefore less broad in its range than Matron's writings, to some extent replicating the language of the working-class movement which undermined the autonomy of women, with its aim to enrol 'the wives and daughters of the men of the Labour Movement'. Articles on women's suffrage, on the industrial position of women, and on the economic causes of prostitution or 'white slavery', which appeared in the general pages of the *Journal*, appear on internal evidence to have been written by men.

The first article by Chalk focused on local issues – housing, education, play spaces for children in Swansea's ageing urban environment – which cried out for women's activism. It began by making the argument made by the Chartist Henry Vincent more than seventy years before, for women's role in politics, the repetition of such arguments over a long period indicating the intractability of gender cultures. A League organiser in south Wales in 1909 had attributed the difficulties of her work to the women being 'tied to their homes dreadfully'.[6] This was recognised by the Swansea activists too, as the author of the column asked working men to take on more responsibility in the home to allow women to attend meetings; like Matron, they recognised that class solidarity across the gender divide was needed if women were to play a part in the movement, and that comradeship needed to extend into marriage and the family.

[6] Christine Collette, *For Labour and For Women: the Women's Labour League, 1906-18* (Manchester, 1989), 83.

In Swansea, as these columns show, the WLL and the Women's Cooperative Guild (WCG) were closely aligned, and shared many of the same personnel. Mrs. Chalk, secretary of the WLL, was also a member of the WCG, and of the National Federation of Women Workers.[7] She was elected to the Swansea Board of Guardians in 1913. Other women followed the same trajectory – WLL, WCG and Guardians. One of the leading women in south Wales Labour politics was Elizabeth Williams (Mrs. David Williams), who combined a number of such roles, as WLL president, as well as Swansea's first Labour Mayoress in 1913.[8]

The League writings balance Matron's view of women's relationship to the labour movement, which did not reflect the position everywhere. For example, in the neighbouring Aberdare and Merthyr valleys, in Cardiff and in other towns, unlike in the Rhondda, women were active in the ILP. According to Matron, the League was 'a case of the women of the middle class bending to help women of the working class'. This was true enough of some of the leadership of the League, but not necessarily of local activists. The existence of the League in Swansea and other centres, and its absence from Rhondda, is a reminder of the variety of social contexts within which Labour politics and women's politics were evolving. The domination of mining in Rhondda meant a politics dominated by the miners' union and its concerns. In Swansea, as in Cardiff and Newport, a more diverse economic and industrial base – dock workers, railwaymen, metal workers, as well as more, and more varied, work for women – appears to have created a political culture which gave some scope for women to organise, while, however, the strength of that organisation

---

[7] Not, as its name suggests, a trade union, the NFWW was an organisation of female social workers for women and children.

[8] Helen Thomas, 'A democracy of working women: the Women's Cooperative Guild in south Wales, 1891-1939', unpublished MA dissertation, University of Glamorgan, 2006, appendix 2.

should not be overstated. These different local cultures are the key to the differences in the political development of women from place to place. [9]

---

[9] See Introduction and chapters 1-4, of Duncan Tanner, Chris Williams and Deian Hopkin (eds), *The Labour Party in Wales, 1900-200* (Cardiff, 2000); in the same volume, Neil Evans and Dot Jones, 'To Help Forward the Great Work of Humanity: Women in the Labour Party in Wales' is a much fuller discussion of these issues than there is room for here.

10. Nora Philipps

An Appeal to Welsh Women (1893)

WOMEN AWAKE!

You have a political duty to perform

Remember

Good laws make it easy, and bad laws make it difficult for men and women to be good.

Remember

That Health and Happiness in town and country depend on good laws; Good laws depend upon Public Opinion; Public Opinion upon yourselves.

Women! We can all help to create sound public opinion, by first obtaining and then diffusing sound Political Knowledge. Women! we have a Political duty, because we have Power; we have power to promote human welfare by supporting by our own sympathy and our work, the great Reforming Party in the State. We have power to fight against disease and vice and crime by supporting the Party that has brought about many reforms in the past and is pledged to grapple with problems of poverty in the future, The Liberal Party, that has given to the people of our country:

    Cheap Bread (Repeal of the Corn Laws);

    Education;

    The Vote,

in the past – and that in the future seeks:

    To lighten the burden of taxation on the poor still further;

    To make education not only free but unsectarian;

    To extend the Political Franchise till it reaches all capable citizens, women as well as men, who abide by the Nation's laws, and help to make the Nation's welfare.

For the sake of Ireland
come forth and Unite!

The Irish have been misgoverned for many centuries. Ireland's industries have been suppressed; her land has been taken from the people, and the Government have been in antagonism to the spirit of the people; and abject poverty, famine and despair have desolated the sister island.

Mr. Gladstone has brought forward a great constructive policy of conciliation, **Home Rule,** which means the giving the Irish a right to manage their own Irish affairs. Come forth and support it!

For the sake of religious Equality
come forth and Unite!

Out of your religious convictions, and for the love of Justice, ask for Disestablishment in Wales. Point out that it is in accordance with the spirit of true Religion, of brotherhood and love of mankind; that it is the divine spiritual right of every human being to seek for truth and to worship according to his convictions and therefore that the Religion of all men should be treated with the same respect; point out that a spiritual body should not be under secular control, and that all State Institutions should be founded on the principle of impartial justice.

A great Liberal Leader has said 'The grievance of the great body of the Welsh People with respect to Church Establishment is the most signal injustice which is left unredressed'. Come forth to redress it!

Women: your sphere is your home!

Yes, but you have a double duty. First of all to your family, and secondly to the wider family, the world of human beings outside, and you fail in one of your most solemn obligations, if you devote yourself solely to your own home and your own children, unmindful of the fact that thousands of poor men and women have no homes, or live in dark degraded homes, and that hundreds and thousands of little children are growing up uncared for, untaught, unthought of, in slums and alleys or the streets of our great cities.

It is your womanly duty to minister to the sick, therefore it is also your duty to raise your voice on behalf of the important Land Laws, Rural Reforms, and other Liberal measures that will prevent overcrowding, bad sanitation and consequent disease.

It is your womanly duty to rescue the tempted and comfort the sorrow stricken; therefore it is also your duty to try to lessen by law the evil of drunkenness, and to support the Liberal measure of Local Option that seeks to make drunkenness difficult by giving power to Localities to reduce the number of Public Houses.

What can you as Women do?

Join a Political Association: - for by union and combination those who are weak become strong, those who are hopeless gain new faith, those who need help obtain the power both of self-help and of helping others.

By means of a Women's Liberal Association you can spread the belief in Liberal principles. You can give to all women in your District, by means of Public Meetings, distribution of pamphlets and social intercourse, a sound knowledge of Politics.

You can persuade them to become interested in the Public business of their country, and make them keen and steadfast workers for Social and Political Reform.

You can enable them through organized associated efforts to secure in all Elections the triumph of the Liberal Party, and you can give them the opportunity of using their influence to keep Elections pure and free from intimidation and corruption.

You can see that all duly qualified women are placed on the register, in order that they may vote at Municipal, Vestry, School Board and County Council Elections, for which they already possess the Franchise.

Women awake, and claim Political Enfranchisement!
In order to do your Political duty well, ask for the right to vote for Parliamentary Candidates. This is the easiest, wisest, best, constitutional method of expressing a Political opinion and exerting political influence.

Out of your Liberalism and out of your womanliness, claim the application of Liberal Principles to womanhood.

Taxation and representation should go together. Capable citizenship gives a title to Political enfranchisement.

Urge these reasons for Woman's Suffrage
1st. That according to the principles of representative Government all those who contribute to maintain the State and the Laws made by the State should have a voice in the making of those laws, by helping to choose the law makers, that is the Members of the House of Commons.

2nd. That the interests of those who have no vote are liable to be postponed to the interests of those who have; and therefore it often happens that their rights are disregarded and their wrongs unredressed.

You may not need a vote for yourself individually, but ask

for it for the sake of the women who must run in the race for life and who are handicapped now by the heavy weight of Electoral disability.

There are over 3,000,000 women who work for wages, and they are underpaid and undervalued in many cases simply because they are women. The result to women of their not having the privilege of citizenship and the power that direct representation gives, is, that they are put at a grievous disadvantage in the overcrowded and callous labour markets of the world.

Claim the Vote

For with it you will have power to nerve the arm of the Nation to protect the weak, to strengthen the will of the Nation to advance in civilization.

Remember

The still small voice the vote may be the conscience of the Nation to move it towards the highest good. Let your programme be:

Home Rule for Ireland
Disestablishment for Wales
Temperance Reform
The Political Enfranchisement of Women
and
Justice for All.

11. Women's Liberal Associations

Rules and Objects of Welsh Women's Liberal Associations (1891, 1893)

Model objects for Welsh WLAs. From <u>The Aim and Object of the Welsh Union</u> by Nora Philipps, 1893.

1. To spread the belief in Liberal principles, and zealously to put the same into practice.
2. To give to all women in this district, by means of public meetings, distribution of pamphlets, and helpful social intercourse, a sound knowledge of politics; to persuade as many as possible to become interested in the public business of their country, and especially to act on Boards of Guardians, School Boards, &c.; to promote Disestablishment and Temperance, and to make them keen and steadfast workers for all social and political reform.
3. To promote all just legislation for women and children, and especially to help forward the cause of Women's Suffrage.
4. To enable women, through organised, associated effort, to secure in all elections the triumph of the Liberal party.
5. To give women an opportunity of using their influence to keep elections pure and free from intimidation and corruption, and to promote as much as possible the election, for all public offices, of men of high moral character.
6. To see that all qualified women are placed on the Register,

that they may vote at County Council and Local Elections, for which they already possess the Franchise.

Rules of the Aberdare Women's Liberal Association. From the Minute Book of the Aberdare WLA, November 26 1891.

I. The Association shall consist of women of all classes who are in sympathy with the Liberal Cause.
II. The Objects of the Association shall be –
    (a) Quiet work for the Liberal Party.
        Advocating and using influence in support of such principles as:
        – Truth and Morality in our public Representatives.
        – Repression of bribery, corruption, intimidation, and undue influence.
        – Absolute Religious equality.
        – Social justice and political rights for all sections of the community.
    (b) Endeavouring to obtain Representatives in sympathy with the objects of the Association, in Parliament and in Local Governing Bodies.
    (c) Promoting the Election of Women on Boards of Guardians and on School Boards, and directing the attention of women who have votes to their responsibility in the matter.
    (d) Promoting the Welfare of Women, by study of political and social questions, and by work for their benefit, educational and practical.
    (e) Establishing Correspondents in every place, whose work will be enrolling members, collecting subscriptions, promoting the objects of the Association, and collecting information for the use of the Liberal Party in registration and other ways.
    (f) Organizing meetings for lectures and discussions on

these subjects.

III The Association shall be managed by a President, two or more Vice-Presidents, a Treasurer, a Secretary and an Executive Committee, all of whom shall be elected annually at a general meeting of members.

IV A General Meeting shall be held at Aberdare annually to elect officers, receive reports and consider plans for future action.

V Members shall subscribe according to their ability to the funds of the Association, 1d. being the minimum subscription.

Footnote. It is hoped that no-one will refrain from joining the association upon the ground that she will be no use, or that she has no time for politics. Every member will be of use, if only in strengthening the [hand?] of those who work, by her sympathy, by her subscription and by her advice. Many women too will have been conscious at Election times of a desire to work in the cause of Liberalism, but have not known how to employ their services. It is hoped that an organised Women's Association will be able to indicate the direction in which such energies can be utilised.

12. Mrs D. M. Richards

The Duty of Women and Wives to try for places on the Parish Councils, &c. (1894)[1]

A missionary once asked the leader of a primitive tribe in India what reason he could give as to why they were as a tribe so slow to climb the steps of civilization and morality. 'Oh', said he, 'that is easy to answer – we have not as yet as a tribe educated our girls, and the boys marry them; and usually nine out of every ten of their children follow the mother, so that it is impossible for us to achieve a thorough-going reform without giving an education to our girls as well as our boys.' Also, one Paolo Mantegazza,[2] an authority who has thoroughly studied the moral, social and religious character of all the women of Europe, says that two things are important in the formation of the female character: firstly, her religious convictions; secondly, her social freedom – the greater her freedom, the greater her virtue. We, the women and wives of Wales, have suffered to a very great extent from a lack of education and social freedom; but we are beginning to awake from our torpor now, though vast areas are yet to be won. But we are now, for all that, on

[1] Leaflet printed about 1894, when local government reform provided more opportunities for women to vote and be elected to Boards of Guardians, and new parish and district councils.

[2] Paolo Mantegazza (mis-spelt as Montogazza in the original) 1831-1910: neurologist, physiologist, anthropologist. Liberal Darwinist, seen as a pioneer 'sexologist'. Some translations available in Britain by the 1880s/90s.

the brink of a new age. Next December, the Parish Councils measure becomes an act, and that should inspire every one of us to take advantage of the measure, and the freedom it offers to us, and I will try to give a brief explanation of our rights as women and wives according to the measure.

Every woman of more than 21 years of age, married or widowed, as long as she has resided in the parish for at least 12 months, or within about a mile of the parish, will be eligible to be elected as an overseer of the poor on the Parish Council, and the Board of Guardians.

Next, I will note the new powers which will come into our possession under this truly Democratic charter:

1. The power to choose overseers for the poor.
2. The compulsory purchase and the compulsory placement of land as allotments and for other purposes.
3. Distributing the parish charities.
4. Ensuring an appropriate water supply, and its transportation to the houses.
5. Lighting the dark street corners of towns and villages.
6. Providing protective fencing in areas dangerous to children.
7. The right to hold meetings in schoolrooms.
8. Building halls in villages.
9. Defending the right of the public to village greens, to roads and paths, and to uncultivated roadsides.
10. Keeping the parish's paths and roads in good order.
11. Getting rid of rubbish dumps and any other nuisances which might harm the health of the public.
12. Providing libraries, reading rooms, wash-houses, and public baths for the villages, &c.

Reviewing these, we see that a woman has particular qualifications suiting her to deal with many of them, such as choosing the overseers of the poor, &c. Are not the majority of the poor, women and children? And unarguably we should have a voice in the distribution of the parish charities, as many of them have been given by women. And who is as affected by the quality and distribution of water as women? This is very definitely a subject on which we need to express our opinion; and so is ensuring that streets are appropriately lit, so that women and children can go out fearlessly and unhesitatingly at night, if circumstances require them to do so. And we can very appropriately give our opinion as to which places are dangerous for children. But however usefully women and wives can deal with the subjects already mentioned, as nearly all the obstructions have been removed, it is undoubtedly as Overseers [of the Poor] that we can act and help and be truly useful.

The poor are always with us, and it is a privilege and a duty to sympathize with the widowed, the old and the disabled. The lambs are also with us, and, as surely as Peter was commanded to feed them, the same obligation is upon us in this age to care for them. Not only those lambs who can feed as they will on rich pastures, but those lambs too who have been deprived of their parents through death, and also many of them through worse things, and have been left along the mountains and precipices of temptation. Do not these call upon us to do our best to rear and nurture them, and make of them worthy citizens of our country and our religion, if possible.

Everybody who has taken the least interest in the question is bound to confess that there are many duties in relation to the poor that no-one can fulfil as well as women and wives. Consider that it is males who have for ages now been arranging what nourishment, clothes and treatment newly-born infants should receive, and the old infirm housebound women. What do men know of those things which they have always considered women's work, such as cooking, washing, mending clothes, sewing, &c.? Would not women be most helpful with matters of this kind? Sitting on the Boards will demand much self-sacrifice and hard work; but there is no privilege without its duties. And as we have demanded the privilege, we must accept the duties pertaining to it.

Women of Wales, let us get to it, seriously – show that we are worthy of this privilege, so that we can claim greater things. Unarguably, many women should sit on every Board of Guardians in the kingdom. But if there is any parish or parishes in Wales for which it proves impossible to get suitable women to stand, let every woman in the possession of a vote ensure that she gives it to the man or men most worthy according to the true meaning of the word.

13. Nora Philipps

Notes on the work of Welsh Liberal Women (1895)

Young Wales, January and February 1895.

i.

Three years ago about forty Welsh women journeyed to Aberystwyth from all parts of the Principality, from places as remote from one another as Corwen and Cardiff, or Narberth and Newport, in order to inaugurate the union of the Women's Liberal Associations which had previously been formed.

The objections to be faced had been amply dwelt upon by those who did not then believe in the possibility of a National Union, and who viewed women's political work with doubt, if not with dismay. It was pointed out by some that, as there were two men's Liberal Federations in Wales, it was obvious that two were necessary; and that as many Welsh public bodies met at Shrewsbury, it was equally obvious that Aberystwyth could not be considered as a suitable meeting place.

But difficulties in the path of the reformer are like fences on the huntsman's track – meant to be got over. High as the hills are between North and South Wales, they are not so high as the aspirations of the dwellers on either side, which combining, enable them to overcome all obstacles; and the first meetings of the Welsh women have been succeeded each year by others, at Swansea in 1893 and at Rhyl in 1894, in which the increase of membership and the awakened interest and sympathy amongst men and women have fully justified the early effort, and have done much to promote that cordial fellowship and hearty cooperation which so far has been a leading feature in the political work of Welsh women.

The Union now numbers 47 Associations and its membership has increased since last spring, when already between 8000 and 9000 members have been enrolled.

Whatever future the Welsh women may have before them – when they shall have interlaced and interwoven their ideals and activities with every Welsh endeavour and every national success – it will always be a great thing to remember that those who came forward first identified themselves from the beginning with all those principles that lie at the very root of progress, and devoted themselves with force and fervour to the reforming efforts made by womanhood throughout the country.

The breadth of the basis on which the Welsh women reared their edifice of social and political endeavour secured their success, because of the diverse interests and individualities that linked themselves together. Those who joined for the sake of promoting some one wing of work which they considered paramount, by thus combining with others, with whose underlying principles they were in harmony, learnt that large lesson of sympathy and genial goodwill which alone can secure the progress of any movement. Thus, for instance, some of the Temperance workers, who desire that the nation by its laws, should help the social effort to lessen drunkenness, have joined the Welsh Union to promote the work they hold important above all others, and by so joining have realised more than before the necessity for Disestablishment and the political enfranchisement of women, by coming in close contact with those who have devoted their lives to the study of these special questions.

Its usefulness
Emerson tells us that 'thoughts are the ancestors of our acts',

and, if this be so, words occasionally may be considered as the parents of our deeds. This must have brought comfort to many a public speaker, and those who believe in a National Union for Wales and the civic powers of women must be greatly encouraged by many recent events. Convictions are catching, and they who declared in 1893 that a National Union could be formed which would combine the North and South of Wales in harmony, now, in 1895, see a further justification of their belief, for a new Union is springing into existence that not only seeks to unite every part of the Principality, but offers equal opportunities of work to both men and women.[1]

Three years ago men were asking why women should be political at all, and now there is scarcely a town that has not women running as candidates for the Board of Guardians, whilst in many villages women have already been elected as Parish Councillors.

It is perhaps not too much to claim that the Welsh Union has been instrumental in helping to awaken women to their responsibilities and in inducing them to undertake them. Ever since it was formed, thousands of leaflets have been distributed, hundreds of lectures have been given, and the Press of the country, commenting on the work, has aroused public opinion, and given a stimulus to the great movement for the civic development of womanhood. At the same time it is to be remembered that some of the staunchest advocates the woman's cause has ever had were to be found in Wales, in the early days of the movement (such a champion, for instance, as the *Cambrian News*[2] has ever been), and this early work smoothed the way for later comers.

---

[1] A reference to the attempt to form the Welsh National Liberal Federation (Cymru Fydd) in 1895, in which women were given equal membership, and which placed women's suffrage amongst its aims.

[2] The *Cambrian News,* published in Aberystwyth, was edited by John Gibson, an active supporter of women's political activities, and of women's suffrage.

The dawn of success

The returns of the recent elections for Parish Councillors and members of Boards of Guardians are most gratifying and decidedly mark the onward march of the women's cause. At Cardiff there were as many as nine women elected to the Board of Guardians, five of whom respectively headed the polls in their various wards; while at Newport six women were among the successful candidates. The extraordinary success of women as candidates for the Board of Guardians is thus much more marked than even their successes as Parish Councillors, instances of which are numerous in many districts both in North and South Wales. In every district there are unmistakable evidences that the claims and qualifications of women for civic duties and for positions of public usefulness are now being recognised.

The women's movement is said to have passed through three stages – firstly, when women's political aspirations were declared 'impossible'; secondly, 'ridiculous', and now at last 'highly respectable'! But women may well compare themselves to the man who, when he was told that a certain task was 'impossible', made no reply till he could answer 'impossible, only I have done it.'

What is it that women have done? They have identified themselves during recent years with every single movement which has for its end and aim the welfare, the better health, and purer happiness of human beings. When men and women come together inspired with the desire to be of service, there is always a moment of difficulty in deciding what practical end can be attained. The difficulty to the ignorant is to find out what *could* be done, and to the intellectual to find out what *should* be done, and amongst the clashings and coercion of conscience, jarred by the waverings and indecisions of judgement, we look to those who seem to have found an answer, glad that they, too, have had to ask our question.

When people are confronted by the apparently totally

divergent opinions as to what would help the world to be better, many are so bewildered that they are almost tempted to say, 'Whilst the opinions of human beings are so opposed to one another, should I not be doing my duty in standing apart, and in doing nothing, just as much as if I took a side when one of two sides must necessarily be wrong, and I am not quite sure which is right'. What answer shall we give them when they ask, 'Is there any great part to be played in the world at this moment? Is there any fine thing to be done? Is there any inspiring advance to be made, and can I play it? Shall I do it? Can I help?'

The history of humanity shows us that certain principles have always conferred benefits on those whom they have touched. What has given us art, literature, morality, cleanliness of mind and person, higher civilization in the country?

We cannot fail to see that two causes have always contributed to these great ends, namely, liberty and knowledge – or, as applied to individuals – enfranchisement and education.

Dean Church has said that, 'the progress of civilization is measured by the utilization of waste'. As man has advanced he has learnt that the things which seem of no value may be of imperishable value. The bare rock when engraved by the hand of the hieroglyphist will enable king to speak to king; the very flint when struck on steel will produce fire; and almost everything that exists has had new uses developed in it accordingly as knowledge has been extended, and freedom to use knowledge has been given to individuals. But it is strange to observe that the very last thing to which value is attributed is to men and women. Here is the ultimate stage of our nineteenth century civilization, when we have found uses for almost everything else, we waste our men and women. We waste many of our men by permitting them to live dark, dreary and unwholesome lives, where neither knowledge nor freedom can be their blessings, and we have no courage to believe because for the moment we do not see how we may make a beneficial use of them.

Still more do we waste many of our women. We curb their energies, we restrain their individuality, we limit their opportunity, we neglect their education; all this we do not so much with a conscious desire to degrade and injure them, but because we have not yet learnt that to liberty and knowledge we owe all the progress, the civilization, the happiness, and morality of humanity, and that out of an extension of these, good must come, and that from their limitation evil, sorrow and wrong inevitably spring.

ii.

Looking to the past, what lives commend themselves to us as the noblest, which we desire to emulate, and should be glad that our children should lead?

There is Mazzini teaching the spirit of fraternity, and liberating Italy. There is Fichte devoting his life to philosophy and rushing forth from his lecture to fight as a common soldier in the ranks for freedom. There is Richard Garrison, giving his life to take the fetters off the African slaves; and John Howard and Elizabeth Fry seeking to lessen the yoke of brutalizing punishment. There is Frederick Dennison Maurice extending learning among the lower classes of London, and telling us that whilst no one recognizes more than he that brute matter must ever be subject to the force of mind, still that our duty to our fellow-creatures less fortunate than ourselves is 'to lend them our brains'.

Further back in history who commands our greatest admiration? Joan of Arc leading a nation in war for self-defence, Columbus discovering a new world, Galileo making us friends with all the stars.

Question as we may, be doubtful, timorous, unenthusiastic as we will, approach the subject from what point of view we like, still throughout history those who above all others commend themselves as beings worthy to have lived, and worthy to be emulated, are those who have done something to give greater freedom and more knowledge to mankind.

It is, therefore, a most invigorating circumstance for those who live and work in Wales to find stirring opportunities of working both for education and freedom, and in seeking the Disestablishment of the State Church by declaring that religion shall be free and unfettered by State control, they may do something to establish the most important of all principles, those of Religious equality and toleration.

Disestablishment

There is a great opportunity for women's work in furthering Disestablishment; and there is no reason why the most devoted adherents of the Church of England should not be brought to view with sympathy the claim of the Liberationists, and thus the struggle would be robbed of its bitterness. The members of the Church of England tell us that they seek to unite 'The Church, the highest embodiment of human goodness, with the State, the highest embodiment of human law', and to obtain, as far as possible, uniformity in the national belief. It must, again and again, be pointed out to them that to attain such an ideal, a Church must be national, and the Church of England in Wales is certainly not national. It is the Church of the few and the wealthy, not of the many and of the poor in Wales. It must be shown to them that their ideal of uniformity in religion cannot be maintained in a country which owes its religious fervour to Nonconformity. The only uniformity that can be obtained in a free, intellectual, enlightened country is the uniformity of fundamental principles; but it is impossible to maintain an external uniformity in which to garb the truth. The great effort for actual uniformity which was made in 1662, when the very 'Act of Uniformity' was passed, resulted in 2,000 of the Clergy leaving the Established Church. All Established Churches try to stereotype and petrify the most fluctuating of all things – human opinion – and the results of the petrifaction necessarily is that those who ask for bread in many instances receive a stone. 'It is generally allowed,' remarks Henry Richard, 'that in the last century the Church fell into a sad condition in Wales'.

Establishment is bad for the faith dependent on it, because spiritual growth suffers from being in any way dependent on secular power, for if the honours and privileges of the State are given to any one Church the worldly people will flock into it, and however many noble and pure spirits there may be in it, they must be hampered by this fact. But the general principle can be often best illustrated by the particular instance. 'Every tree is known by its own fruit', and the establishment of the Church of England in Wales has brought about a bitter antagonism amongst those who should be working in harmony and in brotherhood together.

The knowledge of the feelings and conditions and history of the Church and the Chapels in Wales, and the study, above all, of human opinions, will bring many to see eye to eye with the advocates of Disestablishment. The aim of women is to emulate the example of the oriental potentate who boasted that he had overcome his enemies, 'by converting them into friends'.

The earnest pleading of women for the liberation of the Church from State control and especially the Disestablishment and the Disendowment of the Church of England in Wales must necessarily do much to help on the work of conversion in others, to the recognition of that underlying principle of justice, upon which the demand is based and which must inevitably help, rather than hinder, the spiritual life of the people.

New opportunities in the Principality
Whatever differences may exist on the religious question, all Welsh men and women must be stirred by the great educational schemes which have been brought to fruition in the

Principality. Those who often work apart will find themselves working together to further the objects which promise to confer such great advantages on the younger generation in the Principality.

Nothing will tend more to harmonize the social life of Wales and do more to soften the extreme and necessary severity of party struggles than the combining of different sects, creeds and parties as often as possible to promote great objects on which all are agreed. In view of this the last mentioned object of the Cymru Fydd League will be of general interest: 'To preserve the Welsh language, foster the cultivation of literature, art, and music, encourage the foundation of a national museum, and ensure the preservation of national monuments and antiquities'.

It is hoped that women will assist in bringing a more sympathetic element into politics, and that mere bitterness and personalities may, in time, disappear under the calming influences of advancing civilization. Nothing will benefit the political world more than an exchange of friendliness between those who differ in opinion, and whenever an opportunity occurs for those who generally work apart to work together, staunch partisans need not fear that their motives will be misunderstood.

There are two kinds of toleration, the first which springs from indifference, and the better kinds from that intense faith, which, being itself secure, can afford to respect the faith of others without fear. Such toleration should be preached and practised by all who care for human happiness and the dignity of public life.

The complexity of duty

The question that will be asked of the members of Cymru Fydd is the same kind of question that is asked of the progressive women. 'How far,' we women have been asked, 'can you do your duty to the State whilst fulfilling your obligations to the home?'

'How far,' the Welshman has been asked, 'can you declare yourselves for Welsh rights and yet faithfully serve the general cause and common interests which you share with all the British citizens?' The question of the complex duties of men and women is one that cannot easily be answered. The mistake that many searchers after political and social reform make is in seeking an impossible simplicity, to regulate the most complex of created beings under the most complicated of conditions – man in society. How comparatively simple, for instance, it is for a woman to be entirely domestic or purely political; how comparatively simple for the reformer to be an individualist or a socialist, how easy to be a nationalist or an imperialist compared to facing the fact that the complexity of human nature and society requires perpetual re-adjustment, an untiring and ever-renewed effort to obtain a perfect balance between antagonisms.

It has taken every existent force to develop man, and only by a combination of all the forces at his command can he do justice to the world in which he lives.

It is not easy, it never will be easy, to decide on his relative duties to himself, his own development, and his duties to society. It will always take the best gifts, the whole brain, heart, and spirit of the wisest man and woman, and, above all, it will ever need tact – the power of touch, attachment – close sympathy and correlation, springing from inward love to all things, to do justice to every side of life.

The awakening of national sentiment

In dwelling on the complexity of social problems, and the relation of the man to the State, and of the part to the whole, it is interesting to note that the rising of many hitherto subdued nationalities has taken place in the very century that has listened to the prophecy of a Federation of the world. The same century that has seen the unification of Prussia has seen the enfranchisement of Hungary. The same era that has witnessed a united Italy has seen Bulgaria, Roumania, and Montenegro slowly awaken as nations.

The generation in our own country that has learnt from one of its sweetest singers that they may look forward to the time

'Till the war-drum throbbed no longer, and the battle-
flags were furl'd,
In the Parliament of Man, the Federation of the
World'[3],

has extended its colonizing fraternities, so that our British empire has been compared to 'a world-wide Venice with the sea for streets'; has witnessed the culmination of Irish aspirations and the onward march of Scotland and Wales towards new measures of self-government. To those who take limited views it is easy to decide which of two ideals (which to many mistakenly seem incompatible) he will chose.

Take the question of Nationality. It would be easy to say 'I am Irish, Welsh, or English, therefore I will be patriotic for Ireland, Wales, or England', or it would be easy to say, 'I care and dare for the Empire, its greatness and glory. I will be no "Little Englander"'. But to be truly great is to care for a passionate patriotism for this great empire – great, not only in extent, but far more in the intent of her civilization, - and yet with joy and pride and devotion strive for the country, that part of the great whole to which we, by special love and human linking of family, language, and religion, belong.

Woman's mission in Wales

In the new life that stirs in the Welsh people, what part can woman play? The first and best answer is, 'The best woman can do what the best man can do', yet it is unfortunately

---

[3] Tennyson, 'Locksley Hall' (1842).

necessary to add, 'when they are not denied the opportunities that the best men have'. Therefore no article on woman's work would be complete unless it contained a plea for the enfranchisement of women which is one of the objects on which Welsh women, from the very beginning of their Union, combined. Those who brought the message from the Woman's Liberal Federation [sic], appealing to Welsh womanhood to support the Progressive Party in that Federation,[4] found a splendid response, not only in the women, but also in the men of the Principality. More Welsh representatives, in proportion to their numbers in Wales than in any other part of the country voted on the Local Government Act of 1894 in favour of qualified married as well as single women having votes for Parish and District Councillors, and amongst the declared advocates of Women's Suffrage are Mr. W. Abraham (Rhondda), Mr. Robert D. Burnie, Mr. W. Rees Davies, Major Evan Jones, Mr. J. H. Lewis, Mr. David Randell, Sir E. J. Reed, Mr. J. Bryn Roberts, Mr. Albert Spicer, Mr. Abel Thomas, Mr. Alfred Thomas, Mr. D. A. Thomas, Mr. Egerton Allan, Mr. A. J. Williams, Mr. Bowen Rowlands, while Mr. Lloyd-George [sic] has recently spoken in sympathy with their political aspirations.[5] In the Woman's Liberal Federation, from its first formation, Mrs. Eva McLaren, Miss Cons, Mrs. Josephine Butler and others pressed forward the claims of women to use their direct influence in politics and be recognized as 'Capable Citizens' by their having the freedom of the citizen, i.e., the Parliamentary vote, granted to them, and after some years of work an overwhelming majority of delegates decided to make Women's Suffrage one of the objects of their Federation.

To those who claim that women to be loyal as Liberals should therefore be less liberal to their own womanhood we

---

[4] The 'Progressives' in the Women's Liberal Federation were those who wanted to include women's suffrage amongst its aims; Philipps was a prominent member of the Progressives. They got their way in 1892.

[5] All those named were MPs for Welsh constituencies.

would give once more the reply, 'We have double duties and our work is manifold'. We are better social reformers if we develop our own individuality and make ourselves worthy items of Society. We are more patriotic if we devote ourselves to improving the country in which we live, and so we are more enthusiastic Liberals if, whilst honouring the Liberal Party for giving freedom and opportunity to men, we seek for womanhood the same good advantages of useful service. Welsh women are rousing themselves to seek and to do justice to the new opportunities thrown open to them. In the newly-founded University sex is no barrier even to the Chancellorship, and there is every likelihood that the men of 'Young Wales' will make the woman's cause their own, and champion her claim for equal rights of citizenship, and so identify the programme of the reformers, men and women, in the way it should ever be identified.

The message of the age

'I am not for the man's right or for the woman's right, but for the human right', said Émile de Girardin.

Never has there been a time in which more important issues were to be decided. Within each common life, a hero's life lies hidden, depending not so much on any one thing done as on the spirit in which life is lived. Each individual has the chance of doing the right thing when it is difficult, of expressing convictions with courage, of showing sympathy amid discouragement with unfashionable views, and of joining the party that is instrumental in carrying out the principles that our conscience directs us to adopt. We read that in the thirteenth century the barbaric life of the unconquered Britons was stirred and illuminated by an outburst of song; that poetry and music dawned once more upon the clansmen as it had done in the days of Aneurin and Llywarch Hen, four hundred years before. 'In every house', says an Englishman in the thirteenth century, 'strangers who arrived in the morning were entertained till eventide with the talk of maidens and the music of the harp'. The sun of a new illumination is now once more shining in Wales, and the study of her history may well encourage an inspiriting advance. A great constructive ideal should now be sought for, that should not only emulate the past but graft in its early promise new branches of development. The love of art that has given music and song as an inheritance to every part of the population should now find a new expression in each building that is erected, so that the architecture of Wales shall be worthy of the spirit of the people. The love of liberty that has been born in the descendants of the fiery leaders of the famous clans should now teach her to strive with equal enthusiasm for the freedom of her daughters as for her sons, so that she may rank high among the nations, not only by the affection of her children, but by the goodness, the beauty, and the stability of her accomplished ends.

14. Nora Philipps and Miss Elsbeth Philipps

Progress of Women in Wales (1896)

Young Wales, vol. 2, no. 15, March 1896.

The work of women in Wales has received a fresh impetus since the press has opened its columns to the questions that especially affect them, and has chronicled their doings in the many spheres of political and social work in which they have been increasingly active. Some newspapers have always been ready to champion the women's cause, even when to do so meant to stand alone and brave ridicule if not contempt, and it has been well for womanhood that the pen indeed is 'mightier than the sword', and that in their arduous crusade that keen but bloodless weapon has been so often and so ably wielded on their behalf. Like a winged arrow, the pen, - the 'plume' of feathery origin, - has given power to every thinker to send a quiverful of his best thoughts to hit even the most distant mark.

Young Wales has recognised from the first that the welfare of a rising nation depends upon the combined efforts of men and women, and when the Editor proposed to devote some portion of his magazine, every other month, to the opinions, work and history of Welsh women workers, those who were invited to take part felt that they must not forgo an opportunity that offered such scope for useful service.

It is very important that the world should know what women

have done in the past. For women's rights are constantly refused them on the ground that they have not hitherto accomplished great things, and are therefore not likely to do so in the future. Not only is it an unwarrantable assumption that what human beings have not done under bad conditions they could not do under better, but, as a matter of fact, considering the disabilities and disadvantages that have hampered and restricted all feminine efforts for many centuries, it is remarkable what abilities have nevertheless been shown.

We cannot wonder at the general ignorance concerning the wonderful achievements of women, for a great many classic histories have been written, which, except for the fact that princesses and pedigrees are occasionally mentioned, and thus the existence of a few females is indicated, would lead one to suppose that the world had been peopled by men only. The result of this has been that one of the most inspiring sources of human energy, that of example, has been lacking to women. But the historian of the future will find, when she makes careful investigation of old records with a view of ascertaining the part that woman has played in the world's history, that there are numerous proofs of her physical, mental and political endowments, which will justify the highest ideals of the most liberal-minded advocates of her freedom.

History has proved to us that man has achieved great heights in art, literature and politics, and that then dark ages followed when much that he had accomplished was apparently swept away; yet every succeeding age reaches a higher step, and the intervening periods of so-called retrogression are but the shadows on a continuous advance.

Women in the past have been permitted to take part in the government of the country, and though for some centuries that right has been almost entirely lost, there is no doubt that when regained it will be more widespread, more effective, and more enduring than before. Their physique at the beginning of this century compared unfavourably with that in preceding ages. An excessive admiration for the graces of woman, her gentleness and softness led to the emphasizing of these qualities, till gentleness became weakness and softness degenerated into flabbiness; yet the new movement for the development of the mental, moral and physical fibres of women, is producing, and will continue to produce, a magnificent type of womanhood, worthy descendants of their most heroic ancestresses.

It is interesting to note that the Celtic and kindred British race were remarkable for the energy and courage of their women, who showed, not only vigour in war, but what at all times is really a greater strength, an aptitude for promoting peace.

We read in Mrs C. C. Stopes' learned little work on *British Freewomen*: 'In the league made with Hannibal it was stated that "If the Celts take occasion of quarrelling with the Carthaginians, the governors and generals of the Carthaginians in Spain shall decide the dispute; but if the Carthaginians accuse the Celts, the Celtic women shall decide the controversy"'.

Caesar tells us that the British women were made use of in Court, in Council, and in Camp, and that no distinction of sex was made in places of command or government. Selden in his chapter on 'Women' in the *Janus Anglorum* reminds us that, 'Boadicea so successfully commanded the British armies as to beat and conquer the Roman viceroy, and no doubt that noble lady was a deliberative member of the Council where the resolution was taken to fight, and that she should command the "forces"'. Tacitus says, 'Under the leadership of Boadicea, a woman of kingly descent (for they admit of no distinction of sex in their royal successions) they all rose to arms. Had not Paulinus, on hearing of this outbreak, rendered prompt succour, Britain would have been lost.'

Tacitus, describing the great battle in which Boadicea engaged, in her last desperate struggle with the Romans, reports her speech. Not being 'unaccustomed to address the public', she called her army to witness 'that it was usual for the Britons to war under the conduct of women, but on that occasion she entered the field, not as one descended from ancestors so illustrious to recover her kingdom and her treasure; but as one of the humblest among them to take vengeance for liberty extinguished, her own body lacerated with stripes, and the chastity of her daughters defiled….They would see that in that battle they must conquer or perish'. Such was the fixed resolve of a woman, the men might live if they pleased and be the slaves of the Romans.

When Anglesey was attacked, the women priestesses dashed about clothed in black, like furies, with dishevelled hair, and with torches in their hands, encouraging and threatening the soldiers, and when all was lost, perishing bravely among the flames kindled by the conqueror.

Human history has been built up by the lives of women as well as men, and in order that they may progress and develop more rapidly in the future their failures as well as their successes must be studied, the silent as well as the self-seeking lives must be understood. We must not content ourselves merely with pleasant gossip concerning kings and queens, nor fire our imagination alone with the clang of warfare, but we must study the conduct of the peaceful and productive classes, whose advance is identified with civilization, and where women have played an equal part with men.

It has been said that the measure of a nation's true civilization is the position that it accords to its women, and this must be born in mind if we are truly appreciate the meaning of the development of our country in the present day.

In order to estimate the progress women have achieved comparison must be made with the past. Seeds have been sown by the thinkers of all ages, but the great part seemed to have fallen on arid ground until some 30 years ago.

In England, as early as the time of Daniel Defoe, Mary Astell had published 'An Essay in Defence of the Female Sex', in which she discussed the social position and education of women, and protested against their subjection to man. At the end of the 18th century, Mary Wollstonecraft gave expression to the new impulse which was gathering force, and pointed out that the first duty of women 'is to themselves as rational creatures, and the next in importance as citizens, in that which includes so many, of a mother'. But the first utterance which showed that women were beginning to realise the importance of obtaining the aid of the law to help their development appeared in the works of Mrs J. S. Mill in 1851. These were followed by John Stuart Mill's *Subjection to Women* [sic], a book which still stands out as the leading work on the whole question of woman's position.

The advance has been very slow in its first stages, yet it may now be extremely speedy, and after the long and patient plowing of the soil, and weary waiting in the chill winter of disapproval, the seed sown by the great thinkers may, in the light of a more civilized day, burst into blossom, and ultimately bring a new wealth of harvest to the world.

The educational movement has been well named the elder sister of the political movement; but, fifty years ago the education of women in England was practically non-existent. It was only in 1810 that Sidney Smith wrote his celebrated article in the Edinburgh Quarterly, 'Why should a woman of 40 years be more ignorant than a boy of 12?' The formation of Queen's College in 1846 by Rev T D Maurice [sic: F. D. Maurice] was the first step in obtaining adequate education for girls. In 1872, closely following in point of time the Education Act, which gave equal opportunities of elementary education to the girl and boys – the Girls' Public Day School Co. was formed. At the present moment women are able to study at all the Universities of Great Britain, although in some instances they are placed at a disadvantage, and neither Oxford not Cambridge will yet allow them to take their degree.

That which might have been expected by the student of Welsh History and Welsh Character has come to pass in a peculiar degree, in matters affecting women. Laws and Customs have been more repressive than in England, but, when the inherent forces in the nation, no longer repressible, have burst forth, action has been more swift and the results more sure. The women of Wales who, only a few years ago, were supposed to be behind the women of England, and were so in many respects, can now uplift their own standard to encourage their sisters across the border. Some sixteen years ago, when English women were making great strides in education, the women of Wales had little or no opportunity in training and culture. Now they have improved Elementary Education, and an Intermediate Schools Act which has helped hundreds of girls who cannot leave their homes to attend the College, the Colleges themselves affording them scope to attain a high level of intellectual proficiency, whilst the University of Wales, incorporated in 1893, fittingly crowns the educational structure of the Principality. Not only are women admitted as students on equal terms with men, but several have been elected to serve on the present University Court, and they are eligible to the highest and most honourable of its offices.

As to political progress, four year ago, when the Women's Liberal Federation had flourished for some years, there were only seven Associations in Wales to whom, for their early endeavours, great honour is due. When a progressive and Women's Suffrage Movement agitated the Women's Federation, a campaign was started in Wales, calling on women to unite for the sake of political progress, and urging them to assist the great Liberal effort that was being made to secure Home Rule for Ireland and Disestablishment for Wales. The result was encouraging. Forty-five new associations were formed during a single year. To secure the solidity and lasting value of such work it is necessary before all things that it should be widespread. It must be the work of the nation and not the work of the advance-guard only, and for this the sympathy of and cooperation of all are needed.

However clear the voice that calls a nation to bestir itself, the concord of many voices alone makes harmony. The leading women of Wales are therefore devoting themselves to two great ends; firstly, to widen opportunities and to obtain better laws for women, so that those who have the ability to be of special service in the government of public affairs may not be debarred on the grounds of sex; secondly, to persuade all women to make greater use than they have hitherto done of the opportunities for education and ennobling social service which have been opened to them by the Pioneers. For example, it is most important that the laws should be altered to allow qualified women to serve on County Councils. Such women as Miss Cons, who was actually elected as an Alderman, are only debarred from particular spheres of useful activity by law, against both public sentiment and general desire. On the other hand, it is equally important that women living in villages should have the courage to become Parish Councillors, and that every Board of Guardians should include sufficient women to do the work in which every good housekeeper, who cares for the poor, could render signal service.

In the work that women wish to do, the help of the press as well as the help of the politicians, and sympathy of the people is needed, but to make this of any use, not only occasional articles from experts, but the cooperation of all is needed.

The world is ready, if somewhat reluctantly, to acquiesce in the fact that there are exceptional women, but it must also accept the fact that there are average women, and on the average woman depends the welfare of the world – just as far as she chooses to support the higher ideal which some more far-seeing sister has uplifted.

The Editors of *Young Wales* are anxious to open their paper to progressive women, and the Editors of the 'Progress of Women' page think that they can best serve the end in view by studying the various movements which combine to make the women's movement. They desire to make known to women their past and present condition in educational, social, religious, philanthropic and political spheres, that, out of the knowledge and sympathy which will ensue, they may cooperate even more closely than in the past to hasten a development which has brought unspeakable blessings already.

The national movement in Wales has identified itself in the woman's cause. The national organisation has pledged itself to 'promote citizenship for women with men' as one of its objects, and the 'Wales that is to be' will be the better, because in it the desires of women as well as of men will have found fulfilment, and because they have served each other with loyalty and sympathy whilst uniting to attain an ideal that all may share.

15. Anna Jones

Women and Religious Freedom (1895)

Young Wales, vol. 1, no. 3, March 1895.

I do not think that we realize sufficiently what an active part the women of Wales took one hundred and fifty years ago in the first beginnings of that great Nonconformist movement which has proved such a tremendous force in the development of Welsh national life. It is not only within recent years that Welsh women have awakened to their responsibilities. They did splendid work in the past, and helped to make their country what it is in the present day. We know that before the Nonconformist revival, owing to the neglect of the Established Church, the people had sunk into practical heathenism. The country was raised from this condition entirely through the energetic efforts and self-sacrifices of men and women who left the Church (which had become corrupt, and therefore useless for the purposes for which it was maintained) and gave themselves up to the great work of furthering the cause of religion and education.

It is a matter of history that they suffered terrible persecution on account of this at the hands of those who were in authority in the Church and among the privileged classes. The women took a very prominent part in this crusade – in fact, in many families they took the initiative, and were the means of winning over their relatives of the other sex. These women were decidedly progressive, for we read of one church at Tonyrefail, in South Wales, being kept together, during these times of persecution, by only eight faithful members, all women, and of how they discharged the various offices connected with it. This Church grew and flourished, and eventually became one of the most important in that part of the country.

No small number of these early Nonconformist Churches were founded by women. Jane Griffith, a schoolmistress, originally from Dolbenmaen, Caernarvonshire, first started services at Dolgelley in the year 1776. She, like all who engaged in the same work, had to endure great persecution. On one occasion, during the holding of a religious service in her house, her persecutors stormed the door, threatening to kill her, but before they could enter, another woman hid her in a flour bin. Owing to constant oppression she was ultimately forced to leave the town, but not before she had succeeded in laying the foundation of a great work.

The title of 'Lowri Williams the Apostle' was given to a remarkable woman who lived as Pandy'rddwyryd, in Merioneth. Through her instrumentality eighteen Churches were established in the western part of the county. She also suffered greatly for conscience sake. Her persecutors once set upon her on the road when she was travelling to Maentwrog, and deliberately threw her into the river. She was so seriously hurt through having fallen on some stones at the bottom of the river that she endured great suffering, and could not move from her bed for a length of time.

These heroines of Welsh Nonconformity are not few and far between, and I wish the space would allow of my mentioning a few more.

We in the present day can hardly realize the enormity of the difficulties they had to contend with in those hard and troublesome times, or of the great sacrifices which they made, travelling long distances over rugged mountains, braving storms and cold, enduring hardship and all kinds of persecution, all for the sake of furthering the cause they loved so much. Every ignominy that could be thought of was heaped upon them, and like all pioneers in the work of reform they were scoffed at and stigmatised as fanatics and heretics.

Many widows suffered at the hands of harsh and tyrannical landlords on account of their having publicly joined this band of reformers. A widow of the name of Margaret Hughes, of Llansanon, Denbighshire, who held a farm, was evicted by her landlord for holding Nonconformist services in her house (she had continued the services after Edward Parry, of the same neighbourhood had been turned out of his home for 'harbouring heretics'). She and her children had to take temporary refuge in a wretched hovel on the corner of a common, which could not even be called a proper shelter from the wind and the rain. But through all her trials she worked more and more for the great cause, and when at last a kind-hearted landlord had compassion upon her and took her as a tenant she again continued the services which had been interrupted by the vindictiveness of her former landlord.

In addition to what she had already gone through she, with a number of others, were set upon and ill-treated while holding a service at the house of a certain Thomas Lloyd, from where they had to flee with their lives. Margaret Hughes fared worse than her comrades for she was pursued and again subjected to ill-treatment. Her clothing was torn from her body, and had not a gentleman who happened to be passing at the time come to her rescue, she would in all probability have been killed. Most of her tormentors belonged, as was usually the case, to the aristocracy and privileged classes.

When we consider how these people, from then on, thwarted and tyrannised over those who were in a kind of servitude to them, we cannot wonder at the chasm that exists in Wales today between the landlord and tenant classes. There was then and is still a distinct difference of language, habits, ideas, and, above all, in the form of religious services which divides these two classes. There were some notable exceptions to this rule. Anne Bowen, of Tyddyn, who belonged to a county family in Montgomeryshire, and her daughter Sarah, were associated with Hywel Harris in his work, his home being a great centre of this movement, and her descendants to this day, from generation to generation, have followed in her footsteps.

We must not forget that we owe much to the women of our own time for continuing and carrying on this struggle for religious freedom. Their names are well known throughout North and South Wales, and they are undoubtedly making their mark upon the history of the times.

Wales has risen to the position it now holds as regards Religion, Education, Temperance and other social reforms, through the efforts of Nonconformity, and we, women of today, should feel that to us has been handed down the duty of rendering every aid in our power towards the final accomplishment of this great work. Every Liberal Welsh woman who is a worker on behalf of the cause which is first and foremost in our national aspirations may take courage from the thought that she is treading in the paths cut out by her noble countrywomen who were in the forefront of the struggle at the start.

We have now reached a crisis in the history of our country. The realization of our hopes and aspirations seems at hand. So we must unite as men and women who have a common cause, and spare no effort to bring about the great end we have so long looked forward to – the Disestablishment and Disendowment of the English Church in Wales.

16. Gwyneth Vaughan

Women and their Questions (1897)

Young Wales, vol. 3, no. 25, January 1897.

We are now entering upon another year. It is thus opportune to cast a retrospective glance over the doings and the non-doings of the time that has gone by. The year of 1896 has witnessed many a battle in the cause of women. Some were bravely fought and won; others were as bravely fought and lost. But I doubt if even those that might be counted among the lost were not after all a moral victory for women. Surely, there ought to have been a more worthy plea than that the wearing of university degrees by women – who had nobly won them – would interfere with the vested interests of men, and I venture to predict that it will not be long before we shall see these old universities – which, by the way, were first brought into a possibility of existence by women – submitting to the just verdict of a mature public opinion.

Politically, the air is thick with women's questions. In the United States we find legislators at their wits' end how best to cramp the possibilities of that most 'dangerous' part of the community known as female. Let us hope it will be their last attempt at law-making without the assistance of their sisters' brain power; who will very probably be able to throw some light on several perplexing problems, the vain attempts to solve which, I am told, are the causes of premature baldness and grey hairs so common among our statesmen.

In France, also, we find that no fewer than five different bills are before the Chamber and Senate, which, when they become law, will confer very real benefits upon the women of that country. Coming nearer home, it is with a glad heart that I feel that the men of my own land are in the vanguard of reform, with a very few exceptions, and those we need not worry about. The men of Wales encourage their mothers, wives, sisters, and daughters, in their highest aspirations after the noble, the true, and the beautiful, and rejoice with them in all their achievements. We have John Bull as usual lagging behind in his own thick-headed fashion, but are we not justified by the histories of other movements in hoping that where –

> The vanguard camp to-day,
> The rear will camp to-morrow.

It is not much more than a hundred years ago that Mary Wollstonecraft wrote her book with the object in view of proving that woman was a human being. It is only about fifty years since John Stuart Mill came forth and pleaded that woman being a human being should have the equal rights and privileges of a human being. Today, at the close of the century we may sum up the outlook by saying that women have their future in their own hands. If we show that we deserve liberty, it will be ours sooner than perhaps many of us think. If our souls are dwarfed and stunted in the future, we shall have only ourselves to blame, because we have not been able to keep the vantage ground gained for us by the noble and self-sacrificing lives of those brave pioneers of our freedom. If I were asked what is our duty in life today, my answer would be – to teach our women the necessity of being able to do at least some one thing well. How few, alas! are able to say that, we can scarcely realise. Nevertheless it is quite true. We send our boys into the world fully equipped for the battle of life, but we allow our girls to be brought up in as helpless a manner as *knowing a little* about half a dozen things can possibly make them. Let us train up our girls as we train up our boys. Let there be no smattering of accomplishments. Give the women some one thing that is real in their lives; surely we have had shams enough and to spare? Let us not rest content until every girl holds in her own hand a bread-winning weapon, for the economic position of women must attain its proper level before it is possible for them to take their places on that higher platform we would fain see them occupy. It is then, and only then, that there will dawn the new and better era for the womanhood, and let me add, the manhood of our country. Possibly some of our sons may not realise that, while struggling for the freedom of our daughters, we have also their cause as near to our hearts. But it is even so. She who is good and noble as a woman cannot be other than good and noble in all her relations to man. Let our motto then be – *Onward and upward.* Be worthy of our freedom, worthy of our rights. Let us be ourselves, but not living for ourselves, but rather for the good that we can do. There is immense scope for work on this round earth for the cool, cultivated intellect, and the warm woman's heart.

17. 'Un o'r ddau Wynne' (Alis Mallt Williams)

Patriotism and the Women of Cymru (1898)

Young Wales, vol. 4, no. 41, May 1898

In after years, may the 26th May, 1898, stand out as the beginning of a new era, in the national life of Cymru. For on that day, in an historical London house, a band of ladies gather, under the leadership of Lady Eva Wyndham-Quinn (a representative of one of the few really old Celtic families of Erin), pledged to support and extend the Home Industries of the Principality.

We all know of the great success that has crowned the efforts of the Irish and Scottish Associations, and it is intended to carry out the Welsh Association on the same lines. Such a society will supply a long-felt want in Cymru.

Spinning and weaving, the most picturesque and graceful of all occupations for women, will be revived. Very old patterns of Welsh flannels, and other dress materials, sought out and brought into use again; knitting, carving, pottery, and any other home work will be assisted, and a depot for the sale of such work provided.

The object of this society: To find employment for poor families in the cultivation of their national talents, in their own home and country, thus providing a check to emigration (the emptying of the old land, the old race) is a most laudable one, and it is to be hoped the women of Cymru will rally round the new Association, and so help to make it a real power for good in the land.

For women's influence is paramount in the world, and hitherto the women of Cymru have not cared to use that influence for their country's weal. They have not learnt even the A, B, C, of patriotism. *That* is a virtue they have not cultivated, - hardly recognize. Facts speak for themselves. They have banished an ancient Celtic tongue – their *mother* tongue – the tongue of saints and heroes and princes, from the drawing-room, the school-room and the nursery. They have allowed the picturesque national dress to die out, though ladies in foreign courts take pride in wearing their national dress on gala days.

They have brought up their children in perfect ignorance of the history, poetry, and legends of their own country.

In a word, they have shown no inclination to uphold the *individuality* of their ancient race. But oh! Wives and daughters of Cymru! – of the pure, native blood, – as distinct from Norman houses and English settlers – shake off the apathy of an inglorious past, and show the world of today – the future, that the heroic virtue is not dead in you, has only been asleep.

18. 'Matron'

i. On Women's Work in the Family, Poverty and Housing

Rhondda Socialist, December 1911
Our Women's Column

Out-Heroding Herod:
The Infantile Mortality of the Rhondda

'Then Herod sent forth and slew all the children that were in Bethlehem from two years old and under'
'In Rama was there a voice heard, lamentation and weeping and great mourning, Rachel weeping for her children and would not be comforted because they are not.'

(Matthew II, 16, 18).

770 babies under 1 year old died in the Rhondda area during the year 1910. Herod slew a score or so, but who 'slew all these?'

The following statistics, taken from the Medical Officer of Health's Report for the year 1910, for the Rhondda area, ought to give cause for present thinking and future action.

During the year 1910, the number of births was 5,628 and the number of deaths under a year was 770. This makes an infantile mortality rate of 137 per 1000. The total number of deaths for all ages was 2,181. Thus one death in every three occurring is that of an infant under twelve months old. More than half the deaths occurring are those of children under 15 years of age.

A comparison with other places in the country is striking. Burnley stands highest on the list with an infantile mortality of 170 per 1000. The Rhondda area comes seventh on the list, and is equalled by Blackburn and Stockport. Compared with other localities in Wales, Rhondda stands highest. Merthyr Tydfil comes next with 134 per 1000; Swansea has a rate of 124 per 1000; and Cardiff a rate of 112 per 1000. The average rate of infantile mortality for England and Wales for 1910 is 106 per 1000.

Causes of death

The main causes which carry off these little ones are classed under the name of lung diseases, debility, diarrhoea, convulsions, prematurity, etc.

These diseases are for the most part preventable. 80 per cent of the infants born are said to be healthy. Nature has so ordained that the race shall have a fair start, and even the babes of weakly mothers are born as healthy as others.

The Report (page 16) says: 'No fewer than 150 of the total deaths were attributed to some form of intestinal trouble and altogether with 94 deaths from "convulsions" and the 180 from atrophy, debility, and marasmus' a considerable portion of them might doubtless have been prevented.'

If preventable why not prevented?

The Health Officer attributes much of the loss to the want of sufficient 'attention and knowledge on the part of mothers and others'.

What up to the present has the Rhondda Urban District Council done to increase the knowledge and displace the ignorance of the mothers? The Council has appointed two lady health visitors! Two Health Visitors for 5,628 babies scattered over an area nearly 17 miles long! One district, supervised by one of the visitors extends from Fernhill to Ton; the other district supervised by the only other visitor extends from Tonypandy to Hafod. Thus, Gelli, Llwynpia, Clydach Vale and the whole of Rhondda Fach are left out. The death rate in these latter places averages 12 per 1000 less and so in the opinion of an indifferent Council may safely be neglected.

It is time this policy of neglect ceased.

A redivision of the districts and the appointment of sufficient health visitors – fully trained and qualified – to cover the whole area is the least a humanitarian can ask for. We believe that much good work has been done by the visitors already appointed, but in order to give them a fair opportunity to educate the mothers, their efforts must be concentrated within smaller areas. Their visits could then be made with greater frequency and longer time spent over each infant. Many of these mothers are very young and quite amenable to instruction and advice concerning their infants. Give them more opportunities to be taught and more teachers.

Cause of poverty

We believe the source of this wastage of infant life lies much deeper than the mere lack of knowledge on the mothers' part. The social condition of the mothers of the Rhondda is far from ideal. The pinch of poverty is felt in most homes where there is a young family. Poverty and high rent mean that the mother, in order to keep the home going, must meet part of the expense by keeping lodgers, or sharing the house with another family. The infant suffers in either case. Its nursery is the kitchen, where all the labour of the house, washing, baking, cooking is carried on. The atmosphere is, as a rule, over-heated, stuffy and ill-ventilated. The average kitchen floor of cold stone slabs is a death trap for infants at the creeping stage. Stone slabs may be the correct thing for an outhouse but are not a suitable material for a living room for human beings. Labour men please note. In connection with the housing problem, we quote from page 75 of the Report: 'No serious attempt has been made to meet the demands of the childless or very small families by the provision of a smaller and less expensive house, consisting of a kitchen, scullery, two or preferably three bedrooms, pantry and the necessary sanitary conveniences. There appears to be no insurmountable reason why the scullery of such a house should not be provided with a bath without increasing the total cost to such an extent as to make impracticable the profitable letting of the house at twenty or twenty-two shillings per month of four weeks.'

The above recommendation of the health officer is worth noting. A small house with a rental of 20/- to 22/- would be preferable to most mothers with young families, to the apartment-letting or lodger-keeping business. When apartments are sub-let it is customary for the landlord to extract his second 'pound of flesh' in the form of a considerable rise in the rent, and the parties concerned are not much better off financially, while considerably limited in convenience.

With a lower rental, lodger-keeping on the part of the expectant mother could in many cases be dispensed with. It is not infrequently the case that the mother is working hard over the wash-tub till the last moment before the birth of her child – a proceeding that can have but one result, that of weakened offspring. Again, the time and attention which under the circumstances are required to be given to lodger-keeping could very well be devoted to the interests of the young child.

A pure milk supply

Another cause of infantile mortality is undoubtedly the lack of a pure milk supply. With regard to the sources of our milk supply, we quote from the Report page 78: 'The greater proportion of the milk sold within the Rhondda is obtained from areas beyond the district, chiefly from the rural portions of Glamorgan, although no inconsiderable quantity is derived from England, especially Somersetshire

'There are in the district 50 cowsheds, many of which

are connected with the farms dotted on the hills skirting the two valleys... These premises, as well as the 155 dairies and milkshops in use throughout the district are periodically inspected by the Sanitary Inspectors, *but no provision has yet been made by the Council for the veterinary examination of the cows for the detection of various forms of tuberculosis and other diseases.*

'The present arrangements do nor admit of the systematic examination of samples of milk for the tubercle bacillus, although the Council in the Act of 1905 obtained special powers for the purpose of discovering and dealing with tuberculous milk sold in the district, as well as cows having tuberculous udders'.[1]

We wish to direct the attention of all who care for the health of infants and children to the latter points. It means that milk containing the tubercle bacillus can be freely sold in the Rhondda area. [...]

The milk supply, the housing conditions, the grinding poverty of the people and the consequent hard, incessant toil put upon the mothers have more to do with the high death rate among infants than either carelessness or wilful ignorance on their part. The unfavourable conditions can only be completely overcome by a Socialist state.

In the meantime, the housing at present so detrimental to infant life can be much improved by a Council actuated by humanitarian motives. Houses take time to build; it would take less time to set in motion the machinery necessary to ensure the purity and freshness of our milk supply. The present state of affairs can only be regarded as 'gross negligence' on the part of those entrusted with the well-being of the community.

In a future issue we hope to deal with the question of a municipal milk supply.

*

---

[1] Matron's emphasis.

Rhondda Socialist, 11 April 1912
Our Women's Column

An Eight Hour Day for Women

'Eight hours work
Eight hours play
Eight hours sleep
Eight shillings a day.'

Men have reached a stage in their industrial history when the sentiment expressed in the first of these lines is an accomplished fact, and the last is within sight. When are women to accomplish a similar ideal in life, and reach the same stage in their progress?

It is frankly owned that the legislation which conferred an eight-hour day upon men, without intending to do so, added to the hours of women's work in the home. An advance which creates such a glaring inequality can only be justified by the reduction of that inequality through the lessening of the hours of labour of the working woman. Very few women have realised the possibility of such a reduction in their working hours. When they begin to believe in the possibility, a move will be made in that direction. Legislation has already fixed the hours of women's labour in factories and workshops, but it is unlikely that legislators will ever interfere with women's hours of work in the home. The effort towards such a reduction in hours must be directed by women themselves. The nature and conditions of women's work in the home is unlike that in any other sphere of labour.

Eight shillings a day
The labour done by the majority of women in their homes is largely unrequited labour – unrequited in the sense that there is no wage paid and no monetary value placed upon

such services. When a women marries she does not, under ordinary circumstances, drive a bargain of the domestic type with her partner. She does not lay down her minimum – so much per week or month, so many evenings out, and Sundays off. On the other hand, he does not ask for guarantees against malingering. The marriage contract, and the work which, in consequence, falls upon the women is accepted not in a bargaining, commercial spirit, but is undertaken under the sense of personal attachment and free social service. It is the case that many men accept the labour of their wives in the home as a contribution which does not count in money value. Some may even fail to see its social and moral value to the community. A deeper insight into the work of women in the home reveals the fact that women's labour fulfils the Socialist ideal of production for use, and not for profit.

Women, therefore, are the pioneers of practical Socialism. If one section of the community can fulfil their duty without pay or hope of reward, in the marketable sense, so can all. The ungrudging, unselfish service of the great majority of women in the home is the prelude to the time when we shall all contribute unselfish, ungrudging service to the common stock.

An eight-hour day for women will come through the introduction of many other much needed reforms, such as convenient housing and the public supply of light, heat and water, which we hope to deal with in another issue.

Some benighted people may be asking: 'What do women want with an eight-hour day?' In an article in the *Christian Commonwealth*, Mr. Vernon Hartshorn is reported to have said with regard to the young collier: [2]

> 'The young colliers read more… That has opened their eyes to the fact that life ought not to mean a monotonous,

---

[2] Vernon Hartshorn, official of the South Wales Miners' Federation, later MP and member of the Labour government's of the 1920s.

weary round toil of [*sic*], unrelieved by any touch of imagination and poetry. They are beginning to want very earnestly the privileges of leisure and freedom from anxiety in order to enjoy life as they feel they can. Life is…. inconceivably cramped and limited.'

What is good for the collier is good for his young wife and sister. These are also inconceivably 'cramped and limited' in mind and in outlook upon life. They have no leisure or freedom from tiring drudgery, and nothing to lift them from the sordidness of the actual, into the hope and exaltation of the ideal.

Women need more leisure to rest their bodies, and more leisure in which to cultivate an acquaintance with the world of literature and the intellect. If the young collier's ideal is large enough to include his women folk as well as himself, he will nor rest satisfied with merely carrying a bigger wage home. His attention must be directed to the question of the women's awakening to their sphere of leisure and culture in the social improvement of the community. The woman must be lifted up along with the man, and the standard of home life raised along with the standard of wages.

*

Rhondda Socialist, 11 May 1912.
Our Women's Column

The Housing Question and the Lessening of Women's Hours of Work.

[….]There is not much poetry in this week's column. One cannot write poetry over the scrubbing of floors, blackleading of grates and the smell of soapsuds. Yet what has been written may cause many women to ask why should we be condemned to this treadmill of work, when by means of the application of some simple inventions our labour could be reduced by one half?

When the inventions and discoveries of Science are applied to the service of humanity, and not held up as sources of profit to the few, these inventions and discoveries will be used to make a home life truly possible.

Then women shall have the chance of devoting their energies to the higher interests of themselves and their children.

*

Rhondda Socialist, 8 June 1912.
Our Women's Column

'Household Gods'

Much of the social salvation of women depends upon their power to discriminate between the essentials of true living and the artificial bonds of custom. Our ordinary and extraordinary household gods are the acretions [sic] of past stupid customs.

Idol smashing is a painful, yet wholesome and essential business. Shall we begin to grow wiser, and try how many of these bits of brass, pieces of china and yards of frilling we can do without? […]

The sight of a woman on her knees at this job [scrubbing pavements] fills one with disgust. Where does the dignity and glory of womanhood come in here? Why should we waste precious life on insensate paving stones?

ii. On Women's Equality and the Political Parties

Rhondda Socialist, January 1912
Our Women's Column

Woman Suffrage:
The Socialist Position and the Promised Reform Bill

The Labour and Socialist Party has always insisted upon Adult Suffrage as the only equal, just and complete solution to the present anomalies of our electoral system.

The Liberal Government has resolved to place the present electoral muddle in order and in doing so has given an undertaking to grant manhood Suffrage. This extension of the suffrage to men is to be backed up by the full force of the Party machine.

Throughout the country there has been no widespread demand by men for Manhood Suffrage. There has been a very strong and growing agitation for Woman Suffrage. Yet the Liberal government refuses to take the responsibility of even the smallest measure of granting the suffrage to women. Under this so-called Reform Bill, women are to be left to the tender mercies of a private member's amendment.

Liberalism means one-sided legislation – more votes for men and a shove back to serfdom for women.

With the hesitating equivocating, half-hearted 'trust of the people' party, we wish to contrast the strong, equitable and sure position of the Labour men. [...]

The Parliamentary Labour Party, at its meeting on Thursday, November 16, when Mr. Ramsay Macdonald presided passed the following resolution:

'That the Labour Party welcomes the announcement of the Prime Minister that it is the intention of the Government to deal next session with the question of electoral reform, reiterates its demand for a complete measure of adult suffrage, and declares that no measure for the extension of the franchise will be satisfactory which does not give votes to women.'[1]

[….] We believe the Labour Party's solution to this burning question is the only solution worth fighting for.

*

Rhondda Socialist March 1912
Our Women's Column

Untitled

A certain Liberal magnate in the Ton and Pentre district is reported to have cursed sulphurously over the advent of a woman suffragist in the locality. What is he afraid of, and if he is not afraid, why does he swear? He is a member of a chapel, too. We commend his soul to his minister, who might do worse that try to reform such a character. Should the Minister fail, the wife of this reprobate might succeed in bringing him to his sober senses. What an outburst over such an ordinary occurrence as the visit of a gentle and cultured lady to the Rhondda!

We, who have met and spoken to this lady, have only the choicest words of commendation of her many good and great qualities. She is richly and rarely endowed, intellectually and morally, with high ideals of what human life should be, and what human beings may become, she sees in the extension of the franchise to women the opportunity of women to help in the attainment of those ideals, and the hope of the elevation of the race that is to be.

But these are evidently not the ideals of the Liberals of the Rhondda towards the human race in general or women

---

[1] This position of the party brought about the 1912-14 electoral pact with the National Union of Women's Suffrage Societies.

in particular. In this crisis they prefer to follow Mr. Asquith rather than Mr. Lloyd George, their own countryman.[2] It is remarkable that while Liberal and Free Church women attended the meetings in large numbers, Liberal and Free Church men were largely absent. The men who during this campaign supported the women's cause, were all Labour men. All honour to them for so doing.

The Labour Party stands to gain more from manhood suffrage than from woman suffrage, yet on this occasion, where the interests of women are likely to be thwarted to suit the prejudices of a man holding the office of Prime Minister, they have nobly resolved to stand by the women and refuse a further concession of political power to men unless women are included. Such self-sacrifice is significant as a sign of the altruistic motives which shall actuate the future democracy.

The struggle which women of all classes are now waging for recognition as citizens of the land they live in has had its parallel in the history of the struggle which the labouring man has had for political freedom. Just as the full fruits of ages of agitation is reaching its perfection in the form of manhood suffrage, and the Labour man could grasp it and hold it, it is magnificent to see a whole party refrain and say, 'No, not yet. Here is my sister, the labouring woman; when you place her alongside we shall eat of the fruit together, and enter upon a fresh struggle to the betterment of the race as a whole.'

*

---

[2] The Prime Minister, Asquith, was an anti-suffragist; Lloyd George, Chancellor of the Exchequer, held an equivocal position – see following section of suffragist writings – but declared himself for a full and democratic measure of women's suffrage.

The Rhondda Socialist, 20 July 1912.

Women and the Liberal Party

In the year 1884 the passing of the Reform Act made it illegal to pay canvassers during elections.[3] It then occurred to some of the men of the Conservative Party to get this important work done by women on the voluntary principle. The move was a success, from the party standpoint, and the Primrose League was founded.

The Liberals, not to be behind, proceeded to form their women supporters into a similar organisation, and the Women's Liberal Federation came into existence in 1886. There are numbers of Liberal MPs today who owe their seats and honours, not to their intellectual abilities or administrative capacities, but solely to the hard work done by women on their behalf. The rule of the political game where men are concerned is, that party work deserves party favour, and brings political advantages. We have yet to see what political advantages women have gained for their self-sacrificing work on behalf of Liberal candidates. The utmost that the leaders of the party have done is to mouth flattering speeches – metaphorically speaking – to tip the women under the chin, pat them on the back, and commend them for behaving like quiet, womanly women.

In all cases where the Liberal party have had the opportunity of dispensing justice or granting privileges and reforms amongst men and women, the women have been treated as an inferior class.

---

[3] The relevant act was the *Corrupt and Illegal Practices Prevention Act* of 1883, which preceded the 1884 Reform Act; the latter extended the franchise among sections of the male working class.

Dispensation of Justice

With regard to the former, we have only to compare the treatment of women political offenders with the treatment accorded to men.

For inciting soldiers to mutiny, Mr. Tom Mann received two months, as compared with nine months for Mrs. Pankhurst and Mr. and Mrs. Pethick Lawrence.[4] Seventy-five women are in prison now undergoing the tortures of the hunger strike in defence of their right to be treated as political offenders. The right of first division treatment is a right due to all political reformers. England and Russia are the only countries where prisoners have been driven to this extreme form of protest in defence of principle.

It is well to remember that Irishmen during the agitation for Home Rule were treated as first division prisoners, even although their agitation was marked by the commission of crimes. The offences of the women have only touched property; they have not injured life in their demand for reform.

The Granting of Privileges and Reforms

The Insurance Act is a glaring instance of the sex discrimination which is being created by the Liberal Government in a scheme intended to relieve the sick and prevent destitution. One would have thought that women who earn less wages, and are equally subject to sickness, would have entered this scheme on an equality of treatment, or at least that the widow would have received some advantage. But no – 10/- for men, 7/6 for women; married men included, married women excluded; the husband recognised, the wife ignored. If women lived in one part of this little island, and men in another part, we might be able to see some small reason for separating the sexes; but

---

[4] Tom Mann, Trade Unionist and labour agitator was gaoled in 1912 for his 'open letter' to British soldiers. Pankhurst and the Pethick Lawrences were the leaders of the militant suffrage organisation, the Women's Social and Political Union (WSPU).

when we remember that husband and wife sit at the same table and warm their toes at the hearth, the distinctions introduced become absurdities. The variations in scales of payment and scales of relief between men and women add enormously to the legal intricacies of the scheme, and will add greatly to the difficulties of administration.

One is left to believe that if the present Liberal Party had been asked to adjudicate in the affair in the garden of Eden, they would have turned Eve out and left Adam in.

Wages Paid under the Liberal Government
Under the Government contract system, the women workers are sweated by the Government contractors. Lord Haldane was responsible for an order whereby the sweated factory workers of Pimlico had their paltry wages reduced, thus robbing a sweated victim of a few more pence a week.

Post Office Clerks
The women clerks in the Money Order Department of the Post Office are at present being threatened with reductions in wages and status under the reforming zeal of Mr. Herbert Samuel.[5] Mr. Samuel has introduced a class of women clerks who shall be engaged at a lower salary, work longer hours, and have fewer holidays than the present staff. The increase in the work of the Money Order Department is due to the examining work of Postal Orders issued under the Old Age Pensions Act. The credit which the Liberal Government is taking for working the Act cheaply becomes discredit when it is done at the expense of underpaying the women postal clerks.

It is noticeable that in the new Insurance Office, no appointments over £110 per annum have been made to women clerks.

---

[5] Samuel was Postmaster General in the Liberal Cabinet.

Women Teachers

The women teachers of the country have also a deep grievance. They are paid at lower rates all round for doing equal work. The women teachers have a miserable yearly rise of £4, as against a man's £7.10s, and on reaching their maximum they are paid £50 a year less than men. Even at the beginning of their career, when the 'family wage' argument won't hold, the girl is paid £25 as against the boy's £40.

We have yet to learn that the booksellers allow cheaper rates, or the railway companies grant reduced fares for girls, or that the general expenses of board and education are in any way less, to make up for their smaller wages.

In conclusion, we would say to all women – if the privileges which the Liberal Party has the power to confer are denied to women, then the power of retaliation is in the hands of women. Let them refuse to help Liberal candidates into honours and office, or to be otherwise exploited by the party for party ends.

*

The Rhondda Socialist, 21 December 1912.

Women in the Labour Movement

'It needs women of my class to help women of your class'. So said Miss Margaret Ashton, of Manchester, a member of the City Council, addressing a crowd of working men and women during the annual conference meetings of the ILP held at Merthyr last year. The phrase stuck. How would it appear if a man of the same social position as Miss Ashton required to tell the average ILP'ers or Trade Unionists, 'It needs men of my class to help men of your class'. The assumption, we fear, would be repudiated, and the speaker told at once to mind his own business. The Liberal Party patronage of the working man is of this type, and has been – and is still – accepted by some working men. But the new Labour movement rejects the proffered help of the middle-class man. The realisation of their own power to effect their own well being has upset Tory and Liberal patronage. The whole value of the working-class uprising lies in the fact that it is not an effort of the middle-class man to help those lower in social status to a higher level, but that the roots of the up growth are in the working men themselves. Men have grown up in the ranks of the workers whose ambition is not to rise out of their class and forget 'the base degrees by which they did ascend' but who remain heart and soul with the workers in their struggle.

But when we examine the women's side of the Labour movement we begin to see the point of Miss Ashton's statement. How many women who have worked in factory or workshop, or who have served their time as a working man's wife, or brought up a family on a working man's wage, and therefore know the struggle, are leading in the Women's Labour Movement? The Women's Labour League, founded to benefit working women, is a case of the women of the middle class bending to help women of the working class. All the names of women prominent in the Labour Movement are women who have come into the movement out of sympathy, and not out of a real experience of the working woman's needs and struggles. They are not women of the working class.

There is something to account for this difference between the Labour Movement as evolved by men and the Labour Movement as evolved by women. The lower economic position of the working women partly accounts for the position. These women cannot afford to pay secretaries, agents and leaders to give their time to organisation, etc. These upper-class women step in; they have money and leisure to bestow, and they do the work gratuitously. But if working-class women are ever to be anything else but a subject class, they must work out their own social and political salvation from within. This is particularly true with regard to the wives of working men.

While progress is being recorded all round, they are still in a primitive state of domestic slavery. Knowledge is wanted; enlightenment, a new hope, that they may being [sic] to see their way to make changes in their domestic affairs which will bring them to more hum and a sweeter condition of life.

It is with the position of these working-class wives in the local Labour Movement I shall now deal. There are five bodies which at present represent the local Labour Movement: (1) The Central Labour College Classes; (2) Branches of the ILP; (3) Trades and Labour Councils; (4) Lodges of the Miners' Federation; (5) Urban District Council.

Labour Classes

The educational classes of the Central Labour College are formed for men and women. How many women are attending these classes throughout the valley? They are few, if any. As to the cause, I do not believe it lies in any mental incapacity in the women to understand the subjects dealt with, or to any deep disinclination on their part to try and improve their minds. Most of the attendance at these classes is due to the personal influence of one man upon another. How much persuasion has been extended to women? Has any encouragement been given them to attend, or has cold water been thrown over any little enthusiasm they might have had?

ILP branches

These are conducted almost with a total disregard to the existence of women in the district or to matters in which women are interested. How many women members are there in the valley? Where are the wives, daughters and sisters of the men who run affairs? Are the women wanted as members? Whether or not, they are needed in order that a serious attempt may be made to grapple with the evil social conditions.

The Lodges

A smile will arise at the notion of a collier's wife attending a lodge meeting, and yet how much of what is settled there involves the lives of the women. Have men any moral right to settle matters which concern the lives of women as well as their own without consulting the women? There are times and occasions when an open meeting of the lodge could be held, and the women concerned consulted in matters.

Trades and Labour Councils

As these bodies are constituted, it seems an impossibility for any working women to become a member thereof. A shop girl, teacher or domestic servant of a Trade Union may, but the whole class of wives are debarred from any activity through these bodies. I have the rules of one of these Councils which are so framed.

Urban District Councils

With all these avenues of labour activity partly or entirely closed to women the obvious absence of women from this public body causes no surprise. It is impossible for any woman to be chosen for election by the organisations which hold the strings. Women of the wealthy and leisured classes are limited, even if their sympathies were Labour and they elected to run as independent candidates. What is needed to make the Labour Party on the Council genuinely representative of the people is one or more women of the working class, whose interest is not the result of pity from a distance, but the effect of life's contact with working-class conditions. It is exceedingly difficult for an individual, however keen, to accomplish any social work as an individual; but united with others of similar aims much can be achieved.

I should like to make an appeal for the women, with an alternation from the words of Miss Ashton. It is this: It needs the men of the working class to help the women of the working class. The women of the working class must be brought into the Labour Movement by their own flesh and blood.

19. 'R.C.'

Swansea & District Workers' Journal, April 1912
Our Women's Column

The Women's Labour League

The Editor has very kindly placed a column of the 'Journal' at our disposal, and has asked me – by way of an introduction – to explain why we want the wives and daughters of the men of the Labour Movement to join the Labour League.

We are frequently told that a woman's place is in the home, that she should stay at home and mind the baby or darn her husband's socks, and that, therefore, the Women's Labour League and such like bodies are not necessary.

The persons who reason in this way never stop to consider whether all women have homes, or whether all homes are fit places for the women and the children to stay in. Thousands, nay hundreds of thousands, of women in this country of ours either have no homes or the 'homes' they have are not fit places for them to live in. In most of our large cities the 'homes' of the poor are but dark, unhealthy workshops, in which the women, and very often the little children too, are doomed to toil, day in and day out, week after week without respite.

Many of the homes in our town are unhealthy hovels, in which a rich man would not keep his dogs, but in which very often two or three families are compelled to exist. Most of the homes of the poor in Swansea are in mean, dirty, often ill-kept and unhealthy streets. The poor are herded in damp, dilapidated and insanitary dens. Should this be? Can women not help to change these horrible things?

Often the husband is out of work for long periods and more often when working, he is very miserably and inadequately paid. How then can a woman keep a home and children decently when she is always short of cash? How can she keep her children well fed and comfortably clad without sufficient money? And who should know best what is 'sufficient' to keep a husband and family upon? Are these not questions affecting women?

Most working men bring home with them their employers' dirt. Their occupations are such that their cloths and boots and bodies get covered with dirty. And, under present conditions, this dirt they bring home with them. Is it no concern of the women, whose work in the home is thus made infinitely harder? But these things cannot be altered unless women take an interest in the making of the laws.

Nowadays hardly a law is placed upon the Statute Book which does not, to a more or less degree, affect women. If women took more interest in politics and the making of the laws they would be able to see that the surroundings of their homes were more pleasant, that the conditions under which they and their husbands and sons lived and worked, were improved.

At present there are no places provided for the children to play in, and they have to play in the streets. Surely, that is a question upon which the working women of our town should have an opinion?

Again, the Education Authority has it in its power to feed the necessitous children every day. Are all the children who require food being fed? And are they being fed properly? These are things which women should interest themselves in.

Are you satisfied that all these things are quite satisfactory? Don't you know – of course you do – that all these things could be bettered and improved? Then why don't you come and assist us to put them right and to get them bettered? These are some of the reasons why we want all the workers' wives and daughters to join the Women's Labour League. We believe that women have public rights and duties, and we believe they should assert the former and perform the latter.

Will you join us? We offer you a cordial invitation to join the Swansea Branch, which meets every Tuesday, at 8pm, in the Gas Workers' Hall (opposite Arcade), Alexandra Rd.

*

Swansea & District Workers' Journal, May 1912
Our Women's Column

Women and the Labour Movement

Although women are deprived of the right of citizenship, this has not prevented them from learning the duties of citizens and performing them as far as they are able. We believe that the Women's Question has its relation to the Municipality and the State as well as to industrial organisation. The women of the Labour Movement and of the Cooperative Guild appreciate this view.

Old narrow ways of thinking have given way to broader views of life. Years ago I held the view that there was no need for me to possess a vote, but I have now come to the conclusion that women are absolutely justified in claiming that they should have a voice in the making of the laws. On carrying my mind back and reviewing the work done by the women of the Cooperative Guild, I find that excellent work has been done. Some of them have worked on Boards of Guardians, and the men at first bitterly resented this encroachment by women on their special preserves. But this resentment and indignation has been lived down, and now expressions such as: 'I don't know what we should do without our Women Guardians', and such like, are often heard. Thus we are forced to the conclusion that men and women must work together harmoniously in order to bring about a better state of things, and we of the Women's Labour League are anxious to do all we can in this direction. We want the wives and daughters of our ILP members to take a real active interest in the work of the League, to attend the meetings and to assist in propaganda work. This cannot be done unless the men of the movement sacrifice a little of their leisure time in order to afford their wives an opportunity of attending our meetings, where they will be able to obtain a keener insight into the aims and objects of the League. By this means they will become possessed of a fund of information which cannot fail to convert even the most indifferent and apathetic.

I know it is difficult to leave home where there are little children, but such difficulties as these can easily be overcome by a little self-sacrifice on the part of our male friends. This is an opportune time to direct the attention of men and women to self improvement and enlightenment upon subjects which affect their political and social well-being. The populace can never hope to attain their proper position as citizens until they fully realise the importance of obtaining as much knowledge as they properly can. Evil fattens upon ignorance. The cultivation of character must be fostered in our people if they are to see that our country is to be governed by representatives of the highest worth. This strength of character can never be produced until we create and encourage a real taste and desire for enlightenment. Hope for the future progress lies in the instilling of the 'truth' into the minds of our working men and women. It is absolutely necessary that women should take an active interest in the work of the municipality and the State, in so far as they are affected by and have to submit to the laws of the realm.

We are entering more and more into the world's work, and every day becoming a force to be reckoned with. Consequently, as our movement increases in numbers so the necessity of training our members in the rights, duties and responsibilities of citizenship becomes more imperative. It is natural to expect that we should meet with many disappointments, but we must not be discouraged. Disappointments must act as a stimuli to more determined action.

Our visions of future happiness for the toiling millions of our population will only be realised if we remain true to our faith and ideals. A great principle has often a very small and humble source. It progresses slowly, apparently uncertain in its course, but finally it reaches its goal.

Our Labour League is gradually developing from a comparatively insignificant source, and is acquiring for itself a reputation for good which can only be sustained by the loyalty of its members. Let us therefore, as members of the Swansea Labour League, do all that lies in our power to help in our humble way to bring about the social redemption of our toiling brothers and sisters.

*

Swansea and District Workers Journal , November 1913

The Women's Labour League

Object
The object of the WLL is to form an organisation of women to work for Independent Labour Representation in connection with the Labour Party, and to obtain direct Labour Representation of Women in Parliament and on all local bodies.

Method

1. The members of the Society will work with the Labour Party, locally and nationally, and help Labour's candidates in local and Parliamentary elections.
2. They will educate themselves in political and social questions by means of meetings, discussions, distribution of literature, such as leaflets etc.
3. They will take an active interest in the work of the Poor Law Guardians, Educational bodies, Distress Committees, Town, District, and County Councillors and Members of Parliament.
4. They will work to secure the full rights of citizenship for all men and women.
5. They will watch the interests of working women in their own neighbourhood, and strive, where possible, to improve their social and industrial condition.

The WLL is about 8 years old, but we are proud to say we are now advancing from our spring time, and that we are now founded upon a rock.

To the outsider, to a woman who, like Martha, is cumbered about everything except one thing that makes all the rest bright and clear, or to the woman who wraps herself up in narrow and selfish prejudices, our movement may seem to have no beauty – no inspiration. It may seem silly for the housewife to hurry with her scrubbing so as to spare time to address envelopes in a dingy back room for some labour election, or to go from door to door in the biting cold or the blazing heat, leaving political leaflets, or asking for signatures to some petition in favour of school feeding, or baths and wash houses for working women. It may seem blind obstinacy for the factory girl to risk discharge from her means of bread-winning, because she will stand up for the rights of her fellow workers, and will not hide her convictions from the foreman who is reducing wages so as to stand well with his master. It may seem at first blush a round-about way of looking after one's husband, and children to send men to Parliament to oppose the negligence of railway directors and colliery owners, or to elect men and women to the Town Council to ensure better sanitary conditions for the home. It may seem undignified for the University women to fraternise with the mill hand, and to defer to the opinions of a so-called social inferior, however sensible she may be.

Those of us who are in the movement feel we are only just learning what life means. Medical inspection of school children brings a ray of Divine hope into a mother's heart, and we women of the Labour League, together with the Cooperative Guild in Swansea, went a step further, and helped to bring a ray into the grey life of the slums by our deputation to the Guildhall, where we pointed out that Medical inspection did not dive down far enough, and that there should be a school clinic established in Swansea. Today we can boast of our success, and we earnestly appeal for more women to come into our ranks and help us to carry on our noble work. 'Unity is strength, divided we fall'. We have no age limit in the League. Its members range from 17 to 70 years. I may state that all are young in spirit, young in enthusiasm and faith and energy. We do no want to organise ourselves separately from the men, but we have found that the best way to cooperate effectively with them is to educate ourselves, to teach ourselves to discuss and understand, and to take responsibility in our own meetings, and thus to increase our powers, and at the same time our powers for the right. The fact that the Labour Party is composed in the main of Trade Unionists, men were coming by hundreds and thousands into the ranks, and the wives and daughters and sweet-hearts were left outside. We saw that a special effort was to be made to reach the women and enlist their support, hence our organisation, 'The Women's Labour League'. We glory in the name of 'Labour'. To us it means that every able-bodied woman shall do useful work for the community, whether as housewife or as worker for wages, and in return she should share leisure, beauty and comfort, not be crushed by the burden of incessant drudgery and senseless anxiety to provide the bare necessaries of existence for herself and those dependent on her care. We cannot do much towards this end as individuals, whether by seeing to our own hearth stones, or by charity visiting amongst our neighbours.

But by political methods we believe we can win freedom, economic and spiritual, for ourselves and for the generation that is growing up around us. To this we consecrate ourselves by our membership of the League, and we work through that for the young sling-giant of the future, 'The Labour Party'. We give a hearty welcome to all to come and join us. We meet every Tuesday night in the ILP rooms, Castle Street, at 8pm. We are holding a Bazaar in the Albert Minor Hall on Thursday and Friday, Nov. 13th and 14th. Please note the date.

20. Mrs Scholefield

Annual Report of Cardiff Women's Labour League (1913)

The League Leaflet, February 1913, Branch Annual Reports

CARDIFF (Sec. Mrs. Scholefield). The branch continues to make steady progress. We have enrolled ten new members recently, some of whom show signs of becoming very active ones. Early in the year the members assisted the shop assistants in their protest against the living-in system and half-holiday agitation, by both distributing and picketing. We persuaded several women not to buy at the shops which were trying to deprive their employees of their rights. We helped the Cathays ILP with the soup kitchen during the coal strike, when over 8,000 meals were cooked and distributed. We helped in the November Election canvassing, addressing envelopes etc. We also contributed 27/6 towards election expenses by holding a social and dance. Dr [Marion] Phillips has addressed two public meetings for us,[1] and we also had Mr. J. Seddon to speak for us. We held a series of insurance meetings. Mr. Williams, Barrister-at-Law, and Miss Douglas-Pennant were the speakers. Two delegates have been sent to the district conferences, held at Swansea and Aberkenfig, and two to

---

[1] Dr Marion Phillips, secretary of the Women's Labour League and editor of *League Leaflet*.

the War Against Poverty Conference. We are affiliated to the local Labour Party and have a representative, who has been elected on the E. C. [Executive Committee] for the second time. We have subscribed 10/- towards the Special Effort Fund of the League, and hope to continue to do so yearly. Our meetings have been varied by very interesting papers on 'School Clinics', 'Open Air Schools', 'Women's Suffrage', and 'Women Workers', by Miss Barker BSc, Miss Foxley, of Aberdare Hall, Mrs. Gibson and Mr. Scholefield.[2] The Labour Party held a demonstration on May Day, when we were able to secure the service of Mrs. Glasier to speak from one of the four platforms which had been arranged. It goes without saying she had the largest crowd around her. She joined in the procession with us and proudly carried our League banner.[3] We hold a coffee supper once a month, and every one present is expected to sing, say or pay. So far they have been very successful and each one has left us with a substantial profit. The Trades Council has started a housing campaign to enquire into the conditions in which working-class people are housed. Some of our members have already given some help and we are hoping to get the service of others. Information has been got which will be useful when the facts are presented to the Corporation. We have one member on the Insurance Committee. We have decided, after the Conference is over, to start and canvass the wives of the members of the ILP, with a view of getting them to take a copy of the Leaflet monthly, and thereby hope to make more members and increase the sale of the Leaflets.

---

[2] Local activists.

[3] Katherine Bruce Glasier (formerly St. John Conway) had a long history in the labour movement, as an activist and extremely popular speaker, for the ILP.

Part IV

The Cause: Writings from the Women's Suffrage Movement

The 1913 Women's Suffrage Pilgrimage. The South Wales Pilgrims met up with West Country suffragists at Bath, and continued together to London. This photograph taken at Street in Somerset shows Miss Jenny Kirkland, a Swansea suffragist (possibly to the right of the bicycles and marked with a cross) with the historian Alice Clark and others. From the Kirkland Collection, reproduced with permission, Archives, University of Wales, Swansea.

INTRODUCTION
BY URSULA MASSON

As the previous sections have shown, the issue of women's citizenship had emerged in the political writings of women in Wales in the last half of the nineteenth century, intertwined with education, temperance, religious and national causes. The suffrage movement had its supporters in Wales from the widespread petitioning of Parliament in the 1860s, onwards. In the 1890s, through the organisation of Liberal women, the cause moved into the mainstream of politics. By 1908, branches of all the major suffrage societies associated with the Edwardian movement existed in Wales. The first appears to have been the Cardiff branch, formed in 1906, of the Women's Social and Political Union (WSPU), the militant 'suffragette' organisation which for many is still synonymous with the suffrage struggle. Reflecting British-wide developments, the WSPU in Wales split, resulting in the formation of the Women's Freedom League (WFL); the Cardiff branch had been formed by May 1908. Thereafter, both the WSPU and the WFL remained small, though active, in Wales. Far larger and more broadly based than these militant societies was the National Union of Women's Suffrage Societies, formed nationally in 1897, when Wales formed part of a western district, with the first distinct Welsh branch formed in 1907 in Llandudno. By 1912, the Cardiff and District society, with over one thousand members, was the largest outside London. In the face of rising militancy, the NUWSS defined itself as law abiding and constitutional, but undoubtedly gained members as one result of the militant campaigns was to raise consciousness of the issue, especially amongst young women, not all of whom could commit themselves to militant activity. In south Wales, from 1910, suffrage societies, overwhelmingly of the constitutional variety, replaced Liberal women's organisation, as the latter increasingly came to the conclusion that the party on which they had pinned their hopes for two generations would not be the vehicle of their enfranchisement.[1]

The first three short pieces in this section arise from that disillusionment. Dr Erie Evans, a founder member of the Cardiff & District Women's Suffrage Society, wrote in the heat of her anger following a political meeting in the town to Ald. Edward Thomas, an old-school Radical supporter of women's rights. Her letter reflects the frustration of women at the humiliating conditions imposed on their participation in Liberal politics, as the party attempted to minimise disruption by suffragettes. The conditions were demonstrated in April 1909, when the anti-suffragist Cabinet minister Lewis Harcourt addressed a ticketed meeting of Cardiff Liberals. Despite the fact that almost 1000 women were members of the Cardiff WLA, and some subscribed to the Liberal Association, women could obtain tickets only through male members, who extracted a pledge of good behaviour from them. Women were excluded from the body of the hall, confined to the balcony, distant from the stage and – in the event of interjections - inaudible to most below. As Harcourt ranged over government policy and issues of the day, he provided ample openings to suffragettes to point out the anomalous position of women, and three hecklers were quickly silenced and ejected.[2] In closing remarks Harcourt and others made reference to the interjections, referring to 'the decencies of public meetings', contrasting the right sort of women – local, and decently silent

---

[1] Ryland Wallace, *Organise! Organise! Organise! A Study of Reform Agitations in Wales, 1840-1886* (Cardiff, 1991), ch. XI; Kay Cook and Neil Evans, '"The petty antics of the bell-ringing, boisterous band"? The women's suffrage movement in Wales, 1890-1918', in Angela V. John (ed.), *Our Mothers' Land: Chapters in Welsh Women's History, 1830-1939* (Cardiff, 1991).

[2] *South Wales Daily News* (*SWDN*), 3 April 1909.

– to indecorous, vocal, strangers. The implication was that women's protest was an importation, and lacked legitimacy. Only the vocal interjections of the militants, and their ejection, was reported by the press; the suppression of written questions was revealed by Evans's letter: Harcourt's respect for local women who observed the 'decencies' did not extend to giving them an answer.

The issues covered by Harcourt gave plenty of scope for moving populist rhetoric: free trade and the 'cheap loaf', 'the Peers *versus* the people', the People's Budget; religious equality and Welsh desires for disestablishment. The irony was not lost on suffragists in the audience, as Ethel Lester Jones's written question, described in Evans's letter, made clear. Evans mentions her promise to be silent throughout the meeting, and her support for free speech: her protestations were an ironic reference to the accusation (made by Lloyd George amongst others) that suffragettes, by interrupting meetings, were attacking freedom of speech. Suffragists pointed out that free speech had traditionally meant the right of public assembly without interference from the authorities, not the silencing of individuals at meetings. But Evans was demonstrating her reasonableness, the more effectively to make her main point, the implications of the new restrictions for women's political participation: support for women's suffrage was increasingly delegitimized by the repressive paranoia of a government in crisis.

The following year, Olive Stephenson-Howell, secretary of the Cardiff WFL echoed this protest at women's exclusion from the rhetoric of 'the people' being deployed most effectively in the Welsh context by Lloyd George. Stephenson-Howell's claim that there was now 'no demand in the country' for Welsh Church Disestablishment was an indication of how far the women's movement in Wales had moved away from the position of the 1890s. Her letter is also evidence of the hostility growing between Lloyd George, as a leading member of the government, and suffragists on all parts of the spectrum, which most dramatically erupted in famously violent incidents at Wrexham and Llanystumdwy in 1912. The statement reprinted here, from the resigning executive committee of the Cardiff WLA (a once very large association which was destroyed in the process) shows Liberal women finally deciding to put their own enfranchisement, and self-respect, first, after they, too, had publicly repudiated what Welsh Liberalism had long stood for.

The suffragist flair for spectacular demonstrations was mainly to be seen in London, since the point was to seize the attention of Britain as a whole, and Westminster in particular. Contingents of Welsh suffragists, militant and constitutional, took their banners up to London demonstrations. In 1913, to remind the country that the vote was desired by the mass of law-abiding women, and not just by the suffragettes whose 'outrages' made the headlines and filled the courts and prisons, the NUWSS organised a Suffrage Pilgrimage, with bands of walkers converging on London from all points of the compass in England and Wales. The north Wales societies took a route through Cheshire and Staffordshire, to enter London along Watling Sreet. The south Wales contingent met up with the West of England societies on the Lands End to London route (see photograph). Both groups first demonstrated on their home ground in ways they had not done before; the north Wales contingent with a peregrination through Bangor, Penmaenmawr, Conway, Colwyn Bay and Abergele. They walked into the towns to hold open-air meetings with banners flying and wearing their cockades and shoulder bags in society colours. In Cardiff, two hundred members of the South Wales Federation sent off their pilgrims with a walk through the town:

> It was with great misgivings that some members agreed to take part in the procession, but afterwards their enthusiasm

was aroused and the desire to do something more in the future. The march was useful in drawing the attention of many people to the existence of our society. That evening some 30 of us attended the mass meeting in Newport.[3]

This rather subdued account is belied by a vivid newspaper report which described the procession through Cardiff, in which the marchers set off from Cathays with a band playing alternately 'The Marseillaise' and 'Men of Harlech'. They 'displayed the brilliant colours' of the society on sashes, cockades and shoulder bags.

'Emblazoned on brilliant bannerettes were the names "Joan of Arc", "Florence Nightingale", "Josephine Butler", "George Eliot", "Elizabeth Barrett Browning", "Elizabeth Fry", "Mary Wollestonecraft", all heroines in the cause of women's emancipation'.[4]

This new form of propaganda established something of a tradition in women's political activism. Thirteen years later, in 1926, the women's peace movement consciously imitated the suffrage pilgrimage with its great Peace Pilgrimage to London. In the 1980s, 'Star Marches' by anti-nuclear campaigners moved the centre of pilgrimage to Greenham Common.

The Pilgrimage accounts reprinted here from the *North Wales Chronicle* are amongst the most extended writings by suffragists from Wales for this period. The *Chronicle* was a Conservative newspaper, and like much of the press had shown little interest in the suffrage movement until the suffragettes began to provide lively copy. Giving space to the constitutionalists to write their own column of suffrage news was cheap, probably increased readership, and foregrounded

---

[3] Cardiff & District Women's Suffrage Society Annual Report 1913-14.
[4] *SWDN*, 14 July 1913.

the respectable side of the movement. It also had a party-political usefulness, as it became clear that the movement was a thorn in the side of the Liberal government, and could be used as a stick to beat Lloyd George. Whatever the agenda of the editor, the women's accounts reflect the aims and ethos of the Pilgrimage. Anyone who has been involved in mass demonstrations or marches will recognise the exhilaration and sense of purpose the women experienced. Perhaps most interesting is the occasional sense – as in a true Pilgrim's Progress – of moving through strange and sometimes dangerous country, encountering 'the other' at every turn, in this case working-class Britain, male and female, hostile or supportive. Constitutional suffragists had experienced hostility and violence or the threat of it at a number of indoor meetings particularly during the crisis of 1909-11. Unlike the militants, they had not courted confrontation in public spaces. Such encounters could be unnerving, but served to strengthen the strong sense of suffragists, in common with the Liberal feminists of the 1890s, that their campaign was essentially selfless. The challenges increased resolve: 'Who, after all, cares for a victory easily won?'

The enthusiasm, or determination, with which Welsh militants embraced struggle and imprisonment is conveyed by two short autobiographical entries from the *Suffrage Annual and Women's Who's Who* of 1913. Mary Keating Hill was a member of a remarkable Mountain Ash family, the Keatings, children of working-class Irish immigrants who made their mark in the world, as her entry proudly demonstrates.[5] She had started her suffragist life in the WSPU, but became a leading figure in the Cardiff WFL. Edith Mansell-Moulin was London-based, and a leader of London-Welsh suffragist activity, who 'moved in top suffragette circles', and framed her political activities in Welsh national identity, and 'the

---

[5] Joseph Keating's autobiography, *My Struggle for Life* (Dublin, 2005, first published 1916), makes no mention of his sister's political activities.

Celtic love of liberty'.[6] From the days of Cymru Fydd, this flattering connection between Welshness, or Celticity, and innate egalitarian democracy, had provided a way of linking women's emancipation to national identity, sometimes in the face of suggestions that the demand for enfranchisement was an English importation which risked undermining Welsh unity. As examples of self-representation of suffragists, both of these pieces can be compared to the later accounts of Rachel Barrett and Lady Rhondda, discussed below, in which the militant prisoner identity is to the fore.

Two pieces from 1916, written by the Conway-born doctor, Helena Jones, are a reminder that the ultra-patriotic turn taken by Emmeline and Christabel Pankhurst on the outbreak of war was not unanimously supported by WSPU members. Some women turned to working for international peace, laying the foundations for the women's peace campaigning which was an important feature of the inter-war years (and which we hope to include in a further volume). Others decided to stick to their guns as suffragists. One such group was 'The Suffragettes of the WSPU', on the committee of which Helena Jones served, and which dissociated itself strongly from the Pankhurst position. Their *Suffragette News Sheet* served as a focus for the group. Jones's contributions were written when the government was beginning to consider franchise reform to deal with the issues of voter registration and entitlement to citizenship, created by the war. Jones saw this as a point of both opportunity and danger for the women's cause. Women's war-time work had entitled them to equal citizenship, and post-war political and social conditions would demand women's contribution, but gratitude to the male soldiery of the nation threatened, she feared, 'to swamp women's just demand'.

---

[6] Angela V. John, '"Run like blazes": the suffragettes and Welshness', *LLafur*, vol. 6, no. 3 (1994), 29-40; *idem*, '" A draft of fresh air": women's suffrage, the Welsh and London', Transactions of the Honourable Society of Cymmrodorion (1994-5), 81-93.

Some women, those over the age of 30, who were householders or married to householders, were enfranchised in 1918. What difference would women's vote make? In the pre-war campaigns the vote had borne a great weight of expectation and symbolism; and militancy, entailing martyrdom and suffering, had been seen by some as creating a new, and finer, species of womanhood. How would these women now transform the world through the exercise of their citizenship? Two pieces of 1918/19, reprinted here, addressed that question. The *Suffragette News Sheet* first published Alice Abadam's polemic 'The Feminist Vote: Enfranchised or Emancipated?', which was then re-issued as a pamphlet by the WFL's Minerva Publishing Co.. Daughter of the High Sheriff of Carmarthen, born at Middleton Hall, Llanarthney, Abadam was most active in the suffrage movement outside Wales, though she occasionally visited as a speaker. After the 1920s she gravitated back to Wales, was chairman of the University of Wales sub-committee on art, and died at Abergwili, Carmarthenshire, in 1940. For Abadam, the vote, properly exercised, had the character of a sacrament – an 'outward sign of inward grace' – language which reflected Abadam's Catholicism, but also a view of enfranchisement as a sacred trust held by Josephine Butler[7] and those she inspired, amongst whom Abadam placed herself. The test of 'emancipation', as opposed to being the mere possessor of a vote, would be women's break with the past dominated by sordid male politics, to create 'a Great Crusade, a Great Adventure … a New Force in a New World', obliterating 'the Old Order now expiring amidst blood, savagery, lust, disease and famine'. The apocalyptic vision of Europe after the First World War was the setting for the triumphalist rise of 'Woman her full self'. Abadam's discussion of male 'fear of the Eternal Feminine' foreshadows the 'sex war' debates

[7] Butler was the leader of the campaign of the 1870s-80s to repeal the Contagious Disease Acts.

of the 1920s – stirring stuff, not untypical of the Upper-Case Effusions of some of the more 'spiritual' women's suffrage writings, usually from the militant movement. Abadam began her suffrage career as an 'Independent Socialist' and supporter of the WSPU, then as a member of the first committee of the WFL. She moved on to the constitutional movement, and was a speaker, much in demand, for a range of suffrage societies. Shortly after publication of 'The Feminist Vote', Abadam founded the London-based Feminist League, the objectives of which were: 'To Restore to Women all they should Have, all they should Know and all they should Be'. Between the wars, Abadam increasingly focused on a social purity agenda, with eugenic overtones.[8]

Gwladys Perrie Williams wrote 'Woman's Opportunity' for the monthly journal, *Welsh Outlook* (1914-1933). Williams's anxieties about how women would use their votes echoed Abadam to a degree: both saw 'woman's' opportunity in her freedom from attachment to the old political parties; for both, women had proven their worth by the contribution to the war effort; and for both, solving the problems of peace would demand women's special skills and resources. For Williams, however, it is the realisation of the nation, not of womankind, which would be the test of women's citizenship in Wales. In contrast to the trans-national perspective of other suffragist writings reprinted here, Williams's is a renewal of the link with the feminism of Cymru Fydd, and perhaps most of all, with her final emphasis on mothers as the reproducers of national identity, with the nationalism of Lady Llanover and Alis Mallt Williams.

The prominence in the suffrage movement in Wales of English women living in the coastal towns of north and south

---

[8] Elizabeth Crawford, *The Women's Suffrage Movement: a Reference Guide 1866-1928* (London & New York, 2001), 1; Marilyn Timms, 'Alice Abadam and inter-war feminism: recovering the history of a forgotten suffragist', unpublished MA dissertation, Ruskin College, 69.

has been noted by historians. Several of the writers included here show that the traffic was not all one way; women of Welsh origin, like Jones and Abadam, were active in the movement more widely.[9] Most closely associated with the nerve-centre of militant activity was Carmarthenshire-born Rachel Barrett. Her fragment of autobiography was deposited with others in the Suffragette Fellowship Collection at the Museum of London. The Fellowship was formed in 1926 to 'keep alive the suffragette spirit'. The autobiographical writings were intended to form a 'Book of Suffragette Prisoners' which was not completed.[10] Brief as Barrett's autobiography is, it vividly conveys the nature of the commitment made by some young women to the cause, at the cost of education, careers, freedom and health. Even when out of prison, Barrett's life 'underground' was a form of confinement willingly embraced; it was 'a definite call and I obeyed'. The provenance of the autobiography is a reminder, that within the identity of suffragist, that of 'suffragette prisoner' was a proudly worn badge, and for many women, perhaps, remained a primary self-definition long after the struggle was over.

Not so Margaret, Lady Rhondda, extracts from whose autobiography, *This Was My World*, are our final word on the subject, taking us into the 1930s: 'it was a blessed relief to feel that one had not got to trouble with things of that sort any more'. She has also provided our first words, the title for this volume, *The Very Salt Of Life,* being her vivid phrase for the impact of the militant movement on young women like herself, otherwise destined to lead bland and proper lives of bourgeois marriage and good works. Rhondda was born Margaret Haig Thomas, daughter of the suffragist Sybil Thomas, previously president of the Welsh Union of Women's Liberal Associations, and the MP and coal-owner D. A. Thomas, later Lord Rhondda. By

---

[9] *The Suffrage Annual and Women's Who's Who* (London, 1913) has a number of examples.

[10] Crawford, *The Women's Suffrage Movement*, 663.

the time she was active in the WSPU, Margaret was married to Humphrey Mackworth, of the local gentry. In the inter-war period, she was a leading figure in British feminism, owner of the influential journal *Time and Tide*, and founder of the equal rights Six Point Group.[11] The entertaining core of the extracts reprinted here is Rhondda's account of her fire-bombing of a Newport letter-box, but the whole story is a revealing, if one-sided and partial, account of the place of women in the political landscape of Edwardian Britain, of the configurations of family politics, and of the new life opened up by the 'thrilling discovery' of the militant movement. Despite her short imprisonment and hunger strike, Margaret was no martyr. Her privileged position locally prevented that, but the evidence of the autobiography suggests that a robust sense of humour, particularly revealed in her accounts of public meetings in the coalfield towns, militated against any feeling of victimhood, even in a cause about which she was passionately serious.

Barrett and Rhondda contributed to an important genre of autobiographical writing of the inter-war years, the suffrage memoir. Produced in greater numbers by former militants than by constitutionalists, such memoirs have shaped the historical understanding of the suffrage movement until quite recently, when more attention has been paid to the constitutionalist contribution. Memoirs written by Welsh suffragists are rare. Elizabeth Andrews briefly recalled the movement in her memoir of the 1950s.[12] However, the variety of writings here, from those written in the heat of anger by the Cardiff suffragists, to the good-humoured recollections of Lady Rhondda, suggest the breadth of the movement, and its place in Welsh women's history.

---

[11] Viscountess Rhondda, *This Was My World* (London, 1933); Shirley M. Eoff, *Viscountess Rhondda, Equalitarian Feminist* (Columbus, Ohio, 1991).

[12] Elizabeth Andrews, *A Woman's Work is Never Done, and other political writings* (Dinas Powys, 2006).

21. Cardiff Suffragists Ditch the Liberal Party: Letters

Dr Erie Evans (1909)

Cardiff, 29 April 1909

Dear Mr. Thomas,

In as much as some members of the Liberal executive saw fit this evening to impeach Mr. Lester Jones' good faith, I should like to bear witness through you as to the exact facts which occurred. Mr. Lester Jones gave me a ticket for Mr. Harcourt's meeting having first extracted a pledge from me that I should be silent throughout the meeting and [burn?][1] the ticket if I could not use it. That pledge it was easy for me to give, in as much as I am strongly opposed to any attempt at interfering with free speech. I was sitting next to Miss Lester Jones. Mr. Harcourt in the course of his speech made reference to the 'will of the people'. Miss Lester Jones wrote out a question to the effect that she would be glad to know how Mr. Harcourt thought it possible for the Government to express the will of the people while women had no votes. She consulted me as to whether she should send it up. I told her it would certainly be ignored and could therefore have no effect except in so far as it [registered?][1] in Mr. Harcourt's mind – but that it could do no harm. She therefore handed it to Mr. Lester Jones asking him to forward it. Mr. Lester Jones handed it either to the Chairman or to Mr. Harcourt himself. The question was ignored, but in

---

[1] The hand-written original is unclear at this point.

his closing remarks Mr. Harcourt indicated that he accepted it as proof of the presence of keen suffragists who had listened without interruption.

I gather from the scene which took place after the meeting that it is the feeling of some members of the Liberal executive in Cardiff that it is illegitimate for a woman to send up written questions at a public meeting.

To quote the words of Mr. Bertram in the House of Commons on March 19th, members 'are not there as representing women, they were there representing the men voters of the country'.[2]

I recognise that owing to our disfranchisement it is illegitimate for women to put <u>spoken</u> questions at public meetings because they occupy time which might be used by a voter. But that is should be regarded as illegitimate for unenfranchised sections of the people to put <u>written</u> questions had never occurred to me. For a written question steals no time from a voter and it rests with the Chairman whether it should be answered or no. <u>Could</u> Harcourt have answered it he would have done so. As he couldn't, he ignored it.

It is well for us to clearly understand what are the disabilities imposed on us by our disfranchisement and if written questions are in truth forbidden, the sooner the position is clearly stated, the better.

*

---

[2] During a second reading debate on an adult suffrage bill.

Olive Stephenson-Howell (1910)

Cardiff, September 29th 1910: 'Chancellor and Suffragettes'
South Wales Daily News, 1 October 1910:

Sir,

In the long interview reported in your today's issue,[3] given
to suffragists, Mr. Lloyd George by his attitude towards the
question of the Conciliation Bill, justifies once again the
militant policy of two of the Suffrage Societies, because it
shows that women, after years of agitation, personal prejudice
and personal convictions still stand before public demand
and justice. Mr. Lloyd George states that this is not the cause
nearest to his heart, and that Welsh Disestablishment comes
first. For the latter there is no demand in the country, and a
member, holding a responsible position, has no right to treat
with comparative indifference reforms which do not happen to
be nearest his particular heart. There is a big demand among
women for their enfranchisement, yet a bill embodying this
demand can only be obtained through a government elected
by men, and if this Government cannot be moved to act on the
principle of justice, then the only road open to women is that
of revolt.

Women contribute some millions yearly to the Exchequer,
and it is possible that if they refrained from paying these, the
way to the road which is nearest the Chancellor's heart might
not be difficult to find.

Mr. Lloyd George speaks of the cause of the people from
whom he sprung, and that he must fight the cause of the
poor and oppressed. Are not women to be included in the
people, and are they not notoriously the worst paid class of
workers and the most oppressed by sweating employers? And
are they not so to a great extent on account of their voteless
condition? If the Chancellor is sincere in his concern for the

---

[3] Referring to the *SWDN* of 29 September 1910.

masses, let him turn his attention to women's demands, and if he has democratic objections to the Conciliation Bill, let him introduce a 'perfect' Bill on behalf of the Government, which would satisfy Mr. Asquith (if possible), as indeed he was challenged to do so by Mr. Snowden MP when the Bill was under discussion in the House. To refuse half a loaf in favour of no bread surely runs counter to any democratic principles; it certainly does to political ones.

*

Cardiff Women's Liberal Association (1911)

South Wales Daily News, 10 March 1911: Cardiff Women
Liberals Defence of Recent Policy

'For the following reasons it has seemed essential to us that
Liberal women shall not work for Parliamentary candidates
who do not desire women's enfranchisement:
1. Because we women are accused of not ardently desiring
   the vote, and Liberal women are spoken of as an example.
2. Because it is believed by many who know that if we
   decided on this refusal our enfranchisement would soon
   follow, and we should then be able to work with our full
   powers for other Liberal principles.
3. Because the full representation of the people is a Liberal
   principle, and cannot be considered to be accomplished as
   long as more than half the population is without a vote.
4. Because if women's enfranchisement is long delayed a
   deterioration of Liberalism is likely to take place.

Because the canvassing work that we are asked to do now for a
candidate who does not believe in our political existence is not
satisfactory, and the Men's Liberal Association is apt merely
to think that it can get out of a Women's Liberal Association
that will, under all circumstances, be willing to work for them
instead of regarding the latter as an equal political partner.

22. North Wales Suffragists on Pilgrimage

Newspaper Reports (1913)

North Wales Chronicle, 13 June 1913, Suffrage Notes (By a Suffragist)

Plans for the great Suffrage Pilgrimage are going well forward and great enthusiasm is being shown by non-militant Suffragists in support of this interesting scheme of propaganda throughout the country. We are often told that 'Women's Suffrage has never been properly before the country'. By that phrase is usually meant it has not been put before electors at election times as a question of first rate national significance. If that is the case it is not the fault of the Women Suffragists, who have now, for some years, devoted a great deal of energy and time to educational and propaganda work in the constituencies at election times. The candidates themselves have not so good a record, but that is not the fault of the supporters of Women's Suffrage. But after all we do not accept Rousseau's dictum that the only time an Englishman is free is during elections, and there are ways and times of bringing questions 'before the country' much more real and significant and valuable than that which is generally understood by the technical phrase.

Suffragists claim that no political question has ever been 'brought before the country' as has this matter of women's political enfranchisement, and the thousands of meetings held in every corner of the land, week in week out, during the last six years, bears witness to the fact. The matter has been put before the country in thousands of newspaper articles, leaders, magazines, reviews; there are at least four weekly papers wholly and solely devoted to Women's Suffrage, and others issued at longer intervals. One might well complain that the country has heard the matter argued 'ad nauseam', but to say that it has never been brought face to face with it is to juggle with words – to put it charitably.

But if the country has not yet heard the gospel of Women's Suffrage, it will at any rate have a good opportunity of doing so in this coming month of July, when, along all the main routes to London non-militant Pilgrims will march to London, holding daily meetings, distributing literature, talking to those who care to listen of the Suffrage question.

The members of the North Wales societies are to do a little 'pilgrimaging' in the Principality before they join their main route at Chester. They will leave Bangor on July 2nd, and on reaching Penmaenmawr they will hold an open-air evening meeting. Conway will welcome them at mid-day, and hear Suffrage speeches. The open-air meeting at Colwyn Bay is arranged for 8pm on July 3rd, and meetings will be held next day at both Rhyl and Abergele.

*

North Wales Chronicle, 4 July 1913, Suffrage Notes, from a Correspondent

The Suffrage Pilgrimage is certainly arousing a great deal of interest, though there are, of course, those who frankly admit that they regard it as an absurd and futile expenditure of energy and enthusiasm. Just now it is quite interesting collecting opinions on the Pilgrimage; it is a new summer pastime, and will probably keep its freshness all through July.

The form of the objection differs, but here is one which

many of us possibly echoed when we first heard the project mooted, and did not yet understand all it meant. 'Walking to London? How foolish. What is the good of these ridiculous processions? The time for processions, if it ever existed, is past'. Now it may be that the time for processions is past. But the Suffrage Pilgrimage is not a mere procession. It is a method of propaganda, a chance for doing real educational work on a scale of unprecedented magnitude and in a manner calculated to strike the imagination and at the same time convince the minds of an immense number of persons, some of whom have never yet considered the matter seriously at all. In numberless villages and small towns where women's suffrage has never yet been preached, or where the word connotes nothing but burning of houses or destruction of letters, the real meaning and aim, and necessity of women's political enfranchisement will be made clear in the time which elapses before July 26th, when the Pilgrims march on London from among the several converging routes.

The well-known author of 'Collections and Recollections'[1] contributed an article last Saturday to the *Manchester Guardian*, in which he rather questioned the value of demonstrations, and with much that he had to say in that article one is quite in agreement. 'A demonstration', he says, 'is literally that which may be proved beyond doubt or contradiction' in the manner in which Euclid demonstrates a mathematical proposition. But an enormous gathering of persons does not, of course, prove anything 'beyond doubt or contradiction' except the numerical strength of those who advance it. But the Suffragist Pilgrimage is not a mere demonstration, though it winds up with an immense one in Hyde Park on July 26th. It is, as has been pointed out, a missionary adventure, a preaching mission, and one of its main objects is the conversion of souls!

It is this fact that will give significance and peculiar value

---

[1] G.W.E.Russell, Liberal politician.

to the London gathering. The thousands who there assemble will bear witness to the strength of the movement throughout the country, and they will hearten each other for future work. But the real impression made on the country will not be made in Hyde Park, but in the wayside villages and in the country towns, north, south, east, and west, through which the Pilgrims have trudged and in which they have day by day borne witness to the faith that is in them and explained the grounds of their belief.

Hard is it to understand the mental attitude of those who think that this is a time when anti-militant suffragists should hold their peace. Never was there a greater fallacy! But one constantly meets it. 'I hope X is not on pilgrimage', writes a friend from the West country, 'for the cause of the wiser suffragists has been ruined by the madness of the militant suffragettes. A Pilgrimage might have done good at one time, but not now'. Oh, strange perversion of the facts, and queer misreading of the situation, and the remedy. None know better than the non-militants that their work is rendered trebly difficult by methods of violence and resort to crime. That is an added difficulty in their path, but it does not constitute a call to leave the path and desert the work. It is a call to greater energy, enthusiasm, resource and earnestness in using the means they believe to be right to attain the end they know to be good.

Why should the 'wiser suffragists' leave the field to the unwise? Why give the enemy cause to rejoice and say 'No wise persons now care or work for this cause'? This surely is crooked reasoning and cowardly counsel. The cause of women's suffrage, furthermore, is not the cause of any section of suffragists. It is 'the common cause' – it is the cause of our critic, of every man, woman and child in the nation. It is the cause of justice, of righteousness, of purity, and of religion. Therefore, it cannot be overcome, it is certain of success. But success will not come without effort, nor without persistent work.

Neither the apathy of the indifferent, nor the ignorance of the uninstructed, nor the wrong-headedness of supporters, nor any other thing can ruin this cause, if we so will it, and that it has not been ruined by arson, or window-breaking, by violence or by tactics of despair; it is one of the main objects of the Pilgrimage to demonstrate.

The pilgrims from the furthermost corners of England and from North Wales are now well on their way to London. From each route comes news of successful meetings; the reception of the marchers has, on the whole, been most encouraging, showing that the cause of women's suffrage is really gaining ground. There has been no lack of interest or sympathy, as has been shown by the huge crowds assembled to listen to the message the pilgrims are carrying from the thousands of men and women who are working for the vote by every lawful means in their power. Their appeal is not to force, but to something far greater, to the hearts and consciences of men and women, and when these are roused on our behalf the end is not far off. The pilgrims are making this appeal. They are putting their case before the people of this country, and are telling them why women are asking for the vote.

Plans are practically settled for the great demonstration in London on July 26th. The bands of Pilgrims will march from London and enter Hyde Park from four different quarters, to occupy at least twenty different platforms. Besides the banners of local Societies and different Federations of the Union carried in the procession, there will be shield-shaped and pennant shaped banners illuminated with mottoes, and if rumour speaks truth, at least one original feature connected with the collection of money that will be absolutely new to London. In all probability the platforms will be arranged in a vast circle with a stationary banner behind and above each one showing what group it represents. Thus there will be a London Society platform, and a North Wales platform, and an Eastern Counties platform, with others for the West of England, the

Ridings of Yorkshire, the North-East, the Midlands, and so on. Each one will have a chairman and two or three speakers, including locally notable Suffragists, and among them all will be scattered speakers from the countries where women are already enfranchised. At a certain time the resolution will be put simultaneously from all platforms, and the evening papers will no doubt announce the amount of fund, collected by all the pilgrims, and offered to Mrs. Fawcett for the autumn propagandist campaign in the constituencies.

*

North Wales Chronicle, 11 July 1913, Impressions of the Pilgrimage, by a Pilgrim

Whatever else the Suffrage Pilgrims are meeting with on the road they are not meeting with indifference. Everywhere as we pass along the people come out to see us and we get many hearty words of encouragement to cheer us on our dusty way.

At Rhyl, as at Colwyn Bay, thousands of men, women and children came down to the sands to our evening meeting, and we could easily have done with six platforms and six speakers, and all would have had attentive audiences. Of course, there is always a section of persons who will jibe and jeer, and some who are "out for a row" and don't care whether they get it at a suffrage meeting or elsewhere so long as they have it somehow.

At Llysfaen, more than 200 quarrymen who had ceased work for an hour, insisted on having a meeting: so two of our members took the floor and made capital speeches. But we find it everywhere the same – the genuine working man is sympathetic with the women's cause. Their difficulties are in many ways the same, and they do not let prejudice and preconceived ideas stand in the way of a fair and sympathetic consideration of the question.

And if the quarrymen of Llysfaen were attentive hearers of our message, so were the 50 mothers from Altrincham whom we found on the railway bridge at Abergele – poor women who had been brought for a few days holiday at the sea from cellar homes in Altrincham, and who formed the nucleus of the meeting we held on the shore. They were going home by train 'presently' but were considerably excited at the prospect of hearing 'the ladies' speak before they went.

As we talked of the difficulties and disabilities of the working women and showed how legislation can affect the home – how housing and the care of children and water supplies are all matters nearly affecting women they murmured 'Quite right, miss; very true'. And they did not tell us to go home and mend our stockings or ask if the husband's shirt was washed. The working women, like the working men of the country, realize what the demand for women's citizenship means and how much it is needed on purely practical grounds.

We are a cheerful company as we take to the road, and the hearty comradeship of the adventure is not the least of its pleasures.

The July hedgerows are gay with wild roses and honeysuckle. Never surely was there such a year for wild roses. We think they must have come out for the special delight of the Pilgrims indeed, and the red, white and green of the wayside seems to repeat, though perhaps in more artistic tints, the colours of our National Union. As we look at them we recall again the meaning of them – red for the burning flame of our enthusiasm, white for the purity of our cause, and green for the ever-springing hope in our hearts of what the women's movement is to do for humanity the world over.

We are finding a certain magic in the Pilgrimage already. Pilgrims find themselves doing things they have never done before and would never have dreamed of doing. They find themselves, for instance, standing on orange boxes on the sands in the middle of a surging crowd or holding forth to a massed crowd of persons in the middle of a big market square.

Someone is urgently needed to speak – there is the waiting crowd and one simply forgets to be self-conscious and only remembers that there is a great message to deliver, a great gospel to preach, and somehow one is speaking and they are listening, and there you are! Certainly if the women never got the vote at all the education gained in trying to get it would be worth the trouble expended. For women are learning the meaning of comradeship as never before. They are sharing high purposes and rejoicing in wider horizons and a freer air.

Stevenson has said that 'to travel hopefully is better than to arrive'. Well, the women suffragists still hope to arrive, but meanwhile they are certainly travelling hopefully along their pilgrim way.

And well they may. All along the route they are being received with real sympathy. In Chester on Saturday night the vast crowds that filled the Market Square made an impressive sight. Never for any political meeting, were we told, had such numbers assembled for years. For a race meeting such crowds were common, but not for a serious political object. We had four platforms, with a sequence of speakers at each, and all obtained a good hearing.

At one platform some little interruption occurred, but the temper of the crowd was really very good, and the general character of the meeting very orderly. A crowd is always of course composite in character, and nobody pretends all its members on Saturday were suffragists, but they gave a fair hearing to the speakers, and that is all that can fairly be asked.

*

North Wales Chronicle, 18 July 1913
The Suffragists Progress. More news from the open road.
Some Lively Experiences.

If there were any doubts in our minds about the value of the pilgrimage (writes one of the Suffragist pilgrims) they must have vanished long ago from every pilgrim's mind who has had even one day's experience of 'the road'. The pilgrimage is teaching us many things, not the least important being the extreme need of such a missionary enterprise if the deeper issues of the suffrage movement are ever to be made plain to the people of this country.

There are still depths of ignorance to plumb and enlighten; there are bitter prejudices and misunderstandings to remove; there is an immense amount of steady, persistent educational work to be done, and we are finding it out as never before.

At every single village and town where a meeting was held we met the same confusion of thought, which showed itself in the inevitable association of women's suffrage with violence and destruction even when our multitudinous banners proclaimed us to be non-militant and law-abiding, and asserted that 'reason, not force' was our motto, and peaceful persuasion our sole weapon. But if the public continues to read with avidity every sensational report of lawless exploits, and refuses to lend an ear to the tale of quiet educational work, it is to be feared the Press will be tempted to meet the demand, and we shall be met as ever with the complaint, 'We never heard of you before. What have you been doing?'

Gratefully, however, do we, Constitutional Suffragists, recognise the service rendered to the cause by the growing number of newspaper editors, who give full and frequent publicity to all the varied educational work which the National Union and the other non-militant societies are doing up and down the country.

One effect produced by the pilgrimage and its spectacular

interest is that hundreds of persons come out to suffrage meetings who have never heard a suffrage argument before, nor listened patiently to a suffrage speech. Experience shows that where men and women will listen to reasoned argument we can gain their sympathy and support more often than not.

What is our despair is the attitude of those who refuse to hear and turn deaf and contemptuous ears to anything we say. 'I don't want to hear anything', 'I won't listen', 'I won't read your rubbishy papers'. These are the greetings we have received more that once, and alas, sometimes from members of our own sex.

What made one sick at heart, as we trudged the two miles along the streets from Burslem to Hanley was the number of jeering girls and women of the poorer classes along the route who had no notion that it is for their protection and their uplifting that we are fighting, and their cause especially we desire to plead. When one could get a group of them quietly and talk to them they listened with interest and surprise, and many a working woman cheered us on the way by her words of thanks and encouragement after a speech, or her smile of greeting as we passed along the route.

Nor was it by any means only the poorer women who showed this ignorance and even contempt. One haughty lady in a village we passed through lifted her nose to the heavens as one pilgrim offered her a leaflet and laconically remarked that what we all wanted was to be dipped in a tar barrel! The obvious retort, of course, was that what she wanted was manners and understanding, but pilgrims learn to be patient and good humoured and not to say all they think. But they do think things all the same!

Our splendid meeting in the village of Tarporley was followed next day by a small mid-day meeting in the little village of Barbridge, where the people are mostly connected with the barge industry, and the women go to and fro along the canals with intermittent seasons of housekeeping within four walls. The homes of these women looked rather forlorn, but a number were attentive listeners as we spoke from the car to a small and scattered audience, which contained among others the Conservative political agent, who is also the secretary of the Anti-Suffragist Society, and a keen debater.

On the steps of the village inn we held an animated but friendly discussion after the meeting proper, discovering ultimately that this champion of the 'anti' cause was really a believer in a limited franchise for women, and therefore a subject for hope and further education. He promised to ask further questions at the Nantwich meeting the same night, and was as good as his word. Such opponents one is glad to meet and to reason with.

Unfortunately, Nantwich provided us with an army of small boys who made valiant attempts to drown the speakers by their shouts, and who escorted us down to the station after the meeting, flinging mud and occasional stones at anyone who happened to be handy as a target. Adult Nantwich was stolid and apathetic. But we commend the town to the care and notice of the Crewe Suffrage Society. It will assuredly prove a fine field for missionary enterprise, and who, after all, cares for a victory easily won?

The Pottery towns gave us a reception which was far from apathetic. At Burslem, a fine meeting was held in the main square, and a resolution in favour of women's suffrage was passed almost without dissentients. The presence of Major Cecil Wedgwood on this and the Hanley platform was a great source of strength to us, and at both places there was a vast number of people ready and anxious to hear suffrage arguments and to support our cause. Crowds lined the streets and we marched in procession to Hanley, and the whole town seemed to have turned out to see us pass. At Hanley, after Councillor Margaret Ashton had spoken to an immense and sympathetic audience, the hooligan element present in the vast crowd asserted itself strongly, and many of us had sufficiently exciting experiences getting safely to our lodgings.

At Stafford also there was rowdyism in the huge meeting in the Market Square. But though Miss Ashton suffered from much interruption, another of our speakers, Miss Cicely Leadley Barr, of Liverpool, had a fine audience, whose attitude was entirely sympathetic, and it was quite apparent that the men and women present were with us. Indeed, a group of men went out of their way to explain that is was only a section of irresponsible youths and hooligans who were responsible for the rowdy element, and a band of chivalrous young men pledged themselves to go on to the Wolverhampton meeting next night and act as bodyguard to the speakers.

Incidentally, a good many eggs some orange peel and a considerable amount of wholesome flour were wasted in the Stafford Market Square. These missiles usually fell upon members of the audience, not upon the speakers for whom they were doubtless intended. The editor of the local paper assured us next morning that our meeting had been a great success, and its effect would be to put the cause of women's suffrage on a new and far better footing in Stafford than it had ever been before.

So we went on our way to Wolverhampton cheered and encouraged, for such a result we all felt was well worth many eggs, some rough jostling and a pound or two of flour.

*

North Wales Chronicle, 1 August 1913:
End of the Pilgrimage. Impressions of a Memorable Day. Remarkable Scene in Hyde Park. (From our Suffragist Correspondent).

Friday evening saw the various bands of pilgrims safely encamped on the outskirts of London.

On Saturday afternoon they were to close in on the city

in the united strength of an invading host, meeting at Hyde Park at 5pm for the great demonstration. But before the huge outdoor meeting on Saturday, Londoners were to have the chance to hear the pilgrims' message in the sectional indoor meetings held on Friday evening. Thus the marchers from the great North Road met at Highbury Hall. Mrs. Philip Snowden and others addressed a most enthusiastic gathering, and largely composed of working men at King's Hall, Southwark. At Kensington Town Hall Mrs. Fawcett presided over another great gathering, and our own Watling St. pilgrims gathered at the Ethical Church, Queen's Road, Bayswater.

It was good to meet again with comrades one had parted from reluctantly in the Midlands, to see their bronzed and cheerful faces, and to join in the chorus of the 'Pilgrims' Song', sung before the speeches began, to the tune of 'The March of the Western Men'.

> And shall they scorn the women's voice
> When we for justice cry?
> We're marching in our thousands now
> To know the reason why.

Councillor Margaret Ashton, of Manchester, spoke in words of passionate and moving eloquence of the great social problems that are crying out for women's help. The pilgrimage, she said, had burnt this in upon the minds of many as never before. To have walked through the streets of the Potteries, for instance, had been to make real and concrete what has been realised only as a general proposition by many before. As an administrator, Miss Ashton has intimate and special knowledge of the helplessness of women to deal with such questions as housing, the infant death rate, the moral problems of our great cities. We must make our voices heard in the legislation of the land if things are to be altered for the better. The words of the second verse seemed to echo in our ears as she spoke, and to emphasise the fact that our claim to citizenship is a claim to service.

And we have heard our country's call,
Can we stand idle by?
If still we may not serve, we come
To know the reason why.

Saturday's demonstration was a thing never to be forgotten. There was first the march through the streets with our bands playing, and pennons flying amid the crowds of kindly and sympathetic men and women who lined the route. In our Watling Street company we have three horse-women, amongst them Miss Vera Collum who has ridden a large part of the way with the pilgrims as special Press representative.

When the four great pilgrim armies had all assembled the spectacle in the Park was indeed a remarkable one. To look around and see the standards and pennons flying from nineteen platforms, to see the nineteen great audiences gathered round the platforms which girdled the Park, to walk round and note the fine spirit of the crowd and watch the perfect organisation and order of the whole was a heartening and an uplifting thing.

We are sometimes told that the people of the nation are angered and embittered by the violent acts of a few women, desperate at the repeated refusals of the government to deal with a matter that goes to the root of moral and social reforms. We are told that the mass of the public are against the women's demand for political freedom, and that their cause is well-nigh lost and dead. Never was there a more mistaken reading of the facts.

Hooliganism we have met with on our march through the country, but that is a symptom of grave social disease, which it is part of our mission to deal with. Misunderstanding and ignorance, and apathy and prejudice we have encountered, but this it is the lot of all reformers to contend with. Everywhere we have gone we have also met with an inspiriting sympathy with our aims, a sense of the innate justice of our demand,

and of the deep need of the State for a new service and a new vision brought into politics.

'The country' said Miss Ashton on Friday night, 'is ripe for this great reform, and we shall never rest till it is granted.'

When the bugle rang out at six o'clock in the Park the resolution in favour of votes for women was put from nineteen different corners of the Park, and carried with ringing cheers, and an infinitesimal amount of dissent, from everyone. There was much cheering and clapping of hands, and no disorder or trouble of any kind, so far as one could tell, moving about in a fairly wide area of the Park.

The people didn't seem to want to go even then, but demanded more speeches and little groups remained around individual pilgrims listening to further explanations and argument. Here and there one met men arguing with each other, and men and women asking questions and signing cards, which set forth their sympathy with the cause of women's suffrage. And it was not only the National Union of Women's Suffrage Societies that was represented in the Park. We were all there, working by different methods for the same great end.

There were the Church League people, selling their paper at the gates, for the law does not allow sale of literature within its borders. There were the members of the WSPU, wearing the familiar colours of the purple, white and green, gaily selling their newspaper within the gates, being bound by no reverence for the law, such as handicapped our strictly law-abiding pilgrims! There were the members of the Women's Tax Resistance League, carrying parasols on which 'No Vote, No Tax' was written in large letters for all to see. There were actresses and nurses, writers and clerics, working women and working men, and we felt that we were all comrades and friends in a great cause.

After the meeting, the pilgrims of the Watling Street Route dined together at an Oxford Street restaurant, and a very merry gathering it was. There were many speeches and much laughter, and a great deal of noise. Miss Vera Collum, who rose to speak after repeated calls from a rowdy section of the company, 'We want the Mounted Column, we want the Mounted Column', roused considerable merriment by saying she couldn't possibly speak without her horse, and besides she'd never made a speech in her life, but said she, as she sat down, 'I write very good news.'

Lady Rochdale said she had had a good many rebuffs along the road but perhaps the worst was when her hostess looked her up and down, and then said in a disappointed voice 'Well, I was expecting to see a really nice working woman'.

Miss Eskrigge, our own particular organiser, refused to address such an uproarious gathering without police protection, and sat down amid much laughter.

Two Balliol students, who had been with the pilgrims for a considerable part of the route, and a student from Ruskin Hall, contributed a good deal of wit and liveliness to the proceedings, and all spoke in warm terms of the education and stimulus and happiness which the pilgrimage had brought to them. It was a fine idea that on Sunday afternoon the pilgrims should go together to St Paul's, thus recognising the essential spirituality of the women's movement which is indeed its driving force and the pledge of its triumph. Some of the pilgrims could not, of course, be there, but many hundreds of us assembled beneath the great dome, and the red, white and green of the colours was plentifully scattered up and down the vast congregation.

The pilgrimage culminated very fitly, and very beautifully in a service held on Sunday evening in the Ethical Church, Bayswater, when Miss Maude Royden gave a moving and uplifting address on the Pilgrim Spirit. No one who listened to her words will readily forget them; but as an inspiration and a call to more single-minded service they will remain with us in the days that are to come – days of steady drudgery, perhaps, and times of depression and slackness. The body of Suffragists known as Spiritual Militants,[2] were present at the service, and their flame-coloured sashes lent a note of splendid colour to the church. Their beautiful flame-coloured silk banner was inscribed with words which may have been taken to heart by those who do not yet understand what the suffrage cause stands for – 'The burning sense of a great wrong is the flaming spirit of God'.

After the service came the final gathering of the pilgrims, as guests of the Spiritual Militants, and in the hall below the church, tea and coffee, friendly talk and last goodbyes brought the day to an end, but very reluctantly did the pilgrims say farewell to their 'comrades of the road'.

In one sense it was the end of the great pilgrimage we were witnessing, but in a deeper sense we all felt that it was only the beginning of much greater and better work which the pilgrim spirit is going to enable us to do.

---

[2] The Spiritual Militancy League: not much known; see Elizabeth Crawford, *The Women's Suffrage Movement: a Reference Guide, 1866-1928*, (London & New York, 2001) 650.

23. Who's Who (1913)

From the *Suffrage Annual and Women's Who's Who* (London, 1913)

KEATING HILL, MRS. MARY

Society: WFL (Hon. Secretary Cardiff Branch); born at Mountain Ash, Glamorgan; daughter of Cornelius Keating, Mountain Ash; married Aug. 15th, 1894 to George Hill of Ludlow, Salop; one son and two daughters; sister of Mr. Matthew Keating, MP for South Kilkenny, Ireland, and of Joseph Keating, author; is descendant of same branch of Keatings as Geoffrey Keating of 'History of Ireland' fame; joined Mrs. Pankhurst in first stages of Suffrage work, was present at first raid on House of Commons; was the leader of the second raid in Lobby; Christmas week, 1906, arrested, sentenced to 14 days, entering Black Maria for Holloway Prison, suddenly liberated, astonished, brother had paid 'fine'; exasperated; another raid at once – Holloway at last, 21 days; Christmas day in prison. Recreations: Speaking (Suffrage and Reforms) and study. Address: 98, Diana Street, Roath, Cardiff.

MANSELL-MOULLIN, MRS. EDITH RUTH

Societies: Forward Cymric Suffrage Union, WSPU and Church League for Women's Suffrage; daughter of David Thomas and Anne Thomas (née Lloyd); wife of C. W. Mansell-Moullin, MA, MD (Oxon.), FRCS; one son, Oswald

Mansell-Moullin, MA, Cantab, FCS; founder of FCSU, which has an anti-Government policy and unites Welsh men and women, their sympathisers and friends, who are working for the enfranchisement of women before any other Cause, and who do not support any political party; was the Organiser of the Welsh contingent in the great 'Coronation' Suffrage procession, 1911; imprisoned in Holloway, November 1911, for going on a deputation to the House of Commons, headed by Mrs. Pethick Lawrence, to protest against the exclusion of women from the Manhood Suffrage Bill; was also on deputation with Mrs. Pankhurst, on Black Friday, and in the 'Battle of Downing Street', Nov. 1910, but was not arrested; speaks at numerous meetings in England and Wales. Tel.: Paddington, 1835. Address: 69, Wimpole Street, London.

24. Dr Helena Jones

Women's Votes in Wartime (1916)

The Suffragette News Sheet, September 1916

A very grave injustice would be done if any widening of the basis of the male electorate were to be made, and the sex disqualification not removed. Sir Edward Carsons's statement (during the debate in the House of Commons on Aug. 14th), that its proposed extension to all soldiers and sailors fighting on the various fronts, had nothing to do with women's votes, because, in the past men had had votes and women had not, is, of course, no argument; it is merely the statement of a reactionary and an extremely useful one to us Suffragists as it shows us the blatant prejudice we are up against. It is exactly what Mrs. Pankhurst has told us in the past (although, alas! she has departed from her first love now and gone over to the enemy), viz., that an extension of the franchise to further groups of men is always more easily imposed upon a male Parliament than the initial step of opening the franchise to women, so it behoves us to protest strongly against any alteration being made in the electorate unless women are included therein.

The following are 5 reasons why NOW is the psychological moment for demanding the admission of women to the franchise:

1. The political machine during the war may be likened to sealing wax to which heat has been applied: it is in a

condition to receive new impressions, such as the entrance of a new sex. After the war it will harden again, and the old difficulties with party shibboleths will be revived.

2. The immense labour problems that will be before the country at the declaration of peace will largely be problems affecting women's work, and should only be dealt with by a Parliament directly responsible to women, and this we cannot get, unless women are placed upon the Register soon enough to vote at the next election.

3. If women had not gone in thousands into munition factories, the men would not have been able to put up a fight; so that even IF fighting for the country should be a basis for registration (a standpoint I, personally, do not take), it would be merely unjust to enfranchise the men who fought and not to enfranchise the women who, by their labour, enabled them to fight.

4. In all this shrieking about fighting and fighters, we are apt to forget the future of the nation. What would have happened to the nation if the women had not kept the homes together? If the men had come back to find themselves homeless, and their children dead from want of care? While the men have been out to gain glory, the women have had the prosaic task of guarding the foundations of the nation. Is not this as much worthy of the vote as any work in the trenches?

5. Woman ought to be directly represented when peace terms are discussed; it is up to her to see that no such disaster as a world-wide war ever happens again.

In conclusion, let me repeat that NOW is the day of salvation for the women. NOW is the time when their claims should be acknowledged, and no supposed right of men to a wider franchise should be allowed to swamp the women's just demand.

*

Women as Citizens (1916)

Suffragette News Sheet, December 1916

There is a ridiculous anomaly today in our land. Women are everywhere being force into the limelight; in professions, in munition factories, on the land, in trams, in Government offices they are taking the place of the men who have gone or are going to the front. They are being cajoled by Cabinet Ministers (even Mr. Asquith himself) who assure them that without them the war could not have been carried on; that but for them the Empire would have fallen to pieces. There is even talk of conscripting them, so indispensable are they to their country. And yet – and this is the anomaly – these indispensables, these upholders of the Empire are still classed with idiots who cannot be trusted to vote.

Therefore, we Suffragettes of the WSPU demand that this injustice should immediately be removed. That no woman may vote is a much more elemental injustice than that any particular class of men is debarred, for the disqualification that prevents a woman voting, *viz.*, her sex, is born with her and remains with her all her life; she can never step over the bar. The disqualification that prevents any section of men voting is circumstantial and can be overcome as conditions alter.

We (the Suffragettes of the WSPU) consider that our business as a Women's Suffrage Society is to obtain the removal of the sex barrier. This is the Alpha and Omega of our present existence. What women are enfranchised and what women are not enfranchised is not our concern for the moment. We demand immediate Parliamentary action so that the women who can qualify under the existing Registration Act will be able to do so now, and in the future (perhaps near future), when the basis of the men's franchise is broadened, women's would then be broadened also. History teaches us that whenever the demand for women's enfranchisement is coupled with that of an extension of the existing male franchise, the latter has always succeeded at the expense of the former; the initiation of a new franchise is always so much more difficult than the extension of an existing one. It is therefore to be feared that those suffrage societies that have yielded to the fascination of 'votes for all men and women' are riding for a fall, for in such a demand there are two distinct reforms: (1) the acknowledgement of women as persons, and (2) the nearly doubling of the present male vote. These are both so far reaching in their effects that in all probability they will never materialize in one Act of Parliament, but once again the men may succeed and the women be left behind. These are the considerations that have led us to persist in the old demand 'votes for women on the same terms as they are or may be given to men' and the only safeguard for women's suffrage will be for a short bill enfranchising women to be passed before any change is made in the existing Franchise and Registration Acts.

25. Alice Abadam

The Feminist Vote: Enfranchised or Emancipated? (1918/19)

You are Enfranchised
Are you Emancipated?

Does the vote come to you as a mere external act and fact, a little detail in advancing democracy, a convenient means of reinforcing your political party, of crushing this measure and pushing that, of enabling you to take a languid hand in the game of politics as played by your men folk, and with their values attached to current questions? Have you no thought of handling your new power as a woman and for women, as a necessary set-off to the fact that it has been exercised for so long by men and for men, and that there is much leeway to be made up?

Inward Emancipation

Or, does the vote come to you as the fitting outward and visible sign of the inward emancipation of one who has long since achieved the freedom of her own spirit; whose eyes open fearlessly to truth, wheresoever found, and whose heart holds no parley with evil, however antique and undisputed? Can you laugh at the cowardice of conventions, and are you ready to expose the twisted roots of customs, though they may have twined themselves in places of supposed respectability?

Hypnotism of the *status quo*

Do you see in its rightful perspective the bad, mad past of dominating men and servile women, allotting the true causes to the terrible effects which crowd the highway of life and call for your healing hand? Are you free from the hypnotism of the *status quo*, and ready to dispel its baneful influence in others, shaking them out of their easy sleep in a Fool's Paradise? Do you feel the spirit of a Great Crusade, a Great Adventure stirring within you? Do you realize you are a New Force in the New World which is destined to rise, clean, sweet and white on the ruins of the Old Order now expiring amidst blood, savagery, lust, disease and famine?

Feminist or Conformist?

Will you use your vote merely as men have used theirs, conforming yourself to their methods and political usages, thereby leaving the world exactly as you find it, or will you use it in the spirit of independence, refusing to be entangled by Parties or traditions, and only bent on building a better world? In a word, are you a Feminist or a Conformist?

On the reply to this question depends your utility as a Builder of Better Things.

New Point of View

The ideal value of the women's vote is that it should be the vehicle of a new point of view, for if the State added even twelve millions of women to the Register, and these voted steadily as men dictated, what would it profit the country as an engine of reform? There would be a larger bulk of voting papers, but no reformation along feminist lines. The Slough of Despond would still remain rotting under its covering of green slime.

Woman's Fulcrum

But even one million of good, sound Feminists voting

with a well-understood aim, and coming into politics as an independent body, detached from Party trammels, and acting as free lances should, suddenly, swiftly, unexpectedly, and boldly, would become that group of indeterminable electors who are notoriously those to be most placated by the anxious Statesman. *Here* would be your power, here the spot on which to place the fulcrum which should move Legislative Assemblies.

Would you measure the utility of a Feminist vote? Then take the measure of men's fear of it. Illustrations of this fear lie around us on every hand. England, plunged in a great war, suddenly woke to the fact that women were an untapped resource, and many advertisements of an utterly new and unaccustomed purport, in largest type, occupied places of honour in the most respectable newspapers. '50,000 Women Wanted'. *Wanted*! Those few words spelt enfranchisement. England's necessity it was which brought justice to her daughters.

Let there be no abject expressions of fulsome gratitude. The vote is given because it is dangerous to withhold it. 'To frustrate this measure', said a Member of Parliament, 'would split the country from end to end'. The realisation of this, and the possible disaffection of millions of women workers, carried this measure through the Speaker's Conference, put a grim determination into the majority of the House of Commons and brought even the Lords along at a smart pace.

The Coverture Vote

For all that, signs were not wanting of a sullen anger at their forced débâcle. Out of the six millions of women voters some five million vote not by their own right, but in virtue of their husbands; a mere coverture vote. To women of any spirit, this condition for qualification of the vast majority of the newly enfranchised could not possibly have been more distasteful, and I can imagine that many a married woman will refuse, until she can hold it in her own right, to exercise the vote, which is as little hers as the 'worldly goods' with which the husband endows her in the lip-service of a pre-violated vow.

Fear of the Eternal Feminine

Even with the German at the gates, nay, over our heads, the principle of female enfranchisement has been established by law grudgingly, and hedged about by conditions that betoken not distrust so much as fear – a deep-seated primitive fear of the Eternal Feminine, especially in the person of the unmarried women, 'unbroken to harness' and free of sex influence. What but this has brought about the result of five million married women voters to one million unmarried? What else has caused the absurdity of the age qualification being placed at 30 except that it would obviously decrease the unfettered vote? In vain was it pointed out that Nature has ordained that a woman of 20 is 'older' than a man of 25, and that it was irrational to reverse the natural order by enfranchising the later maturing male at 19 and the earlier maturing female at 30. The truth was unwelcome and unanswered. The real motive of this disqualification was and is 'Fear, Little Brother, Fear!'

Belittling the Woman's Victory

Still, its faults notwithstanding, the passage into law of the Reform Bill, establishing the principle of woman's franchise, so long and ardently fought for, is a 'famous victory'. It is amusing to note the attempt which has been made in many directions to lessen the importance of the women's victory by passing it over as a thing of no moment, not worthy to be named in the same headline with 'P.R.'. Even newspapers of standing have resorted to these transparent tricks, the ancient stock in trade of the industrious minimiser of Fleet Street.

Above all things, woman, especially in the hour of her triumph, must be kept severely in her place.

> God bless the men and all their male relations
> And keep the women in their proper stations.

This anxiety that our enfranchisement should pass *sub silentio* into that back yard, where lie the things that must never command brass bands and fifes, or raise eyes of pride and vain-glory to Westminster Abbey, is evident in many quarters of private as well as public life. A learned barrister lately put the matter in a nutshell with one masterly word, indicating the meek and chastened spirit in which we were to take the trivial incident of our enfranchisement: 'Such questions as women's Suffrage must be as NOTHING at the present time', he writes. Ah! my sisters, slip off your gyves softly; no unseemly rejoicing as if you had, forsooth, anything to complain of before; go about as though nothing unusual had happened; do not grieve man's lordly soul with a hint, however distant, of his defeat, but hide such joy as you may feel under a pleasing exterior of indifference to those paltry matters which concern women only. Yes, Judith's unseemly success is to be labelled 'unimportant', but the man who does so has failed to comprehend the difference between an evil and its cure, that is, war, and the only basis of a permanent world peace.

The larger scope of Woman's Enfranchisement

Quite apart from the rights and wrongs of this or that war, people of all shades of opinion are agreed that regarded in the abstract, apart from the motives with which it may be undertaken, as a thing *per se*, war is a terrible occurrence. The slaughter, torture, maiming, loss of treasure, shortage of food, the ravaging of Nature's smiling face, the destruction of priceless collections of art and science, of the 'frozen music of architecture', the drink, crime, and immortality, the breakdown of the decencies of life and the rude scattering of humanity's garnered fruits, are merely the history of men's sole rule in constant repetition. We have seen it, and our foremothers have seen it in every age since first the man wrested from the woman the control of the State. Phaeton in his pride seized single-handed the Chariot of the Sun and set the universe in flames. There is nothing new in a war-ravaged world, it is the logical outcome, the ever recurring result of world domination by the fighting sex.

The recrudescence of the same fact with the same features, arising from the ever same cause, cannot be so significant, so vitally important as the introduction of a counter principle; that is the beginning, however small, of part government by the non-fighting sex; the balancing of the Destructive Death Dealer by the Constructive Life Producer.

Viewed thus, it will be seen that woman's emancipation is by far the most important happening of the day. Be assured it is the only force which will eventually end all war. That nothing else will, let the many thousand war-blotted years of male sway testify.

'The earth', says Shelley, 'is a tomb'. If it were only that! Rather is has been a slaughter house. Physical struggle, destruction, and death, have been the only final solution of differences of opinion or interest apparent to the male psychology. Such are his limitations; and never, perhaps, has his absence of intuition, and even (in some directions) of reasoning power, been so striking as when he fails to discern the meaning, the inwardness, and the far-reaching scope of woman's advent to power. So blurred is his inward vision that he passes by without recognition that which is the one authentic harbinger of permanent peace. He does not understand the root reason of his own miseries, and therefore does not estimate at its true value that counter force which is destined to dispel them as surely as the Constructive checks the Destructive, the Anabolic balances the Catabolic, producing perfect equilibrium, and the centripetal leads back to the still centre of sweetest and deepest life the erring fury of the Centrifugal.

Woman her full self

With these thoughts before us, it is impossible to over-estimate the importance of woman being her full self. Her whole power as the *opposite* to man is needed. The world is sick well nigh unto death for the womanly touch, and that not in sentiment but in *power*. The Constructive Feminist has to be no man's shadow. She must be herself – keen of vision, strong, independent, courageous, and free to the very soul of all taint of sex servility. So, and only so, can she save a stricken world. She is out to reverse hideous evils, war, drink, prostitution and many another curse. Let her take as her watchword, 'Not by sex alone shall woman live'; for the lack of understanding this has been the serpent's inmost coil. Let her bathe her spirit in Freedom and wash away in the waters of a new baptism the dark accretions of her long sex slave existence.

It is the consecration to this Greater Feminism in its purity and unconquerable strength which will fit her to be the Priestess of the future endowed at last with the power to carry out her inward vision.

O Femina gloriosa! Procede, prospere et regna.

26. Gwladys Perrie Williams

Woman's Opportunity (1919)

Welsh Outlook vol. vi, 1919

Woman is today faced with her greatest opportunity. The heavy burdens and responsibilities of War she bore with courage and skill; the problems of peace and reconstruction will make even greater demands on her fortitude and resource. Housing, health, education, the provision of a better standard of life for those who grind and toil for the production of the country's wealth – all these problems must have the woman's hand to help in their shaping. Her great opportunity lies in the fact that for the first time she has political expression. She is not bound by the shibboleths of old party distinctions, empty enough in 1914, but sheer dry husks now. Unlike her men folk she is not tied to the chariot wheels of any one party; she is free to support the measures which are in the highest interests of the community, whichever political group may have sponsored such measures.

This is true of woman throughout the kingdom, but it has a special significance for us in Wales. Wales has been for so many years the battle-ground of conflicting political groups, all of which claim to act in the interest of Wales. Conservative and Liberal for 50 years fought over the question of religious equality. They still fight each other, tradition exacts it of them. Nationalism in this tug of war is in danger of being torn to shreds. These heterogeneous elements prevent the 'Welsh Party' from being anything but a species of Debating Society, since the members are tied by the separate parties, from whose platform they stepped into Parliament.

A real Welsh Party, with a policy based on Welsh nationalism, a policy that would make Welsh national needs its first and foremost consideration, irrespective of the tenets of any existing political party; a policy that would coincide with that of the Labour Party if it coincided with the requirements of Wales, with that of the Liberal or of the Conservative Party, if the interest of Wales so demanded, that is the only thing that will save Wales from being torn asunder by the ever increasing factions which seek to govern it.

Our men-folk, partially blinded by the prejudices of past bitter struggles often fail to see all the issues. Nationalism for many of them has lost its meaning; they confuse it with Chauvinism. In their yearning for a broader *international* conception – that of the brotherhood of man – they forget that the basis of internationalism must be sound nationalism.

The highest ideal of world brotherhood should have its roots in real love for one's own country, pride in its traditions, faith in its destiny.

There are welcome signs, particularly among the young Welshmen of today, of dissatisfaction with the various policies which fight for the cloak of Welsh nationalism. Groups of these young Welshmen have pledged themselves to the furtherance of the true interests of Wales, the preservation of their language and native culture. However well they plan their movement is foredoomed to failure unless the women of Wales are ready to act as the 'flame-bearers' of Welsh traditions. Their power in the State is a force to be reckoned with, for they form more than half the electorate. Our women have proven themselves, during four and a half trying years, in every way qualified for admission to full citizenship. Let them use their newly acquired political power to weld together a United Wales, to obtain for her that recognition as a national entity, without which her full development is impossible. Administrative work is no new thing to the Welsh woman, nor is she unaccustomed to handling a vote. Nonconformity has given her all the opportunities, on a smaller scale, which a benevolent State at last bestows upon her. She is perfectly ripe for political organisation. It is the hour of her great opportunity. What will she do? Will she put *Wales* first, or will she subordinate it to the considerations of one of the political parties which have our men in their grip? On her answer depends the political future of Wales.

The influence of woman is infinitely deeper and more far-reaching than when reckoned in terms of voting strength. There is a power which can strike at the root of all movement, and that power is in the hands of the mothers. Men may plan and evolve ambitious schemes for the national development of Wales, but the ideals of the future are in the mother's keeping. Hers is the supreme power, the power that no political organisation in itself can equal. The measure of her power is the measure of her responsibility, for the Wales of tomorrow depends on the mother of today. There are still, alas, homes where children are brought up to regard their native language as something inferior, and their race inheritance as something to be carefully hidden under an artificial crust of English veneer.

The need for a national atmosphere in the home was never greater, for no programme of national development can hope for any but ephemeral success unless the foundations are securely laid in the home.

The future definition of the term Wales depends on the attitude of Welsh women of today. In the darkest hours of the history of the race, the women never faltered, never failed. What will they do now?

27. Rachel Barrett

Autobiography [1] (c. 1924)

I was born in Carmarthen of Welsh, Welsh-speaking parents.
I lived there, or in that neighbourhood, until I was grown up
and for some years after. I was educated at a private boarding
school in Stroud; later I won a scholarship into Aberystwyth
College and worked there for my degree of B.Sc. London. I got
my degree in 1904 after I had taught Science and Mathematics
for three years at Carmarthen County School. In 1905 I became
science mistress at Penarth County School and taught there
two years, and it was during this time that I became interested
in the new movement for woman suffrage.

In 1906, like everybody else, I read in the newspapers of
the campaign of the militants and felt from the very first that
they were doing the right and only thing. I had always been
a suffragist – since I first began to think of the position of
women at all – but with no hope of ever seeing women win
the vote.

In the Autumn of that year Mrs. Martel[2] spoke in Cardiff. It
was my first opportunity of joining the WSPU and I signed a
membership card at the end of the meeting.

---

[1] A type-written fragment in the Suffragette Fellowship Collection at the
Museum of London (ref. 57.116/47); reproduced by permission of the
Museum.

[2] Nellie Alma Martel was active in the suffrage movement in Australia, and
from 1905 a speaker and activist for the WSPU in Britain.

Soon after, Adela Pankhurst[3] came to Cardiff as WSPU organiser and I helped her in her work, speaking at meetings, indoors and outdoors, and falling into great disfavour with my headmistress who considered all public work of that kind unsuitable for a woman teacher, more especially when her science mistress was reported in the local papers as drenched with flour at an open-air meeting at the Cardiff docks.

In July 1907 I resigned my post as Penarth and entered as a student at the London School of Economics, intending to study economics and sociology and do some research with a view to getting my D.Sc. in Economics. During the summer I worked with Adela Pankhurst in Bradford and in my first by-election at Bury St. Edmunds with Mrs. Pankhurst, Mrs. Martel, Gladys Keevil, Ada Lamb, Elsa Gye and other stalwarts.[4] In the autumn I studied as an internal student of London University at the School of Economics but found the time to attend innumerable WSPU meetings and to speak at many of them During the winter vacation I helped at the Mid-Devon election, and on my return to London Christabel Pankhurst asked me to give my whole time to the movement and to become an organiser. I was sorry to give up my work at the School and all that it meant, but this was a definite call and I obeyed.

I was sent to Nottingham to organise a campaign there, which lasted some weeks; there were several by-elections, and, when it was over, and I went back to Nottingham to resume work there, I collapsed completely and realised that I could not go on. I resigned my post as organiser and the next year was spent recuperating in various places, including a sanatorium. In the autumn of 1909 I was better and went to

---

[3] Third daughter of Emmeline Pankhurst, and generally lesser-known sister of Christabel and Sylvia.

[4] For brief biographies of all of these women see Elizabeth Crawford, *The Women's Suffrage Movement: a Reference Guide 1866-1928* (London & New York, 2001).

Bristol to work with Annie Kenney[5] as a voluntary worker. I agreed to take up organising again and I was sent to Newport, Mon.. There I worked for some time organising meetings, speaking, raising funds and taking part in protests at meetings, organising militancy; in fact doing the routine work of a WSPU organiser.

When the truce to militancy was decided upon during the time of the Conciliation Bill I was sent to the constituency of the chief opponent, Mr. Lloyd George. There I interviewed his supporters, organised meetings and finally led a deputation to him of women from his constituency. We were received at his house in Criccieth where we spent 2 ½ hours around his dining table arguing hotly. We left, I more convinced than before of his determined opposition to the WSPU and the insincerity of his support of the suffrage, and the other women (mostly liberal and not WSPU members) with their eyes very much opened.[6]

Not long after this I became organiser for Wales with my headquarters in Cardiff. From there I organised a deputation of leading Welsh Liberal women to Mr. Lloyd George. I went to London with the deputation but did not accompany them on the interview as I thought it wiser to remain in the background.

In the spring of 1912 after the raid at the headquarters and Christabel Pankhurst's escape to Paris, I was chosen by Annie Kenney to help her to run the national WSPU campaign which had been put into her hands by Christabel. In the autumn I was asked to take charge of the new paper *The Suffragette* – an appalling task as I knew nothing whatever of journalism.

---

[5] A leading figure in the WSPU, Kenney came from a Lancashire working-class family, and had briefly worked in a mill, which was made much of for propaganda purposes; organizer in the west of England from 1907.

[6] This is the meeting between 'the Chancellor and the Suffragettes' referred to in Olive Stephenson-Howells' letter to the *SWDN* , 1 Oct. 1910, reprinted above.

However, after terrible struggles and some mistakes I was able to carry on to the satisfaction of the editor in Paris, whom I went over to see every now and then and to whom I often talked on the telephone when I could always hear the click of Scotland Yard listening in. In April 1913 on Wednesday morning when we were making up the paper a group of CID men appeared and the staff of the paper were arrested together with Miss Kerr, Mrs. Sanders[7] and Annie Kenney. The police seized all the materials from printing the paper both at Kingsway House and the printers – but, owing to the efforts of Gerald Gould and the *Daily Herald*, *The Suffragette* appeared that week as usual though in a slightly attenuated form.

I appeared in Bow Street police court after a night in Holloway and was then remanded on bail. At the Old Bailey trial in June, I was sentenced to a month in the third division. I spent the first night in Holloway and started the hunger strike at once. Early the next morning, without being told where I was going, I was taken to Canterbury prison. There, in spite of my struggles, I was made to wear prison clothes until an order came from the Home Office giving me permission to wear my own. I was taken to the Infirmary and, after a fight, my finger prints were taken. I was released on licence after a 5-day hunger strike and went to 'Mouse Castle', the house run as a nursing home for 'mice' by Dr Flora Murray.[8] In about 3 weeks time, when I went out, I was re-arrested. This time I was in for 4 days – and then again to Mouse Castle. When I had recovered I was smuggled away from there and later, getting in in disguise, addressed a meeting at the Memorial Hall. The

---

[7] Harriet Roberta Kerr, Beatrice Sanders; the arrested group were tried and imprisoned for conspiracy to cause damage.

[8] This takes its name from the 1913 Prisoners' Temporary Discharge Through Ill health Act, otherwise known as the Cat and Mouse Act: hunger-striking suffragist prisoners would be released before they became dangerously ill, but would be re-arrested to complete their sentence once they appeared in public, apparently fit enough to be active. The government 'Cat' thus cruelly played with the suffragist 'Mouse'.

detectives were waiting for me in the body of the Hall and, after a hard struggle in which a group of members tried to defend me, I was re-arrested on leaving the hall. This time I did the thirst strike as well as the hunger strike and was released after, I think, 5 days feeling very ill. I escaped from Mouse Castle to the house of a friend and then went to Edinburgh to a nursing home where I remained under treatment, until December 1913. Then I returned to London and was smuggled into Kingsway House under the eyes of the detectives. I had one of the rooms there fitted up as a bed-sitting room and I lived there until May, bringing out *The Suffragette* as before, never leaving the office and taking my exercise on the roof.

In May, as my health was suffering a little from the confinement, I got away for a holiday abroad and, while I was away, the office was again raided. I saw Christabel in Paris, and it was arranged that, owing to the difficult position of any printer who printed *The Suffragette*, we should bring the paper out in Scotland where newspaper law was not the same as in England. Accordingly I went to Edinburgh, lived there under the name of Miss Ashworth, the police having apparently lost all trace of me, and again brought out the paper until the last number appeared on the Friday after war was declared between this Country and Germany.

28. Margaret, Lady Rhondda

This was My World (1933)

[…]

I did not read much political stuff. Politics interested me, they always had (they were talked half the time at home, since my father was in Parliament); but, though I considered them and puzzled about them a good deal, I did not, for all their fascination, attempt to study them. What was the use of taking the trouble to know and understand something in which one could have neither part nor lot? How, indeed, failing the right to practise politics, could one ever really hope to know them except superficially from the outside? And to know things from the outside never interested me. It is true that some of the girls I knew worked mildly in subordinate capacities for the National Liberal Federation or the Primrose League, or helped their fathers or husbands. But I never had much use for acting as a substitute for someone else, or in a permanently subordinate capacity. No, politics were not for my touching.
[Ch IX, 96-7]

[…]

So little did I know about myself or what was inside me when I married that during my engagement I withdrew from a local branch of the Liberal Social Council, to which, as my father's daughter, I belonged, on the plea that as I was marrying a man who came of a Conservative family I must now become a

Conservative. That was the traditional and correct thing for wives to do. My mother had changed her party affiliations (the other way about); every other woman I knew had done it. It never occurred to me that there was anything in my heart to prevent me following the same course. It is true I cordially disliked the Liberal Social Council, since it seemed to me to have been deliberately formed to exploit in the interests of the party that sensitive and responsive nerve of snobbery which lies – whether hidden or not – in each one of us, and which has always seemed to me one of the most unattractive bits of all the human make-up […] I do not doubt that my dislike facilitated my resignation. [...].

Such meekness lasted an uncommonly short while. Within four months of my marriage I had joined the Pankhursts' organisation, 'The Women's Social and Political Union', and shaken, as my pledge of membership bade me, the dust of all the parties from off my feet, until such time as 'the vote is granted to women on the same terms as it is or may be granted to men.' And when the Franchise Act of 1928 came and set me free of my pledge, I had too long regarded parties from outside to feel that I could ever again walk inside one.
[Ch IX, 109-10]

[…]

The militant suffrage movement was a thrilling discovery. It supplied the answer to a thousand puzzling problems. And it gave the chance of activity. A cousin, Florence Haig, a contemporary of my mother's, an artist who lived in Chelsea, had been caught up into it, and when she came out of prison, we, much interested all three of us to hear all about it, asked her down to Llanwern. That was in the early days of the suffrage movement, when the whole idea of prison was still very much of a novelty. The result of her visit, so far as I was concerned was the determination to walk in a Suffrage Procession to Hyde Park. I was within a month of being married at the time, and had a certain difficulty – though really not so very much – in persuading my future husband that there was no harm in the plan. My mother accompanied me, (a) because she did not think an unmarried girl should walk unchaperoned through the gutter, (b) because she believed in votes for women. In the event I thoroughly enjoyed the procession, which she did not. She came of a generation which took the gutter and casual street insults hard.

I do not remember that at that time I had thought the thing out at all. I had been brought up, it is true, in a home which believed in votes for women, but up until that visit of Cousin Florence's the fact had meant, so far as I was aware, very little to me. And when she came I went into the militant movement instinctively, thrilled with this chance for action, this release for energy, but unaware that this at last was what I had, all unconsciously, been seeking for, and, at first, totally ignorant of, and unconcerned with, the arguments for our cause. It was a temperamental, not in any sense an intellectual conversion.

Having made up my mind, however, I had to discover why I believed what I did. Throughout the following year I got and read every book and every pamphlet for and against suffrage. I had drawers and drawers full of pamphlets; the house was thick with them… My intellectual assent was complete, but it came second, not first. […]
[Ch. IX, 118-9]

One sometimes hears people who took part in the suffrage campaign pitied. And indeed one knows that there were those to whom it was a martyrdom, who gave everything they had – health, and even life – for it. […] But for me, and for many other young women like me, militant suffrage was the very salt of life. The knowledge of it had come like a draught of fresh air into our padded, stifled lives. It gave us release of energy, it gave us that sense of being of some use in the scheme of things, without which no human being can live at peace. It made us feel we were part of life, not just outside watching it. It made us feel that we had a real purpose and use apart from having children [....] It gave us hope of freedom and power and opportunity. It gave us scope at last, and it gave us what normal healthy youth craves – adventure and excitement. Prison itself, its loneliness (I only tasted it once), its sense of being padlocked in, was indeed sheer taut misery – and there was a lot of dull drudgery too, as there is in all work; but the things people expected one to mind, speaking at rowdy street-corner meetings, selling papers in the gutter, walking clad in sandwich boards in procession, I for my part thoroughly enjoyed, and I suspect that most of my contemporaries did the same. We were young, after all, and we enjoyed experience. These things might frighten us a little in project, but they satisfied the natural appetite of youth for colour and incident.

*

After the procession in Hyde Park I determined to join the Pankhursts organisation, the Women's Social and Political Union, but was held up in this resolve for three months by the fact that my father, who had considerable foresight and realised pretty well what joining that body was likely to mean, was inclined to oppose the idea. However, I finally decided that he could be no judge of a matter which concerned one primarily as a woman. Prid[1] meanwhile had, travelling by a slightly different road, arrived at the same conclusion. [...] She and I met one autumn day in London, and, full of excitement, went off together to Clement's Inn and joined.

Whereupon it occurred to some of my father's Merthyr constituents that it would be a pretty compliment to my father to ask me to come and address the local Liberal Club on suffrage. Since I had never spoken in my life save for that one

---

[1] Elizabeth Pridden, her best friend from school days.

Welsh sentence of my childhood and an occasional 'Thank you very much' when the constituents cheered my father's family, I felt, not unnaturally, a little nervous. Moreover, it was obvious that the opportunity of getting inside a Liberal Club must be used to full advantage. So I wrote to Annie Kenney, one of the leaders of the WSPU, and asked her to accompany me, and persuaded the secretary of the club to allow her to speak too. Also I asked Annie Kenney how one learnt to speak. 'Tell them' replied she, 'firstly what you want, secondly why you want it, and thirdly how you mean to get it'. It was a simple formula for an inexperienced speaker, and for years I based every speech upon it.

Unfortunately just before we went up to Merthyr there had been an incident at Bristol in which someone had threatened Mr. Churchill with a whip, and the Liberals were much enraged. Moreover, the executive of the club, in inviting us, had rather overlooked the point of view of its younger members. It should not have done so. They arrived in large quantities – the little hall was in fact packed to capacity – and they brought with them gongs, tin trumpets and other musical instruments, herrings (a great many herrings) and tomatoes. In fact, the only four really unpleasant things that were missing – I met them all later – were flour bags, eggs, squibs and the evil-smelling carbon bisulphide gas.

It may be supposed that, with so many musical instruments in the room, speaking was not so easy – in fact, so far as being heard was concerned, it was impossible. The chairman implored us to give up the meeting and make our escape through a way at the back of the platform. But Annie Kenney utterly refused to do anything of the kind. It appeared that if one closed any meeting in less than one hour from the time of its opening, one was apt to give the impression to the enemy that it had been broken up, and that one had been forced to fly. Such a course, it was explained to us, was never so much as contemplated in suffragette circles. So Annie Kenney and I stood together at the front of the platform and took it in turns to speak. No one could hear us, we could not hear ourselves – if I wanted to make Annie Kenney hear I had to bawl at the top of my voice into her ear – but honour was being satisfied.

A herring is a floppy thing, there is nothing much to it unless thrown very hard; and a ripe tomato, though messy and damaging to clothes, does not hurt at all. For my part I was uncommonly relieved not to have to make a speech that anyone could hear, and, not being in the position of chief responsibility, I was pleasantly exhilarated by the whole affair. At the end of a short hour, the chairman, with infinite relief – but of course entirely inaudibly – declared the meeting closed. Walking with slow dignity, we left the platform and hall by the back way he had suggested.

*

Following the conviction on my part that it was essential that our local town, Newport, should be converted to suffrage, and that the best way to achieve this result would be hire the largest hall in the town and get Christabel Pankhurst to come and speak to its inhabitants. […] I booked the Temperance Hall. Christabel Pankhurst refused to come, but Mrs. Pankhurst accepted the invitation. I had never heard or seen either of them, and should have preferred the one nearest to my own age. But so long as I got a Pankhurst I did not greatly care which. So far so good. There were, however, other difficulties. To begin with every young hooligan in the town threatened joyously to come and break up the meeting; and further it seemed that one had to find a chairman and stewards. Stewards materialised from somewhere by some kind of magic, but they were not stewards who had ever stewarded at, or so much as attended, a public meeting before. As for the chair, since there was no one else to be found, I decided to take it myself. I had only spoken once in my life – at Merthyr – and in the

circumstances I could scarcely feel I had been initiated into
the art of speaking. Moreover, what I did know about the
possibility of rowdy meetings did not help or encourage me.
The only thing I knew for certain was that I did now know
enough to keep a rowdy meeting in order.

Well, the evening came. The crowd came – packing the hall
to overflowing. The rowdy youths came. And one other factor
I had scarcely reckoned upon came – Mrs. Pankhurst. She
held that audience in the hollow of her hand. When a youth
interrupted her she turned and dealt with him, silenced him,
and without faltering in the thread of her speech, used him
as an illustration of an argument. The audience was so intent
to hear every word that even when one little group of youths
let out that aforementioned evil-smelling gas it did no more
than cause a faint stir in one small corner of the hall. As Mrs.
Pankhurst continued the interruptions got fewer and fewer,
and at last ceased altogether. Even when at the end came
question-time, members of the audience were uncommonly
chary of delivering themselves into her hands. That meeting
was a revelation of the power of a great speaker.[…]
[Ch. X, 120-25].

X – was a fair-sized mining village. One member of the
Newport branch of the WSPU lived there, and she appeared to
begin with to welcome the idea of an X – crusade. So one day,
early in the afternoon, we set out – three of us: Prid, who was
staying with me at the time; Miss C-, an elementary school
teacher and an enthusiastic local member, and I. Our plan was
the usual one. We would prospect the town; decide upon the
best place for an open-air meeting; hire our lorry; chalk the
streets with the announcement of the time (probably 7.30) and
place of the meeting; call on the leading inhabitants and ask
them to make a point of being present, have some high tea and
a short rest-pause, and then hold the meeting.

[…] Directly we began chalking the streets […] we realised

that X-'s reactions to militant suffrage were likely to be militant. When we returned to Mrs. H.'s house for tea [...] we were followed by a crowd which filled the whole of the square outside. After tea I had occasion to cross the square to a house on the other side. I returned with my hat and purse-bag gone and my hair pulled down my back. We began to look forward to the meeting with some trepidation. However, together, the three of us struggled through the crowd to the appointed place, at which we found the lorry waiting. And we struggled through the meeting. I doubt if the crowd heard much of anything we said; and I do dislike rotten eggs more than any other kind of political missile I know; the smell of them clung about us till we bathed, and as for our motor veils, we burnt them. However, I will say that the bundles of *Votes for Women* sold like hot cakes; we had not one left to take home. Which was something.

[...] The station was a quarter of a mile away, and the meeting was impatiently waiting for us to get down off the lorry, obviously looking forward to considerable further entertainment, and more inclined for real mischief than I have ever seen a crowd. Someone – the usual friendly person that exists, thank goodness, in every nasty crowd – told us of a short cut to the station, through some narrow back gardens, and explained the way. So we got down, managed somehow to dodge our pursuers, jumped a couple of small hedges, and ran through rows of cabbages to the station. But the crowd, though it had missed the way we had taken, knew nicely that we were making for the station. We got there first, but by a few moments only; it was close on our heels [...] The little local station was empty, not a porter, not a station-master – nothing. Nothing but the crowd. We ran on to the platform and over the footbridge. Our pursuers followed. And then one of us had the idea of taking refuge in the ladies' waiting-room. 'They won't dare to come in there', we said. It was a particularly stupid plan, because the crowd was in no mood to respect the notice

'Ladies'. And in any case one should always face a crowd in
the open, and never run from it. An English crowd (but this
was a Welsh one, which is not quite the same thing) seldom
does much damage out of doors, but a small enclosed space is a
trap in which two or three temporarily mad youths may do real
harm. Still, the 'Ladies Only' did keep them hesitating for a
minute or two, and then they began to get over their hesitation.
In another minute they would have been in. Miss C – started
to charge them with her umbrella. Prid and I dashed at her and
reft it from her. To use force when you are in a minority of a
hundred to one is sheer lunacy. To make them angrier than
they were was madness [...]

And then we heard a new sound [...]. And there, guarded by
a posse of police, appeared my mother, come to tell us that the
car was waiting outside [...] The youths fell back; we pushed
out of the waiting room. The police made way for us through
the crowd [...]. My mother, her head erect and her cheeks pink,
walked sedately first. The crowd, afraid to do more, kicked her
as she went by. Following close behind her, and now secure
in the protection of the police, I kicked back. Outside, looking
the picture of misery, sat our old chauffeur. Still guarded, we
stepped into the car and drove off.
[Ch. XI, 139-43].

There were many families in those days in which the militancy
of the women caused bitter divisions. But ours was never
one of them. The fact that my father was actually a Liberal
Member of Parliament might have been expected to present
its problems, but somehow, it seldom did.

My mother, who, though she has a conscience like a rock, is
good at tactful compromise, always managed to work loyally
for him during election time, though she did have her occasional
difficulties in combining her loyalty to all sides. During one
election [...] my father went down with influenza, and she [...]
had to appear at all his meetings to apologise for his absence.

At one of them one of the Under-Secretaries of the recent Ministry was to be the star turn. When the speakers reached the crowded hall they saw seated in a prominent position in the front row a couple of well-known local suffragettes. My father's agent was much perturbed and decided to have them turned out. My mother took him aside and pointed out to him quietly that this was unnecessary, as the orders of the WSPU (whose word with all its members was law) were that only Ministers of cabinet rank were to be interrupted. However, he much fussed, and heartily loathing all suffragettes, was not convinced, and preferring to be on the safe side said that he would eject them all the same. 'If you do' said my mother, 'I walk off the platform'. They remained.
[Ch. XI, 148-9]

Various small acts of militancy had been performed by our local branch, but we had not done anything very spectacular or been particularly successful. I decided that we had better try burning letters. As it happened, burning letters was the one piece of militancy of which, when it was first adopted, I had disapproved. I could not bear to think of people expecting letters and not getting them. I had come round to it very reluctantly, partly on 'the end justifies the means' principle; but chiefly on the ground that everyone knew we were doing it and therefore knew they ran the risk of not getting their letters; and that it was up to the public to stop us if they really objected, by forcing the Government to give us the vote.

However, when it came to the point it was obvious that in the case of a local district, at some distance from headquarters, burning the contents of pillar boxes had, tactically, much to recommend it. Acts which shall damage property without risking life and which shall not involve the certain risk of being caught are, as anyone who has tried them knows, much more difficult to perform than they sound. Even to cut a telegraph wire, when it has to be done secretly on a moonless night, and when one considers that telegraph wires are frequently to be reached only across hedges and ditches, are almost always above one's reach, and that an ordinary wire-cutter has little or no effect upon them, is a very difficult thing for the novice to attempt. Setting fire to letters in pillar boxes was amongst the easiest of the things we could find to do, although, as I was presently to discover, even that presents its difficulties if one is well known in the locality. So one summer's day I went off to Clement's Inn to get the necessary ingredients. I was given, packed in a rather flimsy covered basket, twelve long glass tubes, six of which contained one kind of material and the other six another. So long as they were separate all was well, but if one smashed one tube of each material and mixed the contents together, they broke, so it was explained to me, after a minute or two, into flames. I carried the basket home close beside me on the seat in a crowded third-class railway carriage, and the lady next door to me leant her elbow from time to time upon it. I reflected that if she knew as much as I did about the contents she would not do that.

Having got the stuff home, I buried it in the vegetable garden under the black-currant bushes, and a week or so later, dug it up and took it one day into the Newport Suffragette Shop to explain to other members of committee what an easy business setting fire to pillar boxes would be for us all to practise in our spare moments. They were uncommonly reluctant to be convinced. Nothing, I assured them, could be safer or easier; one pushed the two tubes in, as one passed the letter box, smashing them on the inside edge of the letter box as one let them drop. It looked to other passers-by exactly as if one were posting a letter. How simple! They were much impressed, but they could none of them see it in quite that way. And I could think of no better method of convincing them of the ease of the operation than by posting the first tubes myself. In an case, as secretary of the local Society I felt it to be rather my duty to lead off.

The thing proved a good deal more complicated than I had supposed. My heart was beating like a steam engine, my throat was dry, and my nerve went so badly that I made the mistake of walking several times backwards and forwards past the letter box before I found courage to push the packets in. Then, as they were rather bulky, I had to force them a bit before they would drop …When I had finished I collected the basket from the Suffragette Shop, carried it home again and re-buried it under the blackcurrant bushes. […]

As the trial drew near it became certain that I should be given the option of a fine. My husband and I discussed the matter *ad nauseam*. He took the line that in view of my promise [to him] I must pay the fine and not go to prison at all. I, on the other hand, whilst I admitted that he had the right to take that view if he chose, felt that it would be very bad indeed for the movement in our part of the country if I did not go to prison, and that I should be letting down the suffrage cause badly. Finally, I persuaded him to let me go – anyway for a bit. Then we had a further long argument on the question of hunger striking. Here again I felt that it would be very bad for our local organisation if I failed to carry out what had by then come to be regarded as the usual suffragette procedure in prison. I was in a stronger position here, for I had made no promise, and finally he agreed to that too. […]

In court I pleaded a formal 'Not guilty', as that was what the WSPU enjoined on everyone who was taken up, but I made no special effort to pretend that I had not done the thing. […]

I was, of course, found guilty ('one month with the option of a fine', I think it was) and sent off to the county gaol at Usk. As a suffragette I was - provided I behaved myself – allowed certain privileges, amongst which the most important were that I might wear my own clothes and take in some books of my own. Hunger striking, of course, was not behaving oneself, but no one could tell if one was going to do that until one got there, although the authorities had had a pretty good idea that

I intended to and before I left Newport the Chief Constable did his best to get an assurance out of me that I would eat. [...]

I had made up my mind that I would not touch food whilst I was in prison. I had further decided that in order to hurry on the time when I should be weak enough to be let out I would refuse drink for as long as I could; but would take it if and when I found my thirst unendurable. [...]

I did not feel particularly hungry, but I did get terribly thirsty. By the end of three days I had reached the stage where I had difficulty in restraining myself from drinking the contents of the slop pail. Incidentally I was perceptibly weaker, and it seemed that the prison doctor was aware of this. So at that point I took some water, and promptly got quite strong again. It was extraordinary the difference that water made. [...] at the end of five days they let me out. I imagine that I could have been kept twice or three times that length of time without much danger to myself. But I lived near Usk, and I suppose the prison authorities did not wish to take any risks with me. [...]

I had been imprisoned under the Cat and Mouse Act and should normally have been re-arrested as soon as I had recovered, to serve a further term. However, my fine was paid just before I was due to go back.
[Ch. XII, 152-61].

At last, when in 1928, the vote came on equal terms, one felt free to drop the business.

It was a blessed relief to feel one had not got to trouble with things of that sort any more. They are essential, of course. They must be done. And I like and respect the women who do them – indeed, the chief attraction of the work to me was that, in the course of doing it, one came across such extraordinarily fine people. Some of the nicest people I have ever known were, and are, doing that work – but it is not really my kind of work: it never has been. I was never much interested in changing the details of laws. I want bigger game than that.

I had loved, it is true, every minute of that militant fight before the war. That had to be done. There are times when to change the law is the quickest – indeed, the only – way to change public opinion. The period of the militant movement had been such a time. But even so that fight of ours was only ostensibly concerned with changing the law. The vote was really a symbol. And the militant fight itself did more to change the status of women – because it did more to alter our own opinion of ourselves – than the vote ever did. In actual fact, in those years we were changing the attitude of a country – nay, of the world; for in that fight England led the way. The other nations followed after. That was infinitely worth the doing. [Ch. XIX, 299-300]

Other Titles in the Honno Classics Series:

Betsy Cadwaladyr: A Balaclava Nurse
An Autobiography of Elizabeth Davis
edited by Jane Williams, with an introduction by
Deirdre Beddoe.

Elizabeth Davis – known in Wales
as Betsy Cadwaladyr – was a ladies'
maid from Meirionnydd who travelled
the world and gained fame as a nurse
during the Crimean War. She was a
dynamic character who broke free
of the restrictions placed on women
in Victorian times to lead a life of
adventure.

978 1870206 914   £8.99

Eunice Fleet
by Lily Tobias

First published in 1933, this is a deeply
moving story about the treatment of
conscientious objectors during the First
World War.

*'This is an important book to be made
available and I found myself wondering
why it had ever been lost.'* Mslexia

978 1870206 655   £8.99

The Rebecca Rioter
by Amy Dillwyn

Set amidst the notorious Rebecca Riots
of the 1830s, this is the tale of Evan
Williams, a young working class man,
struggling to come to terms with the
injustice and social inequalities of the
world he lives in. His rebellious actions
have dramatic consequences not only
for himself, but inadvertently, for the
woman he loves.

'powerful and engaging' Karen Rosenburg, The Women's
Review of Books

978 1870206 433   £8.99

A Woman's Work is Never Done
by Elizabeth Andrews, edited by Ursula
Masson, with a forword by Glenys
Kinnock.

Elizabeth Andrews was one of the most
influential female political activists of the
early 20th century. This new collection
brings together for the first time her
memoir with many of her political
articles from the 1920s-40s.

978 1870206 785   £8.99

Other titles in the Honno Classics series

Iron and Gold
by Hilda Vaughan
Introduction by Jane Aaron
*A skillful retelling of the best
known Welsh Fairy Bride
folktale, 'The Lady of Llyn y
Fan Fach'.*
> ISBN 978 1870206 501
> £8.99

The Small Mine
by Menna Gallie
Introduction by Angela John
*A Valley community, in
particular its women, struggle
to come to terms with the tragic
death of a young collier.*
> ISBN 978 1870206 389
> £6.99

Strike for a Kingdom
by Menna Gallie
Introduction by Angela John
*The secrets and tensions of a
close-knit mining community
are exposed in the reprint of this
'outstanding detective story',
set at the time of the miners'
strike in 1926.*
> ISBN 978 1870206 587
> £6.99

A View Across the Valley:
***Short stories by women
from Wales c1859-1950***
edited by Jane Aaron
*'A ground-breaking collection
of Anglo-Welsh short stories...'
Liz Saville, Gwales.*
> ISBN 978 1870206 358
> £7.95

**Queen of the Rushes: A
Tale of the Welsh Revival**
by Allen Raine
*A masterful novel, set at the
time of the 1904 Revival, by one
of the most popular authors at
the turn of the century.*
> ISBN 978 1870206 297
> £7.95

**Welsh Women's Poetry
1460 - 2001: An Anthology**
edited by Dr Katie Gramich
and Catherine Brennan
*This ground-breaking volume is
the first bilingual anthology of
Welsh women's poetry.*
> ISBN 978 1870206 549
> £12.99

About Honno

Honno Welsh Women's Press was set up in 1986 by a group of women who felt strongly that women in Wales needed wider opportunities to see their writing in print and to become involved in the publishing process. Our aim is to develop the writing talents of women in Wales, give them new and exciting opportunities to see their work published and often to give them their first 'break' as a writer.

Honno is registered as a community co-operative. Any profit that Honno makes goes towards the cost of future publications. To buy shares or to receive further information about forthcoming publications, please write to Honno at the address below, or visit our website: **www.honno.co.uk**.

Honno
'Ailsa Craig'
Heol y Cawl
Dinas Powys
Bro Morgannwg
CF64 4AH

All Honno titles can be ordered online at www.honno.co.uk or by sending a cheque to Honno, MyW, Vulcan St, Aberystwyth. SY23 1JH
FREE p&p to all UK addresses